INTEGRATED EDUCATION IN CONFLICTED SOCIETIES

INTEGRATED EDUCATION IN CONFLICTED SOCIETIES

Edited by
Claire McGlynn, Michalinos Zembylas, and Zvi Bekerman

palgrave
macmillan

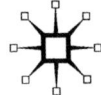

First published in 2013 by
PALGRAVE MACMILLAN®
in the United States—a division of St. Martin's Press LLC,
175 Fifth Avenue, New York, NY 10010.

Where this book is distributed in the UK, Europe and the rest of the world, this is by Palgrave Macmillan, a division of Macmillan Publishers Limited, registered in England, company number 785998, of Houndmills, Basingstoke, Hampshire RG21 6XS.

Palgrave Macmillan is the global academic imprint of the above companies and has companies and representatives throughout the world.

Palgrave® and Macmillan® are registered trademarks in the United States, the United Kingdom, Europe and other countries.

ISBN: 978–1–137–28097–8

Library of Congress Cataloging-in-Publication Data

Integrated education in conflicted societies / edited by Claire McGlynn, Michalinos Zembylas, and Zvi Bekerman.
        pages cm
    Includes index.
    ISBN 978–1–137–28097–8 (hardback)
        1. School integration—Cross-cultural studies. 2. Social integration—Cross-cultural studies. 3. Multicultural education—Cross-cultural studies. 4. Peace education—Cross-cultural studies. I. McGlynn, Claire. II. Zembylas, Michalinos. III. Bekerman, Zvi.

LC214.I58 2013
370.116—dc23   2013023762

A catalogue record of the book is available from the British Library.

Design by Newgen Knowledge Works (P) Ltd., Chennai, India.

First edition: December 2013

10 9 8 7 6 5 4 3 2 1

Contents

Part 4   Moving Forward—Developing and Sustaining Support for Integrated Schools

Acknowledgments

We want to express our deep gratitude to the Northern Ireland Council for Integrated Education that provided the venue and support in Belfast (March 2012) for the conference that produced the chapters of this edited collection. We are grateful to Palgrave Macmillan for undertaking this project and particularly to our editor, Burke Gerstenschlager, for providing support through all the stages of this effort.

Many thanks are also offered to our respective institutions for their continuing support and encouragement by providing us with the "space" to conduct our research and writing: the School of Education, Queen's University Belfast; the Open University of Cyprus; the Melton Centre for Jewish Education; and the Truman Institute for the Advancement of Peace at the Hebrew University, Jerusalem.

General Introduction

Interrogating the Meaning(s) and Doing(s) of "Integrated Education"

Zvi Bekerman and Michalinos Zembylas

The chapters in this volume are all the fruits of the first conference, the Integrated Peace Education: Global Network for Practice and Research, held in Belfast in March 2012, of the international network of academics, practitioners, and nongovernmental organizations,. The volume is a new addition to our longstanding and collaborative endeavor on the theme of sustained peace education efforts in societies that have suffered from protracted conflict, introduced in *Addressing Ethnic Conflict through Peace Education: International Perspectives* (Bekerman & McGlynn, 2007) and the award-winning *Peace Education in Conflict and Post-Conflict Societies: Comparative Perspectives* (McGlynn, Zembylas, Bekerman, & Gallagher, 2009). Yet, this volume is different in that it focuses on the developing field of *integrated education* in conflicted societies, where children who are more normally educated apart are deliberately educated together. We bring together papers that approach the development of integrated education in a variety of geographical and sociopolitical sites—Catholic and Protestant in Northern Ireland, Palestinian and Jewish in Israel, and Greek Cypriot and Turkish Cypriot in Cyprus as well as examples from Macedonia, Bosnia, and Croatia. In all of these societies integrated education has been difficult to initiate, complex to sustain, and has aroused the suspicion of the local historically divided communities; nonetheless, those involved believe it to be essential in contributing to the healing of the wounds that afflict their societies, easing the path toward integration and inclusion.

On the Challenges of Social Cohesion, Integration, and Inclusion

For long, the lack of social cohesion has been considered as the main problem afflicting societies, creating social instability and conflict. The lack of social cohesion is also seen as a threat to national and international stability. It is mostly found among what are considered to be groups belonging to "other" (e.g., minority) cultural groups; their cultural differences, accompanied at times by territorial conflicts, are assumed to be the basis of the social tensions. Thus, social cohesion is assumed to be the "answer" to these differences and tensions; "other" groups must adjust to the majority's social and cultural norms so that the society becomes cohesive.

Within the semantic field of social cohesion, we find other words that might describe the complex social processes that are taking place; these words are "integration" and "inclusion." *Integration* seems to be a rather older concept with practical connotations (e.g., access to work, education); *inclusion* is a more recent word and seems to imply higher expectations, ideals, goals, which, if achieved, should help us all, majority and minority, "abled" and "disabled," overcome estrangement. For the most part, those perceived in need of integration are expected to adopt a set of values and worldviews hailed by the majority or the powerful group as the pillars of their civilization. Mostly, therefore, integration and inclusion seem to be unidirectional. Migrants, indigenous people, and the disabled are integrated into the residents/citizens—the abled, the hegemonic. At the wide sociopolitical level, integration and inclusion seem not to be working well; social cohesion is not really being achieved and the threat is out there. The foreigners, the disabled, the enemies, so we are told, refuse to join and conform.

There are various theoretical considerations that try to explain strategies used by "others" (minorities, indigenous, migrants), when encountering majoritarian contexts. Berry (1997), for example, uses two dimensions—identification with the host culture and identification with group culture—and defines four strategies used by minority groups in negotiating the encounter. These are integration, assimilation, separation, and marginalization. Esser (2010), using a theoretical model based on Berry's approach, distinguishes between two entangled features—the individual (e.g., language) and the social (e.g., labor market). These features, he argues, are interrelated for together they influence the social integration of the individual and the system integration of a society. Rudmin (2003) has posited, critically, that the integration construct, as it develops through acculturation theories, does not seem to allow for much progress regarding minority policy articulations, for not all cultural aspects are open to code switching (e.g., religion), making integration at multiple levels if not impossible at least difficult.

When considering possible solutions, governments and international organizations have pointed at education as one of the main arenas in which the lack of social cohesion should be dealt with. Educational institutions are expected to help overcome social divisions and thus contribute to social stability and peaceful development. Within educational discourses it is also, mainly, strategies of integration that are discussed as being possibly the best ones to be considered when attempting to overcome societal tensions.

Though not always recognized or acknowledged, at the least educationally, where many of the countries represented in this volume are today, the United States of America was over 60 years ago. It took over one hundred years of struggle to reach the 1954 unanimous Supreme Court opinion in *Brown v. Board of Education*, which overturned the *Plessy v. Ferguson* 1896 Supreme Court decision finding Louisiana's "separate but equal" law constitutional. The primary concerns that the psychological briefs submitted to the court in the Brown case over half a century ago are surprisingly similar to present concerns in areas of intractable conflict as the ones discussed in this volume; the solutions offered were also based on the "contact hypothesis" principles. These concerns had to do with the potential psychological impact of segregationist practices that, as was argued, could seriously damage both the populations involved in the segregative system, Afro-Americans and Caucasians (Zirkel & Cantor, 2004). Educational integration seems to have been expected to help overcome these dangers and help better society.

Views are divergent, however, as to whether the Brown decision has fulfilled its promise. The discouraged point out that even today, while not state imposed, many school districts remain segregated by race (Guinier & Torres, 2002). Even in integrated settings, students of color find themselves resegregated through academic tracking or social interactional boundaries (Tatum, 2003). They find themselves disproportionately represented in poorly funded schools (Glickstein, 1996) and, for those students who do make it to college, their dropout rate is much higher than the rate for white populations (Bowen & Bok, 1998; Steele, 1997). The optimists point to the tremendous growth of students of color in the percentage of college graduates (Bowen & Bok, 1998) and to the fact that many educational institutions are involved in developing strategies that will further support the development of students of color through a variety of tools such as affirmative action and a multicultural curriculum. These steps, as well as others, all try to readdress racial disparities in order to attain the primary goal of Brown's decision to offer equal access to educational opportunities (Wells & Jones, 1998).

While the results on school integration may not be conclusive, there is a growing impression that scholars are becoming more and more critical, if not about the essentials of the Brown decision, then about its implementation. This criticism is so strong, that some have recently argued that racial disparities would have been better served if Brown had upheld the *Plessy v. Ferguson* decision of 1896 that provided for "separate but equal" settings. As evident in today's reality, educational settings are still separate but unequal (Bell, 2001; Bifulco, Ladd, & Ross, 2009).

It is worth mentioning in this context that research in a parallel stream in integrated education—that which relates to the inclusion of children with special educational needs in mainstream educational institutions—and which is seriously considered in some of the chapters included in this volume, though showing neutral to positive effects, is also not conclusive (Polat, 2011; Ruijs & Peetsma, 2009). The effects of educational integration on the academic achievement of children with special education needs seems to be slightly positive and there are very few reports that find any negative effects of inclusion in the achievements of children with mild to moderate special education needs. Integration is found to have neutral to negative socio-emotional effects on children with a similar degree of special educational needs as on the ones mentioned above (Bakker & Bosman, 2003).

In the countries included in this volume there has been a long tradition of the use intergroup encounters/dialogues as a tool to improve relations and mutual perceptions among the groups in conflict. The "contact hypothesis," which was presented in its first widely accepted outline by Allport in 1954, stands today as the basis of most educational efforts toward integration. The contact hypothesis suggests that intergroup contact—when occurring under conditions of status equality and cooperative interdependence, while allowing for sustained interaction between participants and the potential formation of friendships—might help alleviate conflict between groups and encourage change in negative intergroup attitudes (Allport, 1954; Amir, 1976; Pettigrew & Tropp, 2006).

A large number of studies have been conducted on intergroup encounters/dialogues, and most of these have tried to assess their effectiveness by focusing on attitudinal change based on pre- and post-measures (Bargal, 1990; Gaertner, Dovidio, Anastasio, Bachman, & Rust, 1993; Pettigrew & Tropp, 2006). A meta-analysis has marked evidence for the benefits of intergroup contact, especially when the contact situation maximizes most, or all of its optimal conditions (Pettigrew & Tropp, 2000). However, what characterizes these dialogue encounters is that they are one-time, singular, two-to-three-day events. Thus, they do not allow for any conclusions to be reached regarding the potential influence of sustained educational initiatives geared toward the alleviation of conflict.

When considering the above, it becomes apparent that integration efforts cannot be considered an easy recipe for the problems of a diverse and conflicted society.

THIS VOLUME

Rather than focus on ad hoc responses to conflict such as short-term educational encounters or programs, this volume investigates a long term, systemic approach and its innovative pedagogies in a range of conflicted societies. These initiatives discussed afford participants long-term exposure to each other's group within an integrated school setting. In this sense these settings can be considered more "real" or at least more present in the reality in which participants interact—their daily lives. Reflecting on these settings, the present volume should help us move away from the utopianism of "contact research" conducted under ideal situations to a more detailed analysis of "contact" of ordinary people in more ordinary situations; schools are indeed a more mundane activity in the lives of children. Research by C. McGlynn, J. Hughes, Z. Bekerman, R. Gavison, and others on the encounters that take place in integrated schools functioning in countries such as Northern Ireland and Israel, though showing some positive results, is yet not decisive, but the present volume, though assisted by this research, wants to reflect not on the work of researchers but on the experience of those directly involved in these educational efforts. Their voices, as it is so traditional in most educational research, have not been heard enough.

The chapters in the book interrogate what can be learned about establishing new integrated schools in conflicted societies from the perspective of those who have been and those who continue to be involved in the development of integrated education. They draw attention to the kind of support that is required by those struggling to establish integrated schools in challenging contexts; explore leadership, specifically the types of strategies, skills, and characteristics that are required for success; and examine the extent to which leadership aspects are common or otherwise across the various country contexts. The chapters ask important questions about what is taught and also how teachers can be given the confidence and skills to meet the challenges of the integrated classroom without shying away from the more difficult aspects of teaching in integrated schools, such as how to deal with controversial issues. All in all, this volume presents integrated education as a broad and constantly developing concept that will not suffer innocence or illusion.

The book is organized into four parts. The first part interrogates the leadership of integrated education, in particular the strategies, skills, and characteristics that are required for success. It examines the extent to which these are common or otherwise. It considers school leadership and the qualities needed to support integrated education, and evaluates the challenges that need to be confronted by both schools and supporting communities.

The second part explores the challenges of establishing new integrated schools in conflicted societies. In particular, the chapters focus on the challenges of establishing new integrated schools and of transforming existing schools. In doing so it also considers the ways in which the biographies of particular schools have influenced their visions of integrated education.

The third part investigates the curriculum and the pedagogy that has developed in integrated schools to respond to student diversity and to historical divisions. It considers the challenges of planning appropriate curricula for integrated education initiatives, explores how difficult topics can be approached in integrated school classrooms, and ponders on the training needs of teachers.

The fourth and final part focuses on what is currently needed to develop and support international integrated education. It reflects on what has been achieved already and what has yet to be done. Furthermore, it investigates the needs of new initiatives for integrated education and the current barriers to the establishment of integrated schools in conflicted societies.

We are told more and more that narratives are powerful tools for encountering and deciphering "realities" in the world; they are powerful in helping us understand ourselves and our positioning and in reflecting on our interactions with others; in short, they are tools that help us find a path. Reading narratives can transport the reader to other places, contexts, situations he or she might not have directly experienced but wishes to understand. Reading other people's stories can help readers understand experiences about which they have questions but which in their own realities are not yet available. Stories help us explore, reflect, and understand.

Thus, this book is a collection of stories, reflective stories, of educators who encounter educational scenes at different institutional levels. What connects these stories is that they are written by educators who share, unfortunately, a common sociopolitical stage characterized by conflict. Not all come from the same geographical area but each of the geographies they inhabit can be described as a conflict or post-conflict society. They also share the fact they are all involved in school initiatives that believe putting children together in an inclusive and respectful context can help alleviate conflict and support mutual understanding. What the authors have, which most researchers lack, is an intimate knowledge of the complexities involved in creating such integrated settings. These authors have lived through the difficulties of starting integrated schools from scratch in political contexts that did not support them and have realized through their long experience that idealistic and romantic perspectives cannot, all by themselves, sustain a real encounter between those who have suffered the results of harsh conflicts. If indeed, as Muriel Rukeyser would have it, the universe is made up of stories, not atoms, the stories in this volume should become the basic units with which to construct better understanding and perspectives for a future with more successful integrative initiatives.

REFERENCES

Allport, G. W. (1954). *The nature of prejudice*. London: Addison-Wesley.

Amir, Y. (1976). The role of intergroup contact in change of prejudice and ethnic relations.In P. A. Katz (Ed.), *Towards the elimination of racism* (pp. 245–308). New York: Pergamon.

Bakker, J. T. A., & Bosman, A. M. T. (2003). Self-image and peer acceptance of Dutch students in regular and special education. *Learning Disability Quarterly, 26*, 5–14.

Bargal, D. (1990). Contact is not enough—The contribution of Lewinian theory to inter-group workshops involving Palestinian and Jewish youth in Israel. *International Journal of Group Tensions, 20*, 179–192.

Bekerman, Z., & McGlynn, C. (Eds). (2007). *Addressing ethnic conflict through peace education: International perspectives*. New York: Palgrave Macmillan.

Bell, D. A. (2001). Dissenting. In J. M. Balkin (Ed.), *What Brown v. Board of Education should have said: The nation's top legal experts rewrite America's landmark civil rights decision* (pp. 185–200). New York: New York University Press.

Berry, J. W. (1997). Immigration, acculturation, and adaptation. *Applied Psychology: An International Review*, 46, 5–68.

Bifulco, R., Ladd, H. F., & Ross, S. (2009). Public school choice and integration: Evidence from Durham, North Carolina. *Social Science Research*, 36 (1), 71–85.

Bowen, W. G., & Bok, D. (1998). *The shape of the river: Long-term consequences of considering race in college and university admissions*. Princeton, NJ: Princeton University Press.

Esser, H. (2010). Assimilation, ethnic stratification, or selective acculturation? Recent theories of the integration of immigrants and the model of intergenerational integration. *Sociologica*, 4(1), 0-0.

Gaertner, S. L., Dovidio, J. F., Anastasio, P. A., Bachman, B. A., & Rust, M. C. (1993). The common ingroup identity model: Recategorization and the reduction of intergroup bias. *European Review of Social Psychology*, 4, 1–26.

Glickstein, H. A. (1996). Inequities in educational funding. In E. C. Lagemann & L. P. Miller (Eds.), *Brown v. Board of Education: The challenge for today's schools* (pp. 122–128). New York: Teachers College Press.

Guinier, L., & Torres, G. (2002). *The miner's canary: Enlisting race, resisting power, and transforming democracy*. Cambridge, MA: Harvard University Press.

McGlynn, C., Zembylas, M., Bekerman, Z., & Gallagher, T. (Eds.). (2009). *Peace education in conflict and post-conflict societies: Comparative perspectives*. New York: Palgrave Macmillan.

Pettigrew, T. F., & Tropp, L. R. (2000). Does intergroup contact reduce prejudice? Recent meta-analytic findings. In S. Oskamp (Ed.), *Reducing prejudice and descrimination* (pp. 93–114). Mahwah, NJ: Earlbaum.

Pettigrew, T. F., & Tropp, L. R. (2006). A meta-analytic test of intergroup contact theory. *Journal of Personality and Social Psychology*, 90(5), 751–783.

Polat, F. (2011). Inclusion in education: A step towards social justice. *International Journal of Educational Development*, 31(1), 50–58.

Rudmin, F. W. (2003). Critical history of the acculturation psychology of assimilation, separation, integration, and marginalization. *Review of General Psychology*, 7(1), 3–37.

Ruijs, N. M., & Peetsma, T. T. D. (2009). Effects of inclusion on students with and without special educational needs reviewed. *Educational Research Review*, 4(2), 67–79.

Steele, C. M. (1997). A threat in the air: How stereotypes shape intellectual identity and performance. *American Psychologist*, 52, 613–619.

Tatum, B. D. (2003). *"Why all the black kids sitting together in the cafeteria." And other conversations about race*. New York: Basic Books.

Wells, M., & Jones, R. (1998). Relationship among childhood parentification, splitting, and dissociation: Preliminary findings. *American Journal of Family Therapy*, 26, 331–339.

Zirkel, S. & Cantor, N. (2004). 50 Years after Brown v. Board of Education: The promise and challenge of multicultural education. *Journal of Social Issues*, 60(1), 1–16.

1

Leadership of Integrated Education

INTRODUCTION TO PART 1

Zvi Bekerman

The first part of this book interrogates the leadership of integrated education, particularly about the skills and strategies required for success. The authors in this part are all pivotal figures in the integration movement both at the school level and at the organizational level that supports integrated education in Northern Ireland, Israel, and Bosnia and Herzegovina. In their chapters, these authors thoughtfully reflect on what it takes to lead integrated education in conflicted societies while evaluating future challenges for both integrated schools and the organizations that support them.

In the first chapter of this part, Mary Roulston chooses to relate to us the many life experiences that, since an early age, shaped her educational philosophy as it is reflected today in the integrated school she leads. She discusses the opportunities she had in her early career to work with all levels of society; and to this variety she attributes the development of her child-centered approach and her empathy for and understanding of children. In Mary's view integration, to be successful, needs to be understood in a very wide sense, one that reflects an all-inclusive child-centered approach. When discussing the many obstacles she had to overcome in creating the Millennium integrated school she leads today, the reader might be impressed by the detailed and complex descriptions Mary offers in all that relates to the hiring of teachers and the need to try and sustain the vibrancy of the school community after the first generation of pioneers leaves the school. Important things do not happen by accident, emphasizes Mary, they need to be strategically planned for them to become accepted and rooted.

Paul Caskey writes the second chapter in this part. As the campaign director of the Integrated Educational Fund (IEF) in Northern

Ireland he has had the opportunity to be involved in the development of the integrated school movement there and it is from a rather macro perspective that he writes this chapter. His story is one about finding ways to finance the integrated movement; it is one that emphasizes the need for creating alliances and coalitions both with governmental and private institutions. Paul believes that integrated education should remain a community-led process; he does not believe it should be imposed on people by the government but does acknowledge that the support of the government is essential for the movement's present and future development. Among the things he has learned, he points at the need not to become frustrated by the complexities of political realities that make legislation amendments less influential that what could be expected. His final lesson is that "we all need to be in this for the long haul."

In the third chapter of this part, Inas Deeb and Nadia Kinani share their experience as leaders of the bilingual, binational integrated Jewish-Palestinian initiative in Israel. Nadia is the present principal of the Max Rayne Hand in Hand Sschool in Jerusalem and Inas functions as the educational director at the Hand in Hand center where she works together with school faculty on developing different aspects of the bilingual model.

The chapter offers an honest, critical, and well-balanced developmental perspective on the complexities of developing integrated educational initiatives in one of the severest areas of intractable conflict known today. Nadia and Inas first offer their perspective on integrated education, as they believe it can be viable in Israel's conflictual setting. They analyze how the bilingual Arabic-Hebrew program is implemented in a country where both languages are officially recognized but where, at the same time, Hebrew is for all practical purposes the only language of civil life while Arabic is devoid of any public importance. They tackle the intricacies of dealing with the controversial national days of remembrance in the school and school community and finally discuss the school community and the negotiations that need to be undertaken for the benefit of the initiative among the main stakeholders—faculty, parents, NGO, and Ministry of Education.

The chapter by Noreen Campbell, presently, the chief executive of the Northern Ireland Council for Integrated Education (NICIE), is the fourth chapter of this part. Noreen has, through her involvement in the integrated school movement, occupied different leading positions—parent, teacher, principal, and today the leader of NICIE, the umbrella organization of the integrated schools. Through her vast experience, she has learned about the need for integrated schools to create an environment of trust in which contentious societal issues can be addressed. She has also become very sensitive to the difficulties encountered by a faculty that is being asked not only to confront a mixed religious students corps but also to teach classes in which students differ also in their socioeconomic status and in their learning abilities; the variations encountered imply the need to develop a continuous program of staff support. Moreover, Noreen discusses the importance of creating a common language through which to express the integrated school ethos as well as developing ceremonies in which to embody this ethos. She believes that being attentive to these needs can secure the success of integrated education and that these characteristics are transferable to other countries in need of developing integrated schools.

In the last chapter of this part, Ljuljjeta Goranci-Brkic reflects on the experiences of the Nansen Dialogue Centre in Sarajevo and its efforts to promote inter-ethnic dialogue and to create inter-ethnic initiatives for integrated education in Bosnia and Herzegovina. In particular, Goranci-Brkic discusses the roles of parents, teachers, students, principals, and politicians in these initiatives for integrated education. This chapter shows most forcefully the immense challenges at the structural level for developing initiatives that promote integration in schools. The initiatives take place at various levels simultaneously involving parents, local authorities, students, and teachers, and show that the process is often slowed down by political power games; yet, persistent efforts to achieve small gains, argues Goranci-Brkic, are clearly better than doing nothing.

1

THE MAGIC OF MILLENNIUM

A MILESTONE TOWARD PEACE IN NORTHERN IRELAND

Mary Roulston

As I reach the final stage of my career in education and take the time in a very busy life to reflect on the journey so far, I am stunned by the strength of feeling that tells me I have been on a journey I didn't plan, through a series of experiences that have shaped my educational philosophy far more than I ever realized at the time, and that my final post as a principal in a grant-maintained integrated primary school setting in Northern Ireland needed me to have been through each and every one of those experiences. I can very clearly see that the ethos of the school and my leadership style has been shaped by the rich variety of posts and experiences I have been fortunate enough to have.

A brief overview of the type of work I was involved in from the age of 16, pre and post qualification as a teacher, demonstrate how each and every environment has had a considerable impact on my personal definition of integrated education. It started with a week's placement in a children's home, when I was a teenager, as part of community service for my Duke of Edinburgh Award, experiencing at firsthand the impact on children's development when they have been institutionalized and have attachment difficulties. For three consecutive summers, I worked in a Colony de Vacances in France with blind children who were in care. Many of the children had additional disabilities such as autism or being deaf and dumb. I have also worked as a "surveillante" (a person who looks after the children and the dormitory before and after school) in a French boarding school and in an international school, in village schools in Northern Ireland, and also in a Rudolph Steiner School. All of these wonderful opportunities have allowed me to work with all levels of society, from the aristocracy to the most marginalized in terms of social class and disability. My child-centered approach, my empathy for and understanding of children, and my ability to work closely with parents and my personal approach to life in general were particularly enhanced by my time at the Rudolph Steiner School.

While my three sons were young I took time out of teaching to be at home with them but I then entered into another defining part of my life journey doing cross-community work through a local parent and toddler group that led to the foundation of a community association I chaired for a number of years and that was successful in accessing European funding to provide a cross-community hall and health facilities. It was through the ups and downs of this work that I really began to understand each side of the Northern Ireland community and, more importantly, that it was possible to work together successfully and harmoniously, at least most of the time!

Before I took up my present post I worked in a village school that, in line with the education system, served a community made up of one tradition only, Protestant. While I loved working with the families and children in this village, I feel it was no accident that I was drawn to the integrated sector and the most incredible opportunity of my whole teaching career—starting a new integrated school and bringing to it both a shared and a personal understanding of what an integrated school should be!

For me integrated education has so many strands. In its most simple, basic, fundamental form it is, in the context of Northern Ireland, about educating Catholic and Protestant children together. However the reality of the type of integrated school I have always sought to develop is much more complex and within this complexity is a kernel of something that is very simple to say but much harder to deliver! The kernel is that all are welcome into the school community and valued as the individuals they are. Therefore Protestant, Catholic, all other faiths and none, all social classes, all cultures, and all levels of ability and disability are actively welcomed.

I understand inclusion in its widest sense in the context of creating an all-ability and child-centered school. Delivering a truly child-centered school means, in addition to the usual shared understanding of putting the children at the center of every decision made and listening to and valuing the children's voice, going the extra mile for those children with considerable barriers to their learning and also for those with complex emotional and behavioral difficulties. It is about welcoming children who are not always welcome in other schools.

One of the real strengths of an integrated school is that children are together from a young age and this shared school, shared nursery, shared classroom environment facilitates friendship before labels and preconceived prejudice can become barriers, and then takes the children on a developmentally age-appropriate exploration of sameness and difference, emphasizing that difference can be as positive, if not more positive, than sameness. At the same time there are opportunities to learn about and celebrate together the diverse religious and cultural events that are reflected in the whole school community.

In the context of Northern Ireland, our first integrated schools were set up within the context of the "Troubles," where civilians, police, and army personnel were being killed and where normal daily life was subject to bombings; bomb scares; families being forced out of their homes; searches; and a very closed in, insular feeling exacerbated by the lack of tourists and visitors; the native population becoming disillusioned and leaving; and also the fear of going out in the evening.

Fortunately Northern Ireland is now on the cusp of a potentially very interesting period of change in education. The peace process has given Northern Ireland society, despite the many starts and stops, a period of a more settled and normalized everyday life. Politicians who, previously, were very vocal in protecting the sector of education associated with their own community and were clearly opposed to integrated education are now making media statements around the need for integrating schools and for sharing. It will be interesting to see what the outcome of this new outlook will be, especially with the added driving force of the economic reality that Northern Ireland can no longer sustain a segregated schooling system. Will the power of an economic shortfall in the education budget bring about the kind of changes that have the potential to be a healing catalyst for Northern Ireland society? Or will the changes be of a more superficial nature? Only time will tell!

Within the Education Reform (Northern Ireland) Order 1989 statutory support for integrated education became enshrined in legislation. As the principal of a new school and having had firsthand experience of struggles before and after the school opened, it still remains difficult to feel a real and true sense of government support, even now when the school is fully established, enjoys an excellent reputation, and is full with a waiting list for some classes.

Going back to the very beginning still brings a smile to my face! Little did I realize as I read a small, provincial newspaper reporting on a number of heated open meetings to establish a new integrated school, that I would, very shortly, be appointed as principal of this new school! Those early days were fraught with an uncertainty that I had never anticipated. Before I start to describe the main events of those early days, I must flag that what I will be describing is not unique within our sector. In fact there is a common thread that will be recognized by any principal who has been on the same journey and for some principals within our sector this journey was even more fraught with difficulties or more prolonged. Indeed, time and time again, the delegates at our Integrated Peace Education conference outlined the details of both early and present-day struggles. As an audience we were united in our empathy, the chord of our common struggles resonating for all.

Reflecting on my earliest memories of the journey, I remain to this day stunned and in awe of those parents who felt so passionate about integrated education that they were prepared to hand over the education of their very precious children to a school that had no reputation, no building, no funding, an unknown principal, and no resources, curriculum, or policies in place! I am equally stunned by my own total belief that it would all come to fruition in time even though all the early signs were fraught with uncertainty. I had given in my notice for the safe and permanent post at the established school I had been employed in and within a very short time two very alarming situations were developing. The first was that although we had a site on which to place a mobile building, we were not going to be allowed to use it and this threw up a major problem. How could the school open if it had nowhere to go? If the school didn't open then I would not have a job!

It was so hard to grasp why we were not being allowed to go onto a site that had previously operated as a car showroom and a furniture business, with all the associated traffic, while ten children and two staff members could not be allowed to use it. This was the beginning of discovering that the opposition, mainly political, to our fledgling school would be fierce and prolonged. This common thread of political opposition came through so strongly from each and every one of the delegates at our Integrated Peace Education conference. It is so disappointing that many politicians elected to be leaders, and government bodies, procrastinate to the point of being obstructive to the real and purposeful change that educators at grass roots level are striving to achieve.

After many afternoons and evenings searching for alternative premises we were eventually gifted a temporary lease on a large, vandalized house outside our catchment area. With only very few days remaining before school officially started there were many manual tasks to do to ensure that our new environment was clean, safe, and welcoming for the start of term. This was a crucial time for the long-term future of the school. We had ten children and we really needed to ensure that all ten children turned up on the first day. Less than ten would have had serious implications for the future of the school and would make all the difference as to whether we would receive government funding the following year.

Therefore this period of time became even busier with the need to reassure and inspire our small number of families. They needed to know that the school was indeed going to open. There needed to be discussions about an earlier than usual opening time so that being outside our catchment area was not going to adversely affect the needs of working parents. They needed to start getting to know me as a person, as an educator, as the principal and sole teacher of this new integrated school. In those very early days I had to remain upbeat and positive, no matter what the hurdles were. The ability not just to listen, but to really hear what the parents were telling me helped me to make the practical decisions that inspired both confidence and relief in the parent body. My ability to be flexible and to use my initiative stood me in good stead and the support I received from my newly appointed classroom assistant and from parents was invaluable. Through sheer necessity I very quickly learnt that this was no straightforward principal post and nothing in the job advertisement or job description could have prepared me for the range and type of duties that needed to be fulfilled in those very early days to ensure that the school opened and once opened did not fall by the wayside. Stamina was a great asset!

As I have already alluded to there was considerable opposition to the school, both overt and covert in those very early years. Planning permission for the site was constantly opposed and delayed. As a result it took us a full three years to get onto site, only to then have to deal with a media frenzy regarding the main road into Belfast that runs outside the school. It would be difficult, perhaps impossible, and certainly a negative step to close a school but a local politician threatened to serve a notice on the school which in effect would close this road. The potential for extremely negative publicity and frustration for the commuters using the road could have had devastating consequences. Fortunately we managed to keep the school and the road open.

Remaining dignified and measured in responses, not being afraid to ask for advice, to know exactly the key points to address, and then to communicate these to the media in a simple, straightforward, and direct manner always served us well.

In that first year I was sustained totally by the children and the sheer joy of teaching such a small class that they were almost like a large family. Some key members of the school board of governors also provided invaluable emotional and practical support. I was also surrounded by a number of organizations that wanted the school to succeed—Belfast Trust for Integrated Education (BELTIE), Northern Ireland Council for Integrated Education (NICIE), Integrated Education Fund (IEF), and the Canadian branch of the International Ireland Funds. Without this umbrella of connections and the feel good factor they generated I would have been overwhelmed by the constant worries in relation to the enrolment numbers, keeping prospective parents upbeat and confident enough to send their children to a school where there were still no guaranteed certainties in relation to funding, site, building, and academic reputation.

In those early years the recruitment of staff, both teachers and learning support assistants, was an onerous business in a number of ways. There was no guarantee for us that the candidates being interviewed were committed to integrated education or even understood what an integrated school was. With falling enrollments across Northern Ireland, permanent teaching posts were scarce, and the integrated sector and the Irish medium sector were the two sectors still growing. The controlled (largely Protestant) and the maintained (Catholic) sector were suffering from the decline in birth rates and to some extent parental interest in integrated and Irish medium education was also having a positive effect. In addition the preparation for recruitment was time consuming. From the drawing up of advertisements, job descriptions, interview questions and answers, a volume of hours was spent shortlisting and interviewing, followed by the associated paperwork after interview. In a small, fledgling school it was a significant pressure to keep teaching, running a school with all that it entails, and finding the additional hours to undertake all of this! On many an occasion I felt I was just about holding my head above water. The reality was that absolutely nothing could have prepared me for the post I had found myself in—not the job advertisement, nor the job description, nor the meeting and long chat I had with another integrated principal before the opening of the school.

However burdensome this was, the future of the school depended on making good appointments and on a number of other fronts. The main business of a school is to educate children, and our parents, quite rightly so, had high expectations. So we needed to appoint teachers who were highly skilled in the core skills of teaching children the primary curriculum. This can be elusive enough during the interview procedure but even more elusive was teasing out candidates who already could or who had the potential to live and breathe in their daily work and relations the core principles of integrated education. We needed teachers who were child centered in their approach; who understood and were able to use positive behavior strategies successfully in their classrooms; who understood that our school had been started and set up by parents who had invested much time and energy to bring to fruition their dream and expected a much greater contact with staff than would generally be the norm; and teachers who were sensitive to all cultures and traditions and open enough and brave enough to explore and bring into their classroom practice and teaching, opportunities for children to explore their own cultural and religious identities and the cultural and religious identities of others.

The biggest struggle we have always felt is that standard interview procedures do not easily facilitate or adequately draw out the caliber of candidates we are looking for. We continue to sense this inadequacy. Over the years we have tried to improve our methodology by introducing a variety of what would be seen as innovative practices within the accepted practices in Northern Ireland for interviewing teachers. We have moved on from selecting questions from a bank of general questions to devising our own questions that are more post and school specific. We have increased the number and range of scenario type questions as they do seem to give a greater insight to candidates' personal qualities and approaches to children. We have given candidates the opportunity to teach the interview panel a new skill and have also used role play and presentations, both prepared in advance of interview and unseen.

To this day we struggle with the whole "integrated"' part of the interview process and how we can meaningfully assess the candidates in this incredibly important aspect of our work. We always ask a straightforward "integrated" question—Millennium is an integrated school. Firstly what do you understand by this and secondly, would you also share with the panel your views on integrating children with special educational needs into mainstream schools? However, it is the question that is, surprisingly,consistently answered in the weakest manner. We have interviewed candidates who have demonstrated a complete lack of knowledge or understanding of what an integrated school is, candidates who have rhymed off a prepared answer verbatim, clearly taken from the NICIE website or some publication or other, yet demonstrate no personal understanding or commitment to the reality and practice of integrated education. At times all candidates have been weak in this area and as a result we constantly reflect and question ourselves about what other mechanisms we can use to tease out the candidates who would be likely to have the openness and personal skills and qualities to be able to embrace our integrated ethos.

Fortunately for us the majority of our appointments have been very successful ones but we are conscious that it only takes one poor appointment to have a considerable negative impact on the day-to-day running of the school and potentially on the future of the school. Employees, at all levels, are the school in the eyes of prospective parents. What they say and do and how they say and do things, their ability to develop positive relationships at all levels are what drives enrollment figures and without healthy enrollment figures any school has a dismal future. It is as simple and as complex as that.

It has been my experience, especially given the way our school grew and developed, that in some ways, in the early days, it was easy and straightforward to deliver the ethos and vision of our school. This was probably due to the constant, regular meetings and conversations as to how to grow the school and also that in a very small, cozy environment, it is much easier for a shared understanding of what is important to take root and to become part of the fabric. Also with very young children there are certain limitations as to the daily outworking of the more thorny issues of integration that pop up in the later years as a reality—how do you teach Religious Education especially as the Catholic children reach the stage of making the sacraments? How do you ensure a fair balance of celebrations and events that reflect the two main religions and traditions and of the other stakeholders in the school who sit outside of these? How do you help children to understand the reasons why there is a divided society in Northern Ireland in a manner that is sensitive, truthful, and transparent? How are teachers skilled up to feeling comfortable working in an integrated school and delivering the integrated ethos? How do you develop an antibias approach at all levels and how do you plan developmentally appropriate activities and experiences for the children that bring to life the core purpose of being a child in an integrated school?

There seems to be some agreement within our schools that there is a point in an integrated school's development where it is possible for the whole integrated aspect of the school to become considerably diluted. The trend seems to be that in the early years the families with the type of pioneering spirit that drives them to set up and commit their children's futures to our schools are passionate in their belief and desire for an integrated experience of education for their children. They so much want something different that they are more than prepared to take risks. Then over time the school begins to develop a reputation in the community it serves and a popularity that may, for some families, be based on anything but the fact that it is an integrated school. Therefore, the deciding factor for prospective parents might be the excellent educational attainments, the holistic approach to education, the open door policy, and the close working relationships with parents, the pastoral care, or the reputation for supporting children with special needs. Couple this with the larger staff team, the even busier nature of the everyday running of the school, staff changes (particularly at leadership level of the staff and the board of governors), and there is the very real potential to lose the initial, integrated vibrancy of the school. From conversations with other principals I think that we should now expect this cyclical trend. First the leadership of the school need to aware of the inherent likelihood of this happening and then to demonstrate the skills of planning strategically for this eventuality on a regular basis in order to determine the optimum timing for an in-depth, whole school community focus on integration.

As a relatively young school we had gone through one of these cycles when it was absolutely crucial to do whole school work on integration. What triggered the need to revisit our ethos and vision? The following realities were the catalyst for the work we undertook. Initially the enrollment figures at school began to grow considerably—we now were on site within our catchment area and we had a proper school building, of sorts! The staff team had grown very quickly. Time constraints and a range of other priorities and new Department of Education initiatives were being allowed to take up our attention at the expense of time being dedicated to our core purpose—integration. I no longer felt that I really knew where the staff stood or where the wider school community stood in terms of a shared ethos and also future aspirations for the school. In addition, our collegiate approach was becoming unwieldy, with the potential consequence of a slowing down of progress in all aspects of curriculum development and more importantly in the delivery of an integrated experience for the children and our families. The children in our school population were no longer four, five, or six years of age and so we needed to look once again at age-appropriate curricular experiences in peace education. Also there were a number of new members in the board of governors.

What approach did we take? I made a conscious decision that this was one area of staff development that I would not deliver or lead. I knew that if I did so, then I would find it impossible not to steer and shape it, and I felt there was a danger that we could spend a lot of time and end up without a truly shared, developed, and whole community ethos. Through NICIE, it was arranged that two experienced facilitators, one from each side of the community, would work through a series of workshops with us to clarify and develop a shared understanding of our integrated ethos. The end result was an agreed mission statement that led us to a school motto. An application was made to the IEF for funding to help with the marketing and the production of the newly agreed school motto and the mission statement that would be explicit to all, including any visitors to the school. We then worked with a design team to develop a corporate image that would be used in the new prospectus and on the new school motto and mission statement boards.

The new motto and mission statement were commercially produced and displayed in prominent places—the front wall of the school, entrance hall, and assembly hall. We then updated our policies to reflect the agreed ethos and vision work. An integration coordinator was appointed, immediately raising the profile of integration and also through our work on integrated practices becoming embedded in the School Development Plan and an Annual Action Plan. A questionnaire was completed by parents and all staff, and the outcomes were used to determine future actions. We made changes to the principal's address on Open Day to ensure that prospective parents had as clear a picture as possible of the ethos of the school with a particular focus on integration—the whys and how it translates into everyday practice. We wrote our first Integration Policy. Time was allocated during staff development days to analyze celebrations and school events, which could be perceived to belong to one side or the other, and tries to ensure a balanced approach so that all religions and cultures within the school community could feel recognized and valued.

In the first five to seven years there were times when I was approached by parents and, depending on what the issue was, the accusation that came was "You are running a Catholic School" or "You are running a Protestant School." The triggers for these kinds of comments from a small but important minority of parents were emotive issues like celebrating Ash Wednesday, introducing the teaching of Irish, holding a street party to celebrate the Queen's Diamond Jubilee, the wearing of sport tops perceived to belong to one section of the community, how the sound for the letter "H" was taught, marking Remembrance Day, taking the children to different places of worship, and preparation for Catholic sacraments. Keeping the school open on St Patrick's Day and celebrating the day in-house brought to my door concerns from both traditions!

Over the last four years parental concern over such issues appears to have dwindled dramatically. It is difficult to be sure why. I like to think we have reached a point where the parents now know us well enough to trust us, to know that we do things sensitively and for good reasons, and maybe we are communicating more clearly to everyone what integration is all about in our school.

So what lessons have I learnt on the biggest, most challenging, and most enjoyable journey of my career? I strongly believe that relationships are the key to everything, both within and beyond the school community. A foundation of trust and friendship will stand you in good stead when you hit a difficult or sensitive issue. I feel you are much more likely to listen to the other and to be heard by the other if there is already a positive, respectful relationship to support both parties. I also believe that recruitment of the right kind of staff is essential——appointing staff who have the right mixture of personal skills, attributes, and attitudes ensures that there are strengths that can be developed and built upon in the future. It is much easier to develop certain skills than to change set negative personality traits. It is also crucial to make plans for your own professional development and for the professional development of the staff. One of the most important areas to develop in any organization is the development of leaders and high-functioning teams—you will not be able to do everything on your own. In order to build up a thriving, respected school community it is also important to know your staff and to use their individual skills wisely. Building links and networking with the wider community can pay dividends on so many levels including the all-important need for resources and funding. Take time to read your community—know their expectations and also be prepared to guide them in new directions when necessary. Make sure that time is spent working with the whole school community to explore and agree on the kind of integrated ethos you value and are striving for. Know that the important things do not happen by accident—they need to be strategically planned for if they are to become rooted and accepted. Be sensitive to, and try to understand the fundamental causes of the misunderstanding inherent in both sides of the community. Lead by example at all times and be prepared to tackle any task to ensure your school thrives. Never forget the importance of marketing the school in the wider community. A willingness to embrace any opportunity that allows you to see other examples of integrated practice in your own country, and further afield, always pays dividends. If you are the principal, make sure you have a mentor to support you when you are struggling. One final piece of advice—do not take up the post of principal in an integrated school unless you have the stamina, perseverance, flexibility, emotional intelligence, and commitment necessary to survive the job.

2

THE INTEGRATED EDUCATION FUND IN NORTHERN IRELAND

Paul Caskey

INTRODUCTION

As campaign director of the Integrated Education Fund (IEF) in Northern Ireland, I have had the privilege of working to support integrated schools for over 12 years. My understanding of integrated education in Northern Ireland today must be placed in the context of Northern Ireland as a contested and divided society, with integrated education being essentially a community response to those divisions. Planned integrated schools, reflecting the main traditions, could help reconcile the community by educating together children of all faiths and none, and encouraging the development of respect and understanding of their differences as well as celebrating what they hold in common. For me, the integrated school would be one characterized not only by religious balance in pupil and staff numbers but also by the school's practice—living out the integrated ethos of the school in terms of the curriculum and extracurricular activities.

Appreciating the political and wider societal division in Northern Ireland is critical to understanding why integrated education did not command widespread political support and why it was largely left to parents to seize the initiative. Separate education served the interests of the churches but arguably also the needs of the main Nationalist and Unionist parties whose votes and power depended on support from different sections of the community. This is not to say that the concept of integrated schools was entirely without any political support, or indeed that of many individuals, most notably the late Basil McIvor and Lord Dunleath. In 1978, Lord Dunleath secured

support for a Private Members Bill in Westminster making it possible
for existing schools in Northern Ireland to transform themselves into
integrated schools—unfortunately no school was willing to avail of
the new legislation.

The campaigning group, All Children Together, grew in the
1970s from essentially a small group of parents interested in educating children together across the community divide. When no existing schools transformed following the Dunleath Act, momentum
increased to establish a new planned integrated school that was to
become Lagan College. It was the visionary and pioneering parents
themselves who established Lagan. It opened in 1981 as a second
level school (post age 11) with 28 children in a scout hall on the
outskirts of Belfast. So began a long and difficult journey to persuade the government that such a school would not only prove viable
but also worthy of government funding. Finding the finances to
help establish and sustain such schools was paramount. In 1985 the
first planned integrated primary schools opened in Belfast, alongside a further integrated college, at Hazelwood in North Belfast.
Once again funding had to be secured from a variety of sympathetic
sources and parents raised money from trusts, foundations, and the
inevitable jumble sales as all costs, capital and recurrent, had to be
found until such time as the schools were recognized as "viable" by
the government and became grant aided.

During the 1980s, individuals such as Brian (now Lord) Mawhinney
became involved. Mawhinney was a direct rule Conservative minister
with roots in Northern Ireland and, crucially, he was responsible for
education. He was instrumental in establishing the 1989 Education
Reform Order that was to place a statutory duty on the Department
of Education to "encourage and facilitate integrated education" and
would pave the way for newly established integrated schools to qualify
for full recurrent funding, even though it was to stop short of providing immediate capital funding for the schools.

I believe the 1989 order was a watershed in integrated education,
its impact lasting to the present day. The order provided access to
recurrent funding for proposed schools that could meet the stipulated
viability criteria of enrollment numbers, religious balance, and appropriate location. In addition, the statutory duty led, in 1991, to core
funding for the Northern Ireland Council for Integrated Education
(NICIE), which had been established in 1987 to act as a coordinating
body for the schools and for integrated education. However, it was
the absence of capital funding that led directly to the establishment
of the IEF in 1992. The IEF would try and bridge the gap between

what was actually needed to support the development of the schools and the support available from the government.

THE EARLY YEARS OF THE IEF, 1992–1997

Despite the passing of the 1989 Education Reform Order parents still needed to galvanize support in local communities for each new school they were striving to establish. Such work invariably incurred costs, in addition to the capital funding required. Both were gaps the IEF would seek to fill; its role would be one of providing grants, loans, and guarantees in support of new school ventures as well as small support grants to parent groups. Thus the IEF was set up in 1992 to be a financial foundation for the furtherance of integrated education. In a very generous act of confidence it was endowed with money from the European Structural Funds, the Department of Education, the Nuffield Foundation, and the Joseph Rowntree Charitable Trust. This provided an initial capital base of £2.375 million.

From the outset the capital base appeared under pressure. The continually growing number of emerging schools must have stretched the limitations of the capital base in securing the loans needed to provide school buildings. It appears that a constructive working relationship with officials in the Department of Education and its newly placed statutory duty to "encourage and facilitate" enabled the fund to secure two major contributions from the department in 1994 and 1995—each of £1 million. However, despite this, the overwhelming financial risk in establishing the schools appeared to be left to the IEF and NICIE.

In 1996, the IEF and NICIE sought a solution to the funding problem through the creation of a new loan facility involving a consortium of local banks called the Club Bank. This was another important milestone. The Club Bank would allow NICIE to take out substantial loans to build the schools in advance of full government funding and the IEF would act as guarantor. The main stipulation was that the loans could only be used to pay for sites and buildings for schools that had conditional approval from the Department of Education. This system was to take a considerable amount of pressure off the IEF, enabling it to look beyond the demands of capital build and to consider other important issues such as the growing need for preschool provision and the needs of more established schools for financial support to expand their resources. However, this new strategic approach soon faced enormous challenges. If government policy in the late 1980s and early 1990s was largely more favorable, the mid-1990s saw something of a reversal. The overall poor state of the school infrastructure in Northern Ireland and increased pressures on education budgets meant government policy shifted toward the transformation of existing nonintegrated schools to integrated status and against new school start-ups. The IEF, while supportive of transformation as one route to integration, saw another route effectively being closed. The enrollment number needed to qualify for recurrent funding for a new integrated school was increased from 60 to 100 pupils in a school's first year and the religious balance criteria was changed; now a school needed to have at least 30 percent of pupils from whichever was the minority community within the school. All this served to make the establishment of new integrated schools more difficult. This was at a time when Northern Ireland was at a critical point in its "peace process" as negotiations intensified leading up to the signing of the Good Friday/Belfast Agreement. The irony was that here were groups of parents actively seeking to establish shared schools for their children but not being supported by many of the politicians who were discussing the possibility of sharing government. The decision by the Department of Education to reject not one, but four development proposals threw down a gauntlet to the Integrated Education Movement and in particular to the IEF—could the IEF offer parents a lifeline by funding the schools independently?

The Independent Years and First IEF Development Plan, 1998–2008

The IEF response was to try and stand behind the parents, support their development proposals, and fund the four schools from whatever resources it had. Although the fund was in a position to just about provide, for a limited period, the necessary finance to support the schools opening as "independents," in doing so it was depleting its capital base, thus jeopardizing its own future. After a difficult period, government policy shifted again, and in a positive direction. The direct rule minister, Tony Worthington, reduced the required first year enrollment to 80 pupils for second level schools. The IEF's position and financial risk-taking were vindicated when all of the four schools were eventually approved for funding by the Department of Education. The four schools came at a heavy price. Almost £4.5 million in fact. The fund's capital base had been reduced to critical levels and financial support could no longer be guaranteed to any future new school start-ups, nor to developing the more established schools. However, for me, the most important fact was that four more integrated schools had been successfully established with the ines-capable reality that without such financial support all projects would surely have failed.

Alongside the day-to-day challenges of supporting these schools was the improving political situation culminating in the signing of the groundbreaking Good Friday/Belfast Agreement between the political parties. The newly formed Women's Coalition helped to ensure that the statutory duty to "encourage and facilitate" inte-grated education was enshrined in Section 13 of the agreement. This led to a series of Ministerial Working Groups on matters relating to integrated education but sadly with little in terms of tangible out-comes. However, the newly elected local assembly minister for educa-tion, Martin McGuinness of Sinn Fein, made an important policy change in favor of integrated schooling by reducing the number of first year pupils required for second level colleges to 50 and for pri-mary schools to 12; 2004 saw the biggest single annual increase in integrated schools.

The desire to present a forward-looking strategy, together with an urgent need to rebuild its capital base, led to the IEF's first for-mal strategic plan in 1998. This set out the fund's aim of raising £10 million to support the development and growth of integrated schools with an objective of reaching 10 percent of the school-going population by 2008. Included in the plan was a strategy for working closely with NICIE to build communications capacity and influence the political scene.

The plan presented a significant fundraising challenge: The £10 million required was to be raised through a Major Gift Fundraising Campaign from, effectively, a standing start. It required a significant investment in professional fundraising staff. Thankfully a major bene-factor, The Atlantic Philanthropies (which operated anonymously at that time), backed the strategy. Without doubt the IEF would not have been able to undertake its Development Campaign without such support. As in the early years of the fund, the impact of external philanthropic organizations was critical. The 10/10/10 Plan charted a course for strategic grant-making: programmes supporting parental demand for new integrated schools, transformation of existing non-integrated schools and support for the development of existing inte-grated schools, and pre-school provision.

IEF trustees set about recruiting a development board with for-mer Trinity Mirror Group chief executive David Montgomery at the helm. It would operate with volunteer groups established in London and Belfast, supported by professional staff, to create a peer-to-peer

network to attract supporters and donors. I feel the introduction
of Baroness May Blood as Campaign Chair in 2002 was a defining
moment. The baroness was someone not only willing and able to use
her influence and standing to open doors but also to walk through
them in order to gain support. Under her leadership the fundraising
drive gathered momentum and the daunting financial targets set out
in the Development Plan started to look achievable.

Naturally, as fundraising capacity developed so did grant-making. Thanks to the continued backing of Atlantic and the small
but growing number of new donors, the IEF was able to launch a
series of grant programs such as "Going for Growth" and "Meet
the Challenge." Parents continued to lead the charge in local communities and the IEF once again stood behind them with financial
guarantees, loans, and grants. Transforming schools also received
additional support. Significantly the IEF also chose to extend its
work to support all schools in Northern Ireland interested in developing cross-community contact, through its Promoting a Culture
of Trust (PACT) program. This was important in terms of not only
supporting worthy and important work but also positioning the
fund as an organization willing to reach out beyond the formal integrated school.

However, by attempting to fill the gap between government funding and what was required to develop integrated schools, was the fund
actually letting the government "off the hook"? Many of the fund's
donors recognized that a "twin track" strategy was needed—have
grant-making on the one hand and an effective lobbying campaign
on the other, both supported by fundraising. If significant policy
changes could be won then the need for the fund could diminish or
even disappear altogether, which I view as the ultimate achievement
for the IEF.

TOWARDS TOMORROW TOGETHER, 2009–2014

The IEF set out its second strategic plan entitled "Towards Tomorrow
Together (2009–2014)" with the vision of a Northern Ireland where
integration, not separation, was the norm in our education system.
The new development plan was open to exploring and supporting
other work beyond its PACT program. The new plan would also significantly increase the fund's broader advocacy work. While funders
and philanthropic organizations could provide support, ultimate success would depend on mainstreaming integration and that would
mean governmental policy change and funding commitments.

The new plan would have to be underpinned by a major and more ambitious fundraising drive but unfortunately it was also launched just before a period of global economic downturn. It was also a time of growing awareness of significant spare capacity in the schools estate. Put simply, Northern Ireland had too many schools belonging to different sectors, many with empty desks or crumbling and outdated school buildings. The IEF recognized that it would become increasingly important to provide evidence that more integration of the education system would make it more efficient. The raison d'être of integrated schools was of course better community relations, not saving money. However, if integrated education could have an economic as well as societal benefit, by reducing the need for separate schools largely catering to only one section of the community, then this could strengthen the IEF's argument.

The fund commissioned two pieces of research that were to have a significant impact—a scoping paper by Oxford Economics entitled "The Case for Shared Education" in 2010 and an independent survey of public opinion by Ipsos MORI in early 2011. Both served to provide further independent evidence of support for a more integrated and shared education system. Their timing also fed neatly into the run-up to local elections to the Northern Ireland assembly. Following the Oxford Economics report a groundbreaking speech by the leader of the largest Unionist party, Peter Robinson of the DUP, argued for a single education system, describing the current situation as "a benign form of apartheid." Some nationalist politicians and commentators viewed the speech as a veiled threat to Catholic schools and a sectarian attempt to remove funding for such schools. However, others acknowledged what appeared to be a seismic shift in thinking and noted the significance of the speech having been delivered by the First Minister of Northern Ireland. Robinson's speech and the political fallout that ensued served to put the issue of integrated and shared education firmly on the political agenda. Consequently, many political parties took positions on the issue in their election manifestos and pre-election literature. Candidates seemed to be starting to formulate policies and ideas that, broadly speaking, were supportive of change while acknowledging the contribution of the various distinct education sectors. I feel the advocacy activities of the fund, along with others, had contributed significantly to shaping the debate on separate education but we had yet to see evidence of policy change. Moreover, the Executive's Programme for Government was launched in 2011 and while committing itself to streamlining the various education authorities into one administrative body called the Education and

Skills Authority, it would retain an important role for the various "sectoral bodies" characterizing the education system. The promise of a new Ministerial Advisory Working Group on Shared Education could be viewed as another step in the right direction but certainly there could be no guarantees over what recommendations such a group might propose.

Meanwhile, alongside the new political debate, the fund continued to fulfill its prime function of supporting parents and schools seeking integrated education. A further grants program had been opened and the demand from existing schools wishing to grow to meet local need was significant. Cuts in public expenditure meant the Department of Education and the various Education and Library Boards were unable to invest significant capital funding in many of those schools that were in a position to grow. Once again the IEF sought to support such projects but fundraising challenges in a difficult economic climate meant not all schools could be granted the money they needed. A slowdown in the number of new school start-ups was evident—not surprising given the difficulties facing the education system as a whole and the likelihood that the government would not be approving any new schools. Hopes largely centered on transformations to integrated status as schools started to come to terms with the need for reorganization and restructuring and the inevitable closure of schools deemed unviable.

The IEF remains open to other potential models of integration that could develop between schools seeking to work more closely across the traditional divide. However the increasing use of the somewhat ambiguous term "shared education" by politicians and educationalists, as opposed to the legally defined "integrated education" has naturally posed challenges for the IEF. What does "shared" mean? How is it to be defined? Does it include integrated education? Is it merely about sharing resources or something more (or perhaps less)? I imagine these questions will continue to occupy the mind in the foreseeable future.

The IEF, as a financial foundation for integrated education, through administering grants and donations, has delivered enormous results to the Integrated Movement. Since 1998, thanks to the support of its donors, the fund has invested over £14 million in shared schooling. Through its grants to new schools, transforming schools, new preschools as well as existing integrated schools, it has helped the number of children in integrated education to increase from 11,910 in 1998 to more than 21,000 in 2011. This is an increase from 3 percent to 7 percent of school children. In addition, thousands more children in hundreds of schools of all management types have been supported in their cross-community activities.

MAIN CHALLENGES

As a financial foundation, the IEF clearly needs adequate funds to enable it to function effectively. The support of the endowing organizations made this possible in 1992. Despite a considerable capital base further funding was needed if the IEF was to meet the major need of providing school buildings in advance of full government support. Thus the support of the Department of Education in making further financial contributions and of the consortium of local banks in the lending process was crucial. The Club Bank arrangement enabled the integrated education movement to carry the financial risk of establishing new schools that had been approved by the Department of Education. However, the need for further funding became critical following the IEF decision to support the independent schools in the late 1990s and even more so when the IEF launched its strategic plans. Proactive fundraising, which can ultimately lead to a diversification of funding channels, has proved vital. The challenge of moving from being an organization using the interest raised from its capital base to make grants and loans to schools to being a fundraising organization was challenging but not without reward. New supporters brought fresh thinking and expertise—which would benefit advocacy strategies as well as grant-making.

Another major challenge facing the IEF was the generally hostile political environment. The integrated education movement was supporting initiatives in the absence of meaningful local political support. The cross-community Alliance Party, smaller loyalist political parties, and the Women's Coalition aside, there was no support for developing integrated education from any of the main political parties. As a consequence, the policy environment was always challenging.

This has meant that the development of integrated schools has remained community-led. While I believe it is vital that integrated education not be something that is imposed on people, qualified government support has clearly served to stifle growth as each new project demanded enormous effort from parents who had to struggle through the uncharted waters of their own local situation, supported by the IEF and NICIE. While the movement has countless pioneers to thank for demonstrating such vision and bravery, I feel that not everyone is a pioneer wishing to take on the formidable task of creating a new school from scratch—other parents are just as likely to accept the realities of separate education despite the regular independent surveys indicating widespread support for change. The road to transformation is equally challenging but in a different way—it takes a brave and courageous group of governors and/or principal and teachers to begin such a journey in what remains a divided society. Therefore a lack of political support has meant that growing and developing integrated education has been a bit-by-bit process rather than a great leap forward.

In financially supporting integrated schools, the IEF was clearly often placing itself at odds with the system and with the policies of the Department of Education, starkly illustrated by the example of the independent schools. The IEF was at times a thorn in the side of the officials, continually challenging the decision making of the department while, on a regular basis, there would be difficult issues requiring agreement such as the practicalities of a school site, accommodation needs, or approved enrollment numbers. Always looming in the background would be the issue of "impact on other schools." New build integrated schools naturally meant less children in a local area enrolling in the traditional Catholic maintained and state-controlled provision. The department tends to take a "neutral" position on such matters, trying to balance parental choice, its statutory duty to encourage and facilitate integrated education, and supporting schools of all sectors. I feel decisions to reject development proposals because of their potential impact on existing provision were difficult for the IEF to accept as this could be interpreted as denying parents the right to have their children educated together and, in effect, forcing children to attend existing nonintegrated provision.

Coupled with political resistance is the challenge of engaging with other education stakeholders keen to preserve their particular ethos or sector and to counter any accusation that separate, single faith–based education may harm social cohesion. I believe moving from separate, parallel education provision for Catholics and Protestants to a more shared and integrated system is unlikely to succeed without engagement and cooperation with other education providers along the way. Despite a track record in supporting schools of all types, I think the IEF's "motives" are still viewed with suspicion in some quarters, and therefore the IEF needs to demonstrate an openness to new ideas on how greater integration can be achieved and present itself as willing to engage with those of different opinions in the process. I don't believe, however, that this means sacrificing its continued support for the integrated model of schooling established over the past 30 years.

For me, especially as I engage with potential donors, the position of the churches toward integrated education is never far away from the discussion. Many are surprised to learn that Northern Ireland has separate teacher training colleges for the Catholic and state-controlled systems, and that the only derogation in fair employment law in the entire European Union is in Northern Ireland in relation to the appointment of teachers in schools. The Catholic Church suspicion is clearly a major barrier to any serious systemic change envisaged by supporters of integrated education. I believe that any significant change in the position of the church will only ever come about by an internally agreed major change of direction, by negotiation and compromise with other sectors, or through a major policy change by the government. Some believe government intervention would be tantamount to imposition and the church would resist such steps strongly. The IEF favors incentivization, not imposition, and that makes sense to me.

Meeting the demand for increasing integrated provision is difficult. Funds are clearly limited and not all applications made by schools or groups can be supported. I feel this can create a degree of resentment among those who are turned down for grants as they understandably feel their particular school or project is worthy of support. Such a problem is clearly not unique to the IEF but I feel it is important that the IEF increases the level of understanding among potential beneficiaries who may hold the mistaken belief that the fund has its own endless resources or is even a government-funded body. Toward the middle of the last decade, the IEF was faced with the difficult decision as to whether it should continue to fund independent schools that had little or no chance of ever becoming fully funded by the government. The IEF provided one school with the opportunity to open independently and campaign for approval and another school with an opportunity to reach viability. However, it became apparent that, despite enormous efforts, neither school could achieve government funding and, unfortunately, it became necessary for the IEF to end its financial backing. It would have been impossible to continue funding both schools with no end in sight. Despite experiencing the sadness of the beneficiaries, and the impact on the communities affected, such decisions had to be taken, and have been the hardest decisions faced by the IEF. I know the donors involved also found these decisions difficult. However, the IEF must act responsibly in managing not only donations but also the hopes and expectations of both beneficiaries and donors, providing professional reporting and undertaking risk assessment of its activities—challenging but vitally important elements of the fund's work.

LESSONS LEARNED BY THE IEF

The first lesson we have learned is not to underestimate parent power! Parents have been at the forefront of integrated education in Northern Ireland. Their passion, dedication, bravery, and vision won the hearts and minds of many influential organizations and people who, in turn, continue to find ways to help them.

Second, we recognize the benefits of external support and fundraising. Integrated schools and the IEF could not have developed without the support of external organizations such as the Nuffield Foundation, Joseph Rowntree Charitable Trust, and the European Union. The continuing support from international philanthropic organizations such as The Atlantic Philanthropies and The Ireland Funds have, together with countless others, made a huge impact and are helping the IEF to become a sustainable financial foundation supporting educational change. However, I feel some people can be very suspicious of well-intentioned "outsiders"; the IEF has learnt that no matter how small the donation, support "at home" adds tremendous weight and power to the message that in turn can even help to convince larger international funders too. Without raising additional funds since its creation, the IEF would have remained limited in its scope and impact, and integrated schools could not have grown as steadily or effectively. Fundraising has provided opportunities to extend the scope of grant-making as well as to contribute to building a wider support base.

Our third lesson is that individuals can make a difference. It is important to build relationships with those you believe can help your work. In fundraising, the IEF has benefited from the support of many individuals—too numerous to mention.

Fourth, we acknowledge the power of smaller parties/groups. In Northern Ireland, the smaller loyalist parties helped not only secure the support of many ex-paramilitary prisoners (helping to dispel the myth that integrated education was just for the liberal middle classes) but the Women's Coalition also ensured integrated education was part of the Good Friday/Belfast Agreement.

Next we recognize the need for communication and lobbying. Funding is needed primarily because of gaps or limitations in government funding; therefore the need to advance changes in government policy, which will ultimately reduce the need for funding in the first place, makes sense. Few donors wish to see the need for their support continuing forever and understandably expect advocacy strategies to address the problem.

Independent research and evidence is vital to gain support. It can help demonstrate the public will for change to politicians, decision-makers, and funders, as well as provide independent evidence that integration works. Demonstrating the added value of integration and the benefits it can bring can help encourage existing schools to change. If you can evidence the potential for economic benefits then you are more likely to secure the interest of policy-makers constrained by fiscal pressures and budgets.

Finally, do not be discouraged! Legislation and political reality can be frustrating. Favorable legislation and policy changes can clearly impact positively on local situations but change is still slow. Despite the Dunleath Act in 1978, the 1989 Education Reform Order, and the 1998 Good Friday/Belfast Agreement there was no sudden shift toward favoring integrated education over separate education. Our final lesson is that we all need to be in this for the long haul.

3

CHANGING OUR REALITY

THE INTEGRATED BILINGUAL ARABIC-HEBREW EDUCATION IN ISRAEL

Inas Deeb and Nadia Kinani

For generations, the continuation of the Israeli-Palestinian conflict has reinforced hatred and opposing senses of destiny, mistrust, and negative stereotypes on both sides (Bar-Tal, 1997; Slone, Tarrasch, & Hallis, 2000; Teichman & Zafrir, 2003). It is little wonder that to this very day, Palestinian and Jewish citizens of Israel live in separate towns and neighborhoods and send their children to separate schools, and experience totally different lifestyles in two diverse societies. The limited occasions on which they meet are primarily for formal services, rarely for communal interaction. Ironically enough, the only site at which both Jews and Palestinians can share the same pain and worry is the hospital, where we are reminded that, ultimately, we are all mortal and human.

Over the last two decades, however, a new educational bilingual (Hebrew and Arabic) and binational initiative has been established in Israel, allowing members of both groups to learn together and experience something like a shared community. The first initiative was the Neve Shalom / Wahat A-Salam School, which takes its name from the town in which it was founded in 1984. In 1997, Hand in Hand: The Center for Arab-Jewish Education (HIH) was founded as a formal nongovernmental organization (NGO) in order to establish bilingual schools, eventually establishing four such schools throughout Israel, and thus creating an alternative to the official, mainstream, segregated educational system. HIH has recently initiated a process to establish new schools, one of which opened in the fall of 2012 as a preschool in Haifa. In this chapter we will analyze how this bilingual Arabic-Hebrew program is implemented in an integrated Palestinian-Jewish educational system, focusing specifically on HIH's Jerusalem school, the Max Rayne Bilingual School. We have chosen to examine five areas that we believe are of particular significance and that we hope may offer some insight and assistance to other educational practitioners, policy makers, and managers who are experiencing similar challenges on their own road to integration and peace. The five areas are as follows: *our understanding of integrated education; the practical implementation of the bilingual model; the controversial anniversaries and marking of national days; the school as a community;* and the *balance of power between key stakeholders.*

BACKGROUND ON AUTHORS AND SCHOOL CONTEXT

Like many other Palestinians from small Arab towns and villages, both authors moved to Jerusalem immediately after completing their higher education and settled into this complicated, mysterious, and charming city. Many young Palestinian couples do not return to the villages and small towns they grew up in, preferring instead to stay in the bigger cities where there are better job opportunities. Both authors were born and raised in the same town, but met for the first time only in 2000 at the bilingual integrated kindergarten that had recently opened in Jerusalem. They brought their young daughters to their first day at the school. They were both in the same class at the bilingual Max Rayne "Hand in Hand" high school. When it began, there were only two classes in the school, with a total of 25 Palestinian and Jewish children and four teachers. The entire initiative was a huge dream, a daunting challenge, too good to be true! There was considerable skepticism, and few people believed it would be possible. Today, 13 years later, the Jerusalem school has 550 students enrolled from prekindergarten through twelfth grade and 75 members of staff.

Nadia could have easily found a teaching position in any of the Arab schools in the city; instead she chose a more demanding direction: teaching at the bilingual school in Jerusalem. She began her professional career at the HIH school in 1999 as the first grade homeroom teacher, sharing responsibilities for all subjects with her Jewish co-teacher. It was Nadia's first experience in co-teaching, in teaching both Jewish and Palestinian pupils, and in developing bilingual and bicultural materials. In fact, Nadia's involvement and contribution to this bilingual initiative was evident in the different stages of her career that moved side by side with the development of the school—as a teacher, as a leading staff, as the school vice principal, and, in the last three years, as the school principal.

From 1992 to 2008, Inas was the Educational Coordinator at the pedagogical training center for Palestinian teachers in East Jerusalem schools. She was very critical of this educational system that promoted mainly teacher-centered pedagogy and allowed little dialogue, self-learning, or pupil-centered methodologies. At the same time, Inas was cautiously observing the bilingual school in Jerusalem where she was an active parent involved in different school committees, learning about the school's strengths and weaknesses. Three years ago, in 2010, Inas became the Educational Director at the HIH center where she works together with the school faculty on leveraging the different aspects of the bilingual model.

THE DEVELOPMENT OF OUR UNDERSTANDING OF INTEGRATED EDUCATION

Integrated education is a broad and constantly developing concept within the HIH context. When the schools were first established, the understanding of integrated education was preliminary and even naïve. In the early years, it meant mainly having Jewish and Palestinian children learn together in the same class; learning the different school subjects in two languages with two teachers who are, respectively, native speakers of those two languages; and learning about each other's heritage and to respect each other's religions and cultures. The desire was to create fully egalitarian bilingual educational environments by engaging both Palestinian and Jewish teaching staff and by the equal use of Arabic and Hebrew in these teaching environments.

However, many important questions and issues regarding the actual implementation of this model were ambiguous and confusing. Teachers lacked the experience or training to teach in the two languages. This was a pioneering endeavor, both pedagogically and societally. Teachers had to prepare their own bilingual materials, struggle with challenging day-to-day issues, and many times take crucial decisions concerning the right teaching practices . With hard work and assertive will, both the school administration and the teaching staff learned from everyone's pitfalls and gained better knowledge and experience with time.

Today, the school leadership perceives integrated education in a more comprehensive and nuanced manner. It has become clearer to the school administration that achieving a fully egalitarian bilingual education is an implausible goal for various reasons, many of which are described in this chapter. Yet, this realization does not hinder the school faculty from striving for increasingly higher achievements at various academic and social levels, and achieving various significant measures toward egalitarianism. It became clear that viable approaches were needed to address the key areas that lie at the core of integrated education in practice, which the remainder of this chapter analyzes.

Integrated Bilingual Education in Practice

To address bilingual education in the larger context, we first have to examine the different key areas mentioned above and understand how each affects the other as they are interconnected. When one of these areas is insufficiently addressed, it will affect the degree of impact of the other components and the general implementation of integrated education in all school aspects. One must first understand the unique status and dynamics of the two different languages—Arabic and Hebrew—inside and outside school limits. Both Arabic and Hebrew are official languages in Israel, but the regular activities of the State of Israel and of Israeli society in general does not take place in both languages. Hebrew is the language of the controlling majority and is, for all intents and purposes, the only language in Israeli civil life. It is the language of the bureaucracy, of higher education, of the majority of local media, and of the labor market. The status accorded to Arabic is still devoid of practical importance in public life. Arabic is important not in general society, but in the lives of an internal minority (Amara, 2005). These facts indeed make the implementation of the bilingual model in schools a more challenging and complex matter.

A central aspect is of course that of the language of classroom instruction. For example, which classes should—or could—be taught only in Arabic, only in Hebrew, or in both languages? What is the educational rationale for having two teachers, each representing her/his culture, religion, and world to a bilingual classroom? In which classes or subject areas should the school have two teachers—Jewish and Palestinian—teaching together at the time? Are there subjects that pragmatism suggests are better taught in the society's dominant language? A related question is the composition of the classroom per subject area. Are there subjects and occasions where it is better to split the class and teach to a mono-ethnical group? And inevitably, what language is finally used in the classroom will also be determined by the number of teachers who are actually fluent in both languages, as opposed to those who can only speak one language, which in this case is true for the Jewish teachers who are fluent only in Hebrew. In the process of trying to achieve concrete answers to these questions on a daily basis in the classroom, the bilingual model undertaken at HIH schools has undergone dramatic changes over the years, specifically with regard to the acquisition of Arabic as a native language among Palestinian pupils and among Jewish pupils as a second language. In the beginning, Arabic and Hebrew were taught without separating the Jewish and Palestinian children, who studied all subjects, including language, together. This approach was agreed upon enthusiastically by the parents and school administration, who did not want to separate the Jewish and Arab students, even if for pedagogical reasons, as they feared it would mirror the separation that exists generally in Israel. However, after several years of teaching both languages jointly, the educators realized that the Arab pupils' level of Arabic as a mother tongue fell below that of pupils in Israeli Arab schools. Moreover, the functional level of Arabic among the Jewish pupils was also lower than could be expected.

It is important to explain that this is not just because Hebrew is the dominant language, but also because Arabic is a diglossic language, that is, the spoken and the literary language are dramatically different, making it almost two different languages. Furthermore, Arabic dialects can differ considerably across Arabic-speaking countries, as well as among regions and cities within countries. Therefore, achieving high levels of language proficiency are challenging not just for those learning it as a second language but even for those for whom it is the mother tongue.

Thus, after the first few years of implementation it was decided to separate Jewish and Palestinian students in some of the language classes in order to strengthen Arabic as a first language for the Palestinian students and as a second language for the Jewish students. At the same time, it is not difficult to acquire Hebrew in school, either as a first or a second language, and both the Jewish and Palestinian students read, write, speak, and understand Hebrew at all required levels. Today the Jewish students in all bilingual schools study Arabic as a second language separately from the Palestinian pupils. The classes are individually tailored to their capabilities, with an emphasis on the spoken language rather than the literary language, enriching vocabulary, grammar, and writing at the appropriate level. After the pedagogical change, internal findings showed a marked improvement in the achievements of Arabic as a first language and indicated that Jewish pupils had also achieved progress in the use of Arabic as a spoken language. Nonetheless, the school and NGO still feel that the level of achievement could be higher and are looking to further improve the pedagogical methodology.

Another pivotal factor in terms of creating both an integrated and bilingual school is the number of pupils from each ethnic group. HIH schools strive for equal numbers of Jews and Arabs in every classroom; however, for a wide range of reasons, this is not always feasible. This factor however plays into the ability of the school and the teacher of a given class to effectively create bilingual students.

An additional question is at what point is it desirable, or feasible, to expect not just that every classroom and every student are bilingual, but also that every teacher is bilingual? All the Palestinian teachers speak both Arabic and Hebrew, while most of the Jewish staff members are not fluent in Arabic. This limits the degree of parity envisioned in the bilingual teaching model. In the current situation, the Palestinian teachers are forced to use Hebrew in classes, at work, in social meetings, and in the ongoing everyday discourse when working directly with their Jewish colleagues. When Jewish teachers attain proficiency in Arabic, then the chances of having a fully egalitarian bilingual lesson will be more attainable. To address this issue the school offers Arabic lessons to staff and parents; however, these lessons, while important, take place on a weekly basis for a few hours, which is not enough to attain fluency. Effective long-term solutions require far more extensive investments of time, training, and resources.

An additional area is the cultural competence of the teaching staff. Even if teachers are not all fully bilingual, which may not be realistic to expect at this stage, they are expected to become sensitive to and be able to acknowledge and respect, and ultimately be fluent in the cultural context of each side. Jewish and Palestinian teachers enroll in this school system with teaching certification for a monolingual classroom. Unquestionably, joining the bilingual school staff requires not only superlative teaching methods that can be used with bilingual children who come from different cultures, ethnicities, and religions, but also the willingness to invest extensive time and energy to learning more about the other, to being open to diversity and for dialogue with the other, and to being able to tolerate ambiguous situations. The school and NGO tackle this important need through efforts such as ongoing dialogue and discussions with all teachers on different controversial topics, and by providing all new teachers an intensive two-day orientation to foster interest in and respect for the other. The school administration matches each novice teacher with another experienced teacher as a coach and mentor. Increasing cultural competence and sensitivity is not easy and many times it can be only achieved to some degree. Therefore, when a teacher, either Palestinian or Jewish, is not able to achieve cultural competence and sensitivity, some decide to quit and go to the regular, segregated school system where they feel more comfortable. There is no academic preparation or certification available to achieve cultural competence, only on-the-job training. The school faculty is therefore pioneers in this field.

Curriculum

In addition to the language of instruction and the composition of the faculty and student body, a bilingual integrated model is defined fundamentally by the way it manages and conveys core questions of culture and community. The Ministry of Education curricula are geared toward specific populations within Israel (secular Jews, Orthodox Jews, Arabs, and so on) and are not geared for a mixed population of Jews and Palestinians. This was felt keenly during the early years of the school's existence. It was therefore decided not to use the Ministry of Education textbooks but instead to create a curriculum congruent with the school's ideology and values. At a later stage the faculty realized that this task was extremely difficult and that there was not enough time to create completely new teaching materials in all subjects. The school does not set out to teach an official version of what is "right"; it aims to facilitate the meeting of and dialogue between the accepted truths of different groups, and thus to show students the complexity of reality and the existence of viewpoints and perspectives that differ from their own and from what they know. The school's unique curriculum is in the process of development and consolidation. Beyond the basic curriculum required by the Ministry of Education, a special educational program has been developed, with the support of the HIH NGO, that addresses the uniqueness of the school and its ideology. A local team of professionals works with teachers and school principals to develop specific materials and curriculum in religious studies, civic education, history, and cultural heritage that represents the unique areas of the integrated model.

Controversial Anniversaries and Marking National Days at School

The school instills among its students and staff respect for the customs and holidays of all cultures, nationalities, and religions represented within it (Palestinian and Israeli, Jewish, Muslim, and Christian), based on the values of tolerance and mutual regard. Marking the National Days is based on the principle that the school is a place for Jewish and Palestinian children to meet together in a framework of equality, in acknowledgment of each other's diversities, fears, and misunderstandings, which will strengthen tolerance and respect and reduce prejudices. The actual implementation of these values and principles within the daily school setting is not easy and requires significant organization and preparation. This is particularly evident in the school's efforts to acknowledge the National Days.

The National Days that are commemorated by the bilingual schools include three government-mandated days: Holocaust and Heroism Day, which pays tribute to the memory of the six million Jews murdered by the Nazis before and during World War II; Remembrance Day, in memory of the Israel Defense Forces soldiers killed in service in Israel's wars; and Independence Day, denoting the establishment of the State of Israel. In addition, the school community holds activities that acknowledge two Palestinian memorial days: Land Day, marking the March 30, 1976, protest in which Israeli security forces killed six Palestinian citizens, commemorated annually in Israel with rallies, conferences, strikes, and demonstrations against the continuing policies of land expropriation; and Nakba Day, on which Palestinians acknowledge the Nakba, the catastrophic destruction of their homeland in 1948 when, in the wake of the war, 750 thousand local Palestinians became refugees and many of their villages were destroyed (Khaldi, 2001).

The National Days begin with Land Day on March 30 and end with Nakba Day on May 15. The HIH staff always approach these days with some degree of trepidation, as these days, with their inherently contradictory meanings to Jews and Arabs, are inevitably challenging. No matter how the administration copes with these days, sometimes the gap in the world views of teachers from both groups is just too great to overcome. The result is that they continue to work and be together, even as they experience dissonance regarding these broader questions. In the framework of our work, the school administration invests significant effort in working with the staff, and especially in strengthening relationships between the pairs of co-teachers who work together in the same classroom. The school staff, veterans, and newcomers, prepare for the National Days in team meetings where their own national and group identity are discussed and in preparatory educational deliberations on the nature of the ceremonies and their educational content as geared for different ages at different levels.

In the authors' opinion, although the concept and ideology behind the school is revolutionary, especially in a society where meaningful integration between Jews and Palestinians is almost nonexistent, it is still very difficult for much of the school community to make significant changes, particularly in relation to the commemoration of the National Days. The administration always emphasizes to the faculty that they should not assume responsibility for resolving the decades-long conflict or place it on the shoulders of parents and pupils.

The school encourages meetings between parents of various classes. Such commitment is felt vibrantly each year, after the Nakba Day ceremony when Jewish and Palestinian parents join the school in an emotional march to one of the confiscated villages and hear the story of the people who lived there and were expelled, deprived of their lands and their homes. A gathering such as this, together with other social events, strengthens relations between Jewish and Palestinian families beyond the day-to-day school practices.

THE ROLE OF PARENTS AS A COMMUNITY

The school views parents as important partners in the decision-making process, and as vital human resource for enriching the educational process and making a change in the community. The school encourages social meetings among the school community to enhance understanding and knowledge of each other's cultures, with parents participating in a variety of forums and committees as a contribution to the school. Parent committees in each class organize joint activities for both children and their parents, and the school's central PTA is an active body that meets frequently and works in conjunction with the staff to promote the school's ethos and address specific problems. Nevertheless, the school administration is careful not to allow parents to interfere in pedagogical matters that should remain under the school's professional supervision.

The role of the parents does not end with participating in different school activities; it extends instead to making real changes and ensuring the future existence of the school. In the last two years, 2011 and 2012, parents offered a helping hand to school administration to ensure that enough Jewish students stay in the school for the middle school or junior high school period to ensure continuation of the model. Last year, 2012, thanks to full cooperation between the school administration, the teachers, and the parents' committees, nearly all the Jewish and Palestinian students went on to seventh grade. This successful experience is evidence that these schools cannot last long without full parental commitment and support.

The intensive changes, developments, and learning that occurred in the endeavor's first decade, have brought HIH to the latest stage of expanded vision and scope. The recent direction taken by HIH of establishing new schools and beginning to work at the adult community level is based on the assumption that the bilingual schools present an excellent educational pathway as well as a viable underpinning to multicultural social life in Israel. Yet, this pathway to shared citizenship can be further fostered with committed adults who can make a change. The NGO and the schools, together with parents, are now planning to systematically enlarge the scope of the organization's influence from the school children into the surrounding community. Vibrant and efficient networking between the different communities/schools is expected to elevate the desired change in Israeli society from the local level of experience to the national level of influence. HIH believes that parents and other interested adults already involved in community activities centering around the schools should institutionalize their activity, so as to create an organized, joint Jewish-Arab social structure in addition to, not in place of, each community's particular life in Israel.

Balance of Power between Stakeholders

The development of the HIH integrated bilingual model cannot be understood without an analysis of the interplay over time between the key stakeholders: the schools, as embodied by the professional management and faculty; the HIH NGO; the parents; and the Ministry of Education. Throughout the development of this model these four players have each been instrumental in developing the model's ideology, pedagogy, and resource base. Naturally each player has their own interests, priorities, and concerns. At different periods there have been varying degrees of alignment between the key stakeholders in the areas of ideology, pedagogy, and resource acquisition. Some degree of competition and conflict is natural; however in our decade and a half of experience, there have been too many risks of the endeavor being suppressed in its entirety. Establishing and implementing such an endeavor requires full cognizance of this challenge and a willingness to invest in managing these dynamics.

Conclusion

Indeed, we believe that integration requires a wide range of policies, practices, and pedagogies for students to learn to live together while attaining their full potential, both academically and socially. It involves building skills, values, and attitudes; constructing a longitudinal process of integration in respect of language, culture, and social norms; and a bi-national curriculum among teachers, who need first to understand the meaning of integration and then be able to transfer this to students. Every day that goes by changes the reality, breaks the regular rigid norms, and brings another sign of success. Integrated education in Israel becomes a reality even for many who still disagree with its cause and mission. We have learned that the bilingual schools cannot exist for long if they are only institutions led by an ideology that fosters multicultural education; they cannot fall behind other schools in terms of scholastic achievement but must attain consistently higher standards in all aspects of education. Undoubtedly, managing this program requires a powerful vision and the ideological commitment of the key stakeholders. To ensure that ideology and pedagogy are on par, the different key areas affecting integrated education must undergo constant evaluation and adaptation. This will eventually ensure stability and growth. Strong staff with pronounced leadership abilities shape and sustain superior educational values and solid school achievements. Every day we remind ourselves—students, parents, and staff alike—that the fact that we live together and are involved in undertaking a great mission for meaningful coexistence between Jews and Palestinians in Israel in the face of ongoing conflicts and complex political situations should not to be taken for granted.

ACKNOWLEDGMENT

We wish to thank two leading people in our organization for their contributions, time, thoughtful analysis, and insights to this chapter—Shalom (Shuli) Dichter, the executive director of HIH, and Rebecca Bardach, the Director of Resource Development and Strategy. Special thanks to Rebecca for the endless hours that she spent working with us to bring all of this together and to convey a deep and honest analysis of our experience in developing the integrated bilingual model at HIH.

REFERENCES

Amara, M. (2005). *The bilingual model in the Hand-in-Hand integrated schools.* Hand-in-Hand Publication—Center for Jewish and Arab Education in Israel, p. 29.

Bar-Tal, D. (1997). Formation and change of ethnic and national stereotypes: An integrative model. *International Journal of Intercultural Relations, 21,* 491–523.

Khaldi, W. (Ed.). (2001). *All that remains: The Palestinian villages occupied and depopulated by Israel in 1948.* Institute for Palestinian Studies.

Slone, M., Tarrasch, R., & Hallis, D. (2000). Ethnic stereotypic attitudes among Israeli children: Two intervention programs. *Merrill-Palmer Quarterly, 46,* 370–389.

Teichman, Y., & Zafrir, H. (2003). Images held by Jewish and Arab children in Israel of people representing their own and the other group. *Journal of Cross-Cultural Psychology, 34,* 658–676.

4

ON THE PEACE LINE

THE EXPERIENCE OF AN INTEGRATED SCHOOL

Noreen Campell

INTEGRATED EDUCATION: BEGINNINGS

As chief executive of the Northern Ireland Council for Integrated Education (NICIE), I am often asked to explain the development of the integrated education movement. There is much interest in what is seen as a unique process in the history of education. Why, there being a choice of publicly funded schools, would anyone embark on the unprecedented, challenging journey of creating a new school? Why would a teacher with a secure career in an established school leave that post to work in a school started by a parents' group, where salary is not guaranteed, and in the knowledge that it might be difficult to return to more established institutions?

My experience in integrated education as both parent and teacher, reaching back to its inception 30 years ago, enables me to suggest some answers. My interest in integrated education stemmed from my concerns as a parent and from my professional interest as an educator. My husband and I had both attended single-sex, Catholic, selective schools. As parents of four boys, growing up in the 1970s and 1980s, our priority was to secure for them an education that did not define them either by religious background or cultural identity and that did not limit their expectations and experiences. It was equally important to us that their school should be co-educational. No school matched those needs. As parents, the development of integrated schools offered a solution to these dilemmas.

As an educator, I was committed to the concept of inclusion. In 1973, I started my teaching career in an all-boys Catholic secondary school. This was a traditional school, hierarchical and authoritarian that, for me, typified the problems of a segregated and selective educational system. Twelve years' experience of this school shaped my educational philosophy and led me to reject the practices I found there.

The pioneering parents and teachers, myself included, who became involved in the establishment of integrated schools did so primarily because we rejected the divisions that existed at every level of society between the two major traditions, Protestant and Catholic. These divisions were reflected in the structures of society, including a segregated educational system, and were expressed through ongoing violence. More than a gesture of rejection, these parents were also proclaiming hope for a different type of society. They wanted their children to be educated together. They believed that in creating an integrated model of education they would show that it was possible for the "two sides" to live and work together, that division was not the only answer, and they were doing so by working together themselves to make their vision a reality.

Characteristics of Integrated Education

In her opening address at the inaugural conference of the Integrated Peace Education Global Network, Claire McGlynn offered a definition of integrated education as the education together, in equal numbers, of children, who are more usually educated separately and that provides opportunities to develop respect and understanding for alternative cultures. As such integration is interpreted as a way of mixing, of living interdependently, and participating fully in a shared society, while maintaining cultural distinctiveness.

This definition captures both the motivation and aims of the early founders of integrated education in Northern Ireland. The underpinning principles of integrated education had been formulated prior to the establishment in 1981 of the first integrated school in Northern Ireland, Lagan College. Spencer (2005) outlines the three main characteristics that became the underpinning principles of integrated schools. He distinguishes between assimilation and integration, emphasizing the importance of equal recognition of the religious and cultural identities of both major traditions. Integrated education was designed to be Christian in character, in recognition that the overwhelming majority of the population was Christian. Parental involvement was to be paramount.

These key principles continue to underpin the rationale for integrated education and have shaped the development of the 40 existing grant-maintained integrated schools. To these characteristics were added the adoption of the principles of all-ability and co-education. NICIE, established in 1987 to act as an umbrella body for the new schools, captured these characteristics in its statement of principles to which new schools subscribed. When this statement of principles was revised in 2007 these characteristics were retained as the defining elements of integration (NICIE, 2012). However, each school—shaped by a combination of founding parents, location, and specific circumstances—interpreted these characteristics in its own unique way.

The Hazelwood primary and post-primary schools were founded in 1985. This extension of integrated education was not without controversy as the founding organization supporting Lagan College, All Children Together, argued that the time was not right for further growth. A new trust, Belfast Charitable Trust for Integrated Education (BELTIE), supported the two new schools. The officers of the trust, the parents' group, and the newly appointed teachers developed a distinctive Hazelwood approach to integration. As parent and educator, I was a part of the process of discussion and development.

The schools were located in north Belfast. In west and east Belfast, there exist large, geographically separated communities of Protestants and Catholics. In north Belfast, religious segregation manifests itself in smaller enclaves, separated by the so-called peace walls, tall barriers that keep Protestant and Catholic communities apart. It was an area marked by regular outbursts of intercommunal violence. More than six hundred sectarian murders had taken place in north Belfast during the "Troubles."¹ The area was also marked by high unemployment and deprivation.

In 1985, the year Hazelwood Integrated College was founded, there was a shift in demographics, with Protestant families leaving the area. Six state, de facto Protestant, schools closed and amalgamated in 1985, reflecting this shift. Despite a number of empty school buildings, the local education authority refused to make a vacant building available to the new school. The first year of the school was spent in warehouse premises belonging to the Co-operative Society. Only pressure from the United Kingdom government in Westminster resulted in the grounds of a recently closed state school being made available at the end of that first year.

The school was opposed by many: the local education authority that had just closed five post primary schools was opposed to its opening; the Catholic Church was opposed to the concept of integration, putting pressure on Catholic parents who were supporting the new schools; and there was no financial backing for the schools other than the funds raised by the supporting trust, BELTIE. It was in such hostile circumstances that both Hazelwood schools were founded.

THE HAZELWOOD COLLEGE "CONTEXTUAL" MODEL

Early discussions between parents, trustees, and newly appointed staff established the distinctive parameters in which the school would operate. The school would engage openly with issues of difference. While being Christian in character, it would reflect this through a value-based approach to education, rather than an overtly ecumenical approach such as had been adopted in the first integrated college, where two chaplains had been appointed as staff members. It would be inclusive: co-educational, all-ability, and welcoming to those with special needs. The school would be child-centered, focused on meeting the needs of individual children. This, it was argued, would lift the ceiling of aspiration for every child and ensure high levels of academic success. Partnership and positive relationships with parents were core to the enterprise. The parents' voice had structural expression through the parents' council and through representation on the board of governors.

Influenced by the ideas of Carl Rodgers, the first principal of the school, and myself, founding teacher and appointed vice principal in 1986, developed an ethos based on a holistic, value-based concept of education. Our aim was to create an environment based on empathy, openness, trust, and acceptance, one that would promote the self-esteem of each individual, one that would create conditions that would allow for the exploration of difference and the development of mutual respect. The aim was to create a school ethos in which all of the strands were interlinked and underpinned by this clear philosophy of education. The same degree of attention was to be given to the construction of the "hidden curriculum" as to the formal curriculum.

The formal curriculum was a given. Although in 1985, the Northern Ireland curriculum had not been introduced, there was an examination system and a set of expectations that defined what was taught. Nonetheless, the Hazelwood curriculum was designed to reflect the underpinning philosophy. Drama, seen as a vehicle for developing empathy, was to be taught to all children until the end of third year. Religious education would be broadly based, teaching the common strands of Christianity. Where necessary, special provision would be made for Catholic students, particularly for preparation for the sacrament of confirmation, and a module of "moral" education was introduced for all to develop a capacity for moral reasoning.

The Irish language would be taught, but as a subject of choice, and another bespoke module, Ulster Studies, was developed to explore cultural background. An element of choice was built into the curriculum through the introduction of a menu of activities on Friday afternoons and an "enrichment fortnight" at the end of every school year, in which student choice was a key factor.

The hidden curriculum, the working structure of the school, was consciously constructed to ensure that the principles of integrated education would be secured and expressed through the lived experience of the individual student. An exposition of the philosophy of Hazelwood outlined this "contextual model" in which the school operated (Rowley, 1993).

This contextual model determined the construction of the learning environment. The principles of equality and integration were expressed through mixed ability classes that were also constructed to reflect the religious balance in the school. There was a focus on the personal and social development of the child as well as on academic development. The code of behavior was based on a "non-punitive" approach—inappropriate behavior was to be an opportunity for learning rather than punishment, and teachers and support staff were to role-model the type of behavior they wished to see. Students and teachers were to be on first name terms, symbolizing the importance of personal relationships in the life of the school (a radical innovation in a conservative education system). A pastoral system based on strong relationships between teacher, child, and parent was developed.

Just as the school aimed to be a microcosm of the society we wished to promote, each class was to be a microcosm of the school: balanced by religious/cultural background, gender, and ability. To ensure effective teaching, classes would be small, with no more than 23 children per class. Pupils would have a voice through a students' council; expression of difference would be encouraged; mistakes would be seen as an opportunity for learning, not punishment; and personal, social, and academic learning were to be seen as mutually supportive, underpinning, and promoting academic achievement.

The crucial role of parents was recognized and a calendar of events was created to give expression to the school's aims and to which parents and the local community were invited. A parents' council gave parents a voice in the school and there was significant parental representation on the board of governors. This open approach allowed parents to engage in debates about school policy, particularly as they related to contentious issues. This open, welcoming approach enabled parents to feel a part of, and included in, the school community. An ongoing program of staff development supported staff in exploring their own bias. Through a collaborative and respectful approach to management, teachers were encouraged to model the values that permeated the school. Relationships were built around personal interactions, as symbolized by the use of first names, rather than formalities of role and hierarchy. Teachers understood that the school used an approach in which roles were replaced by relationships.

Early experience taught us that in order to create the safe space in which students could deal with controversial issues, it was necessary to create that same safe space for staff to reflect and to build trust with each other. The ongoing violence on the streets, impacting as it did the lives of our students, ensured we could not avoid divisive issues. There was much debate on how we might deal with these. Equally there was much debate about teaching and learning. There were many debates about the practice of all-ability versus streaming, and about a policy of inclusion that worked to keep students in the system rather than exclude them if they were difficult.

HAZELWOOD COLLEGE: THE STUDENTS' EXPERIENCE

It was the intention of management that our students would love school, that they would feel a sense of belonging and loyalty, that they would feel safe and respected. We aimed to create a community in which students had a voice and felt accepted regardless of their background. We believed that the mission of Hazelwood as an integrated school was important; we wanted our students to share that sense of mission. The sense of playing a larger role was critical in supporting students as they negotiated the conflict of loyalty between home, neighborhood, and school. Leaving an area that felt constantly under threat, to come to learn alongside the "other,'" demanded courage from families and from young people. The school recognized this and gave the students an opportunity to explore the conflict of loyalties that might emerge.

Opportunities were created to engage with students about conflict: the school was an open house to world media and that media had uncensored access to students. At the time of the first ceasefires in 1994, a French TV production company spent four months filming the school and broadcasting from the school every day. This often created a controversy and the subsequent debate was encouraged and facilitated. This exposure to the media and to a range of visitors underlined to all that our work had societal importance. The National Commission on Education, established to identify characteristics of successful schools, selected Hazelwood College as an example of such a school (National Commission on Education, 1996). They commented on the ethos, which they found to be clear and unambiguous and which united staff, students, and parents in a shared sense of mission. They noted that this ethos was put into practice on a daily basis through the college structures. They found staff-student relationships open, friendly, positive, and characterized by trust and respect. The use of ritual to celebrate both the achievements of integrated education and the individual achievements of students and staff was recognized as a factor that contributed to the success of the school (National Commission on Education, 1996). It was this set of embedded values and approaches that enabled Hazelwood to navigate the many years of "troubles" that impacted significantly on the area in which the school was situated.

A SCHOOL TESTED, 2001–2002

During the first 20 years of the college, many violent events tested its strength. The year 2001–2002 was such a one. This dispute was centered in the Ardoyne area of Belfast, a nationalist area separated from Protestant neighbors by a peace wall. A conflict developed, and quickly escalated, between the residents of a loyalist area that lay on the route to the entrance of a local Catholic primary school and the pupils and parents of the school. In June 2001, loyalists began to blockade the Catholic primary school. Riot police were deployed to escort children through the picket line. Tensions escalated and nightly rioting became routine across north Belfast affecting many of our Hazelwood students. The standoff continued until the end of school term. Talks between residents from the two parts of Ardoyne took place over the summer, but no agreement was reached. The protest resumed on Monday, September 3, the first day of the school term. Rioting followed and spread to other areas including the area where the Hazelwood schools are situated.

On the morning of September 4, a Protestant boy was knocked down and killed by a Catholic parent leaving off her children at the Hazelwood Integrated Primary School. Tension gripped the area. Parents brought students home early from school, fearful of the repercussions of a killing characterized as murder by the local Protestant population. Hazelwood College had to manage panicking parents to avoid a mass exodus from the school, and to ensure that school buses ferried children home safely. Ironically the school had added a new bus run that same September, a route that went through Ardoyne, the area most affected by the ongoing rioting.

After ensuring the safety of the children, the next challenge was to ensure that the issues on the street were dealt with in a way that would allow students to express their feelings, to hear the anger and hurt that existed, and to do so in the safety of, and with respect for, the school ethos. This required that all staff be vigilant and supportive, in particular those teachers taking the class with both cousins of the dead boy and nephews of the driver of the car. The school community had to be reassured. The school had to manage the impact of the funeral of the dead boy and of the ongoing riots, a nightly feature in the area. My notes for a special assembly convened included the following:

> As we watch what is going on in north Belfast, and many of you are experiencing the rioting and sectarianism close at hand, we in Hazelwood again find ourselves in a special position. We have here a community based on acceptance and trust. We accept each other…we accept that we have different backgrounds, beliefs and opinions. And because we know and trust each other, we are able to be friends, to work together…to listen to each other, to differ in our opinions… I want you to be sensitive to each other and the pressure that individuals may be under. I appreciate that many of you feel the hurt of your communities and you may feel under stress. If you need support, seek it from myself or other members of staff.

On September 28, seven Hazelwood students were injured when a concrete block was thrown at their school bus. Again an immediate response to reassure parents and children was necessary, with the additional challenge of handling media interest. During the following months, violence continued in north Belfast and on November 11, during riots in the Protestant Tigers Bay area, a 16-year-old boy was killed by a pipe bomb he was handling. His friends in the college were traumatized by his death. After negotiations, the blockade was called off on November 23, and the situation on the streets became quiet for some weeks.

However, the new school term started with confrontations outside the Catholic primary school during the afternoon school run, which turned into widespread sectarian rioting across north Belfast. On January 11, a loyalist splinter group issued a death threat to the teachers and other staff working in Catholic schools in north Belfast. On January 12, a 20-year-old Catholic man, a former student of

Hazelwood Integrated College, was murdered—a sectarian killing—as he arrived for work at a postal sorting office; the college faced another crisis that reverberated through the whole school community.

The school responded in a range of ways: practical arrangements were put in place, such as a critical incident response procedure; additional security was employed when threats were issued against Catholic teachers; and police were present at the start and end of the school day when threats were ongoing.

Throughout this period, college staff worked to ensure that sectarian tension did not impact the school. A program of staff training was arranged, delivered by the staff of NICIE, to support staff in responding to student needs. This included a bus tour of the areas in which nightly rioting was taking place, and a day devoted to exploring strategies for dealing with contentious issues. Other agencies were called on for support including a group working with families damaged by the "Troubles" that provided a counseling service for children who either self-referred or were referred by teachers. A youth support group arranged a bus trip to a reconciliation center for those children traveling on the school bus that daily crossed Ardoyne bringing Protestant and Catholic students from both sides of the peace lines to school. The aim of these additional interventions was to acknowledge the pressures on our young people, to create a space for students to reflect on their experiences of living through endemic violence, and to give them the opportunity to get to know each other at a level that would enable them to withstand pressures of division and sectarianism.

A whole school trip to watch the Belfast Giants ice hockey team was organized, and more than six hundred children attended, along with parents, with cheerleaders from the school opening the game. This was enormously successful in reaffirming the school identity and in recognizing and celebrating its resilience.

A visit of 20 students from Denver, United States, during the worst phase of the violence reinforced the normality of school life. Weekly assemblies provided opportunities for all to reflect on the pressures some students were under, to acknowledge the impact of the ongoing conflict, and to reaffirm the mission of the college. Typical of the content of such assemblies was that of the first assembly of 2002 when as principal, I said: "Our environment has not come about by chance. It has developed because each individual in the school contributes to it. The more we are aware of our responsibility to protect our ethos, the stronger the ethos will be." Students were challenged to take a lead in speaking out against violence and sectarianism, sometimes to controversial effect.

The local radio, for example, was permitted to interview students from areas caught up in violence. During one interview, some students spoke of their personal experience of rioting, and the controversy this caused is captured by O'Connor:

> The broadcast caused the school some difficulty, and gave a number of people unholy delight, including an official of the Catholic schools' umbrella body, CCMS, who thought it questioned the worth of twenty years of integrated education ... Hazelwood principal, Noreen Campbell, went on air later to defend the pupils and the school. Her argument, in the main, was that the openness of the teenagers proved the value of the school's work. The most remarkable feature of the broadcast was that local sectarian tension and the fraught issues of policing and police bias were discussed calmly, without anyone shouting anyone else down or being stung into a hostile reaction. (2002, p. 137)

This ongoing effort to enable students to speak openly about their experiences culminated in the organization of a special day for all third year students held in May 2002, the first of what was to become an annual event, *Speak Your Peace Day*. This carefully constructed event brought students together in small groups for workshops delivered by youth workers and teachers. The day culminated with groups sharing with their peers a symbol of importance to them, brought into the school for this purpose. Many students had brought political symbols, flags, and emblems associated with their area. It was inspiring to watch 14-year-old boys and girls listen while another in the group displayed and spoke about a contentious symbol. The respect they gave each other, the respect they showed for what was for them an object of fear and hatred, was moving. This was a day when students and teachers learned the difference between the use of a symbol as a weapon and as a badge of identity. This day exemplified trust and openness and the best of the Hazelwood environment.

The year 2001–2002 was one of the most difficult years faced by the college. As it responded to violence in the community, the school continued with its main work, preparing students for exams, implementing curricular strategies, developing resources and approaches, dealing with day-to-day school life. The school came through this year stronger for a number of reasons: the strength of the values embedded in previous years; the dedication of staff who balanced providing extra pastoral support with a focus on everyday work; the students who handled competing loyalties in a mature and reflective fashion; and the parents who, despite all pressures, continued to support the college.

LESSONS LEARNED

The geographical position of Hazelwood College ensured it was not possible to ignore the violence and sectarianism pervasive in north Belfast. The school had to create an environment that allowed contentious issues to be addressed, that promoted understanding and acceptance, and that also ensured educational excellence was embedded. The adoption of a model of progressive education enabled Hazelwood to embed such an environment. In my opinion, this progressive approach was protected by the integrated nature of the school. As only the second college to be established, the fact of integrated education was considered an oddity in itself and the characteristics peculiar to Hazelwood and integral to its approach—first name terms, all-ability classes, nonpunitive approach to behaviour management—meant these approaches avoided the hostile scrutiny they might otherwise have received.

I think this approach created the accepting ethos that was critical to the success of the school. But this approach was demanding for teachers. As an integrated school, we were asking staff, who had been educated in a segregated system and shaped by the experience of living in a divided society, to deal with issues peculiar to teaching in an integrated school. Just as it was recognized that the act of "integrating" is a daily practice, so it should be recognized that supporting teachers in embedding integration also demands continuous attention.

As a progressive school, staff was being asked to teach classes mixed not only by religion, but also by class and ability; asked to teach in a different way; and expected to role-model the way we wanted students to be. Without a doubt, the time, thought, planning, and support that went into the task of staff development was insufficient. A continuous program of staff support, engagement, and development is necessary when such demands are being made. Hazelwood did not provide this in a structured and sustained way; it is a credit to staff that they performed at such a high level despite this failing.

The ethos of Hazelwood College was constructed. A culture was developed and was underpinned by the use of language that shaped, framed, and validated it. The development of rituals and celebration reinforced and embedded this culture. This conscious use of ritual was commented on in *Success against the Odds*:

> Our fieldwork suggests that the role accorded to ritual in Hazelwood is both more explicit and direct than may be the case in most other schools. Our fieldwork was topped and tailed by two ritualistic events, the presentation evening and the Assembly for Peace. Both

events highlighted the twin themes that run through so much of
the Hazelwood experience: the priority attached to high expectation and achievement through a comprehensive educational strategy;
and the priority attached to reconciliation through religious integration... Once again we see how decisions about the day to day activities
in the school, and here specifically in relation to ritual, are consistent with an agreed set of principles that underpin the school ethos.
(Gallagher, Osborne, Cormack, McKay, & Peover, 1996, p. 222)

My experience tells me it is possible to create a culture of acceptance
and of high expectation. It is possible to develop an ethos that allows
students and teachers to reflect on what shapes them and their peers
and to explore contentious issues in a peaceful and respectful way.
Experience also tells me that such an ethos must be constantly revisited and reaffirmed. Equally such a culture must be underpinned by
a capacity for reflection and a commitment to innovation. A capacity
for risk taking and a willingness to challenge are vital ingredients.

I believe the Hazelwood model is transferable because it is based
on universal principles and is informed by a long tradition of progressive education and by an understanding of human nature, informed
by the work of Carl Rodgers and others. The model works both in
terms of breaking down boundaries, enabling a greater exploration
of self-identity, and of enabling academic success. The model works
because it was developed and owned by those involved in founding
the school in response to specific challenges.

A follow-up report, *Success against the Odds Five Years on*, identified key factors in the success of Hazelwood: a distinctive mission and
a clear sense of ethos and purpose; a child-centered and inclusive set
of principles; a commitment to academic excellence and high achievement; a recognition of the differing needs and aspirations of pupils
and the different forms success can take; strong and positive relationships between staff and pupils; a commitment to ritual as a way of
building community; and an environment that is welcoming to all
(Gallagher, 2001).

I believe that the characteristics identified are transferable to any
country and are applicable to any school seeking to meet the needs of
all of its children.

REFERENCES

Gallagher, A. (2001). Hazelwood College. In M. Maden (Ed.), *Success
against the odds—five years on: Revisiting effective schools in disadvantaged areas* (pp. 205–228). London: Routledge.

Gallagher, A., Osborne, R., Cormack, R., McKay, I., & Peover, S. (1996). Hazelwood Integrated College. In National Commission for Education (Ed.), *Success against the odds: Effective schools in disadvantaged areas* (pp. 200–230). London: Routledge.

Hamlyn, Paul. (1996). *Success against the odds: Effective schools in disadvantaged areas.* London and New York: Routledge.

Northern Ireland Council for Integrated Education (NICIE). 2012. "Statement of Principles." Accessed 16 May, 2013, at http://www.nicie.org/aboutus/default.asp?id=27

O'Connor, F. (2002). *A shared childhood: The story of the integrated schools in Northern Ireland.* Belfast: Blackstaff Press.

Rowley, T. (1993). Contextual education: The Hazelwood model. In C. Moffat (Ed.), *Education together for a change* (pp. 52–61). Belfast: Fortnight Educational Trust.

Spencer, A. (2005). *The development of education in Belfast: A planning study for 1984–89.* Belfast: Privately published.

5

INTERETHNIC DIALOGUE AND COOPERATION FOR INTEGRATED EDUCATION IN BiH

THE PRACTICE AND EXPERIENCES OF THE NANSEN DIALOGUE CENTER SARAJEVO

Ljuljjeta Goranci-Brkic

Since the end of the war in the 1990s Bosnia and Herzegovina (BiH) has been considered a deeply ethnically divided society, where ethnicity determines almost all aspects of life: cultural, social, political, and economical. This chapter reflects on the experience of the Nansen Dialogue Center in Sarajevo (NDC Sarajevo) and its mission to promote interethnic dialogue and to create interethnic initiatives among ethnically divided communities in BiH. In particular, the roles of parents, teachers, students, principals, and politicians in the initiatives for integrated education are examined.

ETHNICALLY DIVIDED DDUCATION SYSTEM IN BiH

The structure of the education system in BiH is extremely complex and inefficient, and it serves exclusively to protect the interests of three national/ethnic groups as determined by the Constitution. In BiH there are four administrative levels of institutional/national bodies that are in charge of education: State level, Entity level, Cantonal level (in Federation of BiH), and Brčko District. These bodies are organized into 13 Ministries of Education that are responsible for education in BiH. Despite declaring support for integrated education and respect for human rights, the relevant institutional forces (politicians, representatives of Ministries of Education, and policy makers) seem to support ethnic segregation and principles that are totally opposed to the very essence of the idea of integrated education! The education system is ethnically divided and it is structured in a way that furthers the divide among students. Division is visible in school curricula, which are not harmonized with the needs of students of different ethnic backgrounds. Thus the curriculum is a source of segregation and discrimination. As a consequence, students are educated and raised in exclusive ethnic settings, and they lack any knowledge and sensibility about/for the other ethnic groups. Owing to such organizational structure of the education system, I believe, the ethnic division and ethnic segregation are becoming stronger and deeper every day.

Regardless of the fact that in some schools students attend ethnically mixed classes, they tend to have negative prejudices about each other, they do not communicate across ethnic divisions, some of them feel rejected by the others, and some do not even hesitate to express open hatred toward their peers from the other ethnic groups. Also, it is usually the case that primary schoolchildren are sent by their parents to travel ten or more kilometers every day to attend mono-ethnic schools, rather than attend a school in the neighborhood that delivers a curriculum for another ethnic group. Education, then, could potentially be seen as a possible source for the future escalation of ethnically based conflict.

THE ROLE OF NDC SARAJEVO

The NDC Sarajevo is a nonprofit, non-governmental, peace- building organization that aims to develop the widest spectra of democratic practices in local, multiethnic yet divided communities in BiH for their integration to the level of functional societies equally beneficial for all their members. As seen by the NDC Sarajevo, the role of the main stakeholders in the schools, such as parents, teachers, students, principals, and politicians, is crucial for any positive change in school and local community. By cooperating with representatives of the various segments and levels of the local communities, the NDC Sarajevo opens a space for using dialogue as a tool for understanding, accepting, and negotiating diversities, especially ethnic, religious, cultural, national, as also political, gender, sexual, age, lifestyle. These processes are necessary preconditions for functional integration.

From the very beginning, the NDC Sarajevo started dialogue activities through dialogue training for the same target groups coming from Sarajevo—a city comprising two entities: Federation of BiH and

Republic of Srpska. Public discussions related to important interethnic issues were also organized. A turning point in NDC Sarajevo activities happened when it was approached by the Regional Educational Department of the Organization for Security and Co-operation in Europe (OSCE) through the OSCE Mission to BiH at the end of 2002, requesting training for teachers in ethnically divided schools in small towns and rural areas.

The main goal of this program for NDC Sarajevo was to provide education in interethnic dialogue, nonviolent communication, and conflict management to schoolteachers who were working in ethnically divided schools in BiH. The pilot training was additionally supported by the Norwegian Embassy in Sarajevo, and its success brought us closer to focusing on this particular activity during 2003 and 2004, while continuing to work in Sarajevo. The training program was additionally funded by the Norwegian Ministry of Foreign Affairs and, at a later stage, also by EU funds.

Besides impressive qualitative and quantitative results the most important outcome of the NDC Sarajevo is the knowledge and perspective gained as a result of its intensive fieldwork throughout BiH. Ethnic divisions, lack of interethnic communication, and basically dysfunctional communities convinced us that we have to respond somehow to such a condition, which can, by no means, be compared with the one in divided Sarajevo. In particular, ethnic segregation in schools is most visible in (?)communities of returnees. This is the reason why NDC Sarajevo has chosen to focus on Eastern and Central Bosnia (Srebrenica, Bratunac, Zvornik, and Jajce). We found particularly hard conditions in a region of Eastern Bosnia and we decided to focus on that area. With limited funds we started to organize roundtables dedicated to interethnic issues in all major towns in the region throughout the year 2005. The participants were municipal officials, NGO activists, teachers, journalists, and also ordinary citizens, the majority of them returnees and Internally Displaced Persons (IDPs). For many of these participants from the returnee and IDP population it was the first time since the war that they sat down together and discussed the issues of ethnic division in their communities.

BRATUNAC AND SREBRENICA—LIVING ON "SURVIVAL MODE"

Holding roundtables provided us with a deep insight into the problems of the referring communities, and at the end of 2005, NDC Sarajevo decided to focus on the particularly problematic region of Bratunac and Srebrenica—the toughest and most challenging regions because of extremely traumatic war past and consequences. Our reasoning was that no functional state is possible if it does not function in local communities, and that the whole society is as strong as its "weakest link." So, what does life in these regions look like? We find that the population is clearly divided along ethnic lines. The level of communication and coordination in everyday life is very low among different ethnic groups. There is a high level of distrust that is combined with an internal group pressuring against interethnic communication. Though the number of returnees is significant, they face a huge level of both formal and informal obstructions. The political actors are under the influence of the political elites from the top parties at the national level and they just follow the "global" politics of their parties rather than create a local one. Also, a strong link between local politicians and local businessmen results in many semi-legal arrangements, and a high level of corruption makes the creation of any development opportunities even harder.

The situation suits those who can maintain local power. So, the basic strategy is the homogenization of the electoral body along ethnic lines. Obstructing the process of return, manipulating war crimes and victims, provoking violent interethnic incidents, threatening, and economic discrimination are tactics used to keep groups homogenized. On the other hand, the political elites of all parties cooperate at a pragmatic level, supporting each other for the sake of staying in power and developing parallelism and imbalances wherever possible, even doubling institutions.

The population, being impoverished and under constant pressure from the elites, perceive the situation in a somewhat fatalist manner, as something "normal." Combined with the characteristics of a traditional society such as submissiveness to authorities, close communal links, lack of critical thinking, limited courage and inability to articulate politically, this creates a vicious circle. Under such circumstances homogenization and acting within one's own group is perceived as the most reasonable action: that is the only way to provide oneself with a means for living. In this regard, preserving the status quo is also seen as beneficial for local population. Throughout these places the population is in a position where they practically operate on a "survival mode." From this perspective many will say "the war was better." And this "survival mode" somehow forces them to accept any immediate solution although it severely disturbs any development of the region.

Therefore, the challenges to create an integrated education in such a context are immense. If you have to unite two mono-ethnic schools into an integrated multiethnic school you must deal with the fear and passivity of parents, the influence of political actors from the field and from the political centers, the teachers and school administrators who will lose their job once the school is united, possible war-criminal suspects who are still living in the community and might be a parent or even a teacher, and, finally, ordinary criminals who benefit from the existing ethnic divisions. You must be ready to face a process that may take many years to progress.

An important outcome of our initiatives is the fact that after our engagement, the young people who were born and grew up in purely monoethnic environment and had no interethnic experience except the atrocities started to communicate across ethnic lines, not only at the seminars but also in their private lives. At the beginning these encounters would take place in isolated places, but gradually they became more public. In each community and school where NDC Sarajevo operates the Nansen Forums of Young Peace builders (NFYP) were established. The NFYP are involved in various extracurricular sections such as forums for school mediation, documentary film section, and young journalist section. The example of open and free interethnic communication even among limited number of young people had a huge impact on the small towns such as Bratunac and Srebrenica. Also, youth nongovernmental organizations (NGOs) started to attract multiethnic memberships, and a multiethnic cultural club was founded, which still serves as a forum for dealing with interethnic youth issues. Nowadays, additionally, several joint projects are being designed.

The most important indicator of change for us is that these processes are not only "our initiatives" but also initiatives that gradually came from the participants themselves. Having recognized their own interests and having overcome ethnical boundaries they are now coming to NDC Sarajevo looking for support for their ideas and looking for means to implement joint initiatives in their respective local communities.

RETURN THROUGH DIALOGUE—EXPERIENCE OF INTERETHNIC WORK IN THE FIELD

NDC Sarajevo operates in three high school centers and two elementary schools in BiH (Federation of BiH and Republic of Srpska):

- High School Center Srebrenica in Srebrenica—480 students
- High School Center Petar Kočić in Zvornik—1,600 students (this is the largest high school in Republic of Srpska)

- Vocational High School in Jajce—400 students
- Elementary School Petar Petrović Njegoš in Srebrenica with field/branch school in Potočari—428 students
- Elementary School Petar Kočić in Konjević Polje with field school also in Konjević Polje—454 students

The Elementary School Petar Kočić is situated in the northeast of BiH, in the Bratunac Municipality. It consists of two buildings: the main one located in a Serb-populated village, Kravica, and the field school located ten kilometers away in the Bosniak returnees' village, Konjević Polje. Both villages experienced extreme atrocities and violence during the war in BiH. Many people were killed; everyone was driven out of their homes by force; many houses were destroyed. As a consequence there is almost no interethnic communication among the population; relations are very tense, always at the edge of conflict, and the school is strictly divided according "ethnic curricula." Although taught by the same teachers, in the Kravica school premises students follow the "Serb Curriculum," while in Konjević Polje students follow the "Bosniak Curriculum"; needless to say, the classes in both schools are mono-ethnic. Considering that the villages are also mono-ethnic, the described situation seems to be convenient for the majority of students and their parents.

However, there are a number of students who live in the surrounding villages, which are populated with other ethnic groups: Bosniak villages around Serbs ones and vice versa. Regardless of the fact that they can see the school building from their houses and that they would be taught by the same teachers, the students from such villages commute up to 20 or more kilometers every day to attend the school that offers their own "ethnic curriculum."

Keeping all of this in mind, in 2006 NDC Sarajevo decided to engage with the communities and to encourage and support the (re)establishment of interethnic communication among students, parents, and among the general population. NDC Sarajevo's approach to the problem could be described as gradual, very cautious, and holistic. NDC Sarajevo entered in the communities through work with school administration and teachers. The administrators and teachers attended a number of dialogue training sessions where they improved their skills in interethnic and nonviolent communication. They also learnt conflict management and about the Forum for School Mediation and Film Section, as well as human rights, especially children's rights. During this process the school administration and teachers became not only supporters of NDC Sarajevo interethnic initiatives and projects in the schools, but also active partners, and valuable agents of change were introduced not only in the school but also in communities. The majority of NDC Sarajevo interethnic extracurricular activities are organized and realized by Bosniak, Serb, and Croat teachers, with the support of the school administration and parents.

A parallel process involved parents. At the beginning we experienced resistance, hesitation, even obstructionist behavior on the part of some of the parents. It took us a lot of time and patience, months of discussions, face-to-face talks, going back and forth. At the beginning it was difficult to ensure support from the parents because of obstructions by the local informal or formal hard-line leaders. Finally, after gaining trust and with the significant help of the school administration, parents begun to support our work. Moreover, they even initiated and started the joint interethnic work of rebuilding some classrooms and cleaning the schoolyard. In these rebuilt classrooms, on the parents' initiative, their children started extracurricular classes–IT and English language. With IT being taught in one village and English language in the other, the students started to commute again, but now they were together, in spite of ethnic differences! This represents an unprecedented practice in postwar BiH; hence it is against the trends of ethnical homogenization. However, this was just the beginning. Supported by NDC Sarajevo, the parents continued to communicate and cooperate through the newly established, multiethnic parents' council. Together with the school staff, they continued to create an environment for their children to be together. Within the school, multiethnic football teams were established, as well as drama and folklore sections.

It is important to say that this is not just a localized, limited-to-school process, but one where the whole community is involved to become—hopefully—gradually transformed by improved interethnic relations. The improvement is best seen during the school day anniversary celebrations. In 2008, for the first time after the war, the population from different ethnic groups came together at such a public event—they even rooted for their (territorial) multiethnic students' football teams. In 2009, an even bigger event took place—it has been organized for the first time after the war in Konjević Polje, the Bosniak returnees' village. People from both ethnic groups celebrated the anniversary and municipal and entity government's representatives were present at the event. Multiethnic groups of students played and performed, celebrating together.

In this process NDC Sarajevo is seen as a provider of a safe and trustworthy space and as a catalyst for enabling communication and dialogue. The credit for such results go to our local partners, school staff, and parents, who are the real agents of change in their communities. Although students still attend regular classes divided by ethnic curricula, and although interethnic communication and cooperation in the region is still very far from favorable, the fact that interethnic activities do take place in and around schools proves that the changes are not just formal and superficial, but substantial and viable.

NFYP—UNITING THE YOUTH

The NDC Sarajevo project consists of three phases of implementation:

1. Education and training for wider selected groups of beneficiaries in interethnic dialogue, intercultural communication, conflict transformation, and human rights.
2. Establishing core groups, consisting of the most involved and active participants; their local engagement, and advanced education both in interethnic issues and designing and implementing community development actions.
3. Transforming the core groups into the Nansen Teachers Alumni and NFYP. These are multiethnic local bodies educated and empowered to take initiatives and actions for the improvement of interethnic relations and general situation in their communities. The bodies consist of students, teachers, school administration, and parents. The aim is to continue their work independently after the project implementation phase.

Through cooperation and through the inclusion of teachers, school administrations, and parents NDC Sarajevo established the NFYP in each school. There are five NFYP, one in each school. The NFYP consist of Bosniak, Serb, and Croat Elementary and High School students who participate in our dialogue training seminars. Each school provides one office or classroom to be used for the activities of the NFYP. These offices or classrooms are officially named Nansen Classrooms. Nansen Classrooms are used for all activities designed and organized by the members of the NFYP in each school.

The NYFP has several achievements to its credit. The NFYP in Srebrenica established an editorial body of the independent school magazine *Argentarija*, a group of young photography artists, and a film section produced a documentary film *Life in Srebrenica*; NDC Sarajevo initiated institutional cooperation between High School Center Srebrenica and Mesna High School from Lillehammer/Norway and it also organized the first exchange visit of students from these two schools from October 17 to October 22, 2011 in Lillehammer/Norway. The NFYP in Zvornik established the school magazine *Drina*.. The NFYP in Jajce established the Forum for School Mediation, and Film Section; it organizes activities in Vocational High School Jajce on a regular basis; and so far they have organized six training programs in peer and school mediation in two elementary schools in Jajce.

In addition, NDC Sarajevo initiated interethnic extracurricular activities: football tournaments with other elementary schools from the Srebrenica/Bratunac region; IT and school mediation class; establishment of a forum for school mediation consisting of Bosniak and Serb students who participated in our educational program. In the Elementary School Petar Kočić, Bratunac, NDC Sarajevo established the following: a Nansen Classroom in Konjević Polje School and a Nansen Parents Council consisting of 14 Bosniak and Serb parents from Kravica and Konjević Polje. This multiethnic group of parents supports, participates, and implements various interethnic activities and initiatives in the Kravica and Konjević Polje schools; interethnic extracurricular classes of English and IT; Nansen Folklore Ensemble—this is the first and only multiethnic folklore group in eastern Bosnia; an interethnic Nansen football team consisting of Bosniak and Serb pupils from Kravica/Konjević Polje.

By 2006 we had covered 40 municipalities, 49 towns and villages, and 54 schools in both the Federation of BiH and Republic of Srpska. Our training was completed successfully by 266 teachers (41 percent Bosniaks, 24 percent Serbs, 26 percent Croats, 5 percent others). The total number of pupils who are indirect beneficiaries is approximately 41,121. The most important outcomes of these activities are that as more teachers start to communicate across ethnic lines, they (re)establish their relations both on professional and personal levels; they start to use knowledge and skills they have received in everyday work with the children, and start to be proactive in the educational process. In many schools teachers started extracurricular activities with ethnically mixed students, which was not the case before our activities.

CONCLUSION

In all of these activities the role of NDC Sarajevo is not being seen as an agent of change but merely as a catalyst and facilitator, a moderator in the process of interethnic dialogue, that should and could enable the very population to act as the agents of change themselves. In our view, that is the only way to produce sustainable results. Only a year after full engagement in interethnic dialogue activities we are starting to see a positive response. Although the process was severely influenced by political "power games" we succeeded in starting a dialogue about some common issues. Therefore, we believe that it is possible for a common interest to take precedence over an ethnic one.

NDC Sarajevo has succeeded so far in breaking through ethnic boundaries among the participants in the process who have started to communicate, even on a personal level. It is successfully reaching out to teachers and school administrators who are now actively working for reintegration. NDC Sarajevo is also working to tone down radical views of the majority of parents, who are now giving their still modest but promising support for the process by their mere willingness to participate.

CONCLUSION TO PART 1

Zvi Bekerman

As with all following parts, this first part strikes us with its complexity. Some of the themes raised might look repetitive but the moment you pay attention to the details in each chapter you realize that generalizations will not work easily. Yes, all authors seem to encounter multiple contextual and historical challenges and realize that conflict is woven into multiple facets of daily life, but in each of the chapters, in each of the geographical areas dealt with, the nuances are not only different but alter when seen from the perspectives of the different actors involved. So much so that even within the same geographical area the perspectives may vary.

Take, for example, the importance of personal background for those involved in the integrative initiative pointing at multicultural experiences as leverage for empathy and understanding. Consider how the concept of integration develops and widens from a restricted perception of integration that includes accounting for those involved in the immediate conflict to an all-inclusive one that accounts for all social classes, all cultures, and all levels of ability and disability. No less important are the statements that point at the relevance of sharpening the educators' senses in all that relates to being attentive and sensitive to the multiple voices of the stakeholders involved in such initiatives—parents, teachers, officers, and children.

As the initiatives develop new challenges arise; integration at an early age might seem easy, for the children appear not much involved in the adult's world of conflict, yet conflict is present and echoed by the parents' presence and the teachers' worries and attachments. As children grow, as they are captured more and more by society's conflictual discourses, and as the daily educational work is in need of introducing them to trickier issues (religious education, historical narratives), ensuring a balanced presentation of all narratives/traditions involved becomes more difficult. For parents sending their children to integrated schools—driven by a pledge to make a difference in a troubled world they want their children not to encounter—taking risks might be easy at first. As time passes, as children grow and parents expect them to be recognized as proud members of their own communities (whose members might not have all gone through similar reflective processes), tensions rise and the ease with which integration was conducted dwindles.

At the macro level these difficulties are augmented by lack of political support, lack of funding, lack of professional training, all making the development of integrated initiatives a difficult challenge. Lay and professional leadership need to maneuver between preferred options while understanding the importance of having integrated initiatives grow from the field and be community-led. They realize that without governmental support they will not be able to grow at the same time as they realize that governmental support can limit the vision of such initiatives. Navigating these uncharted paths, coupled with other educational considerations—general ones such as the position of integrated schools within school districts, demographic considerations, and so on—has made the development of these initiatives demanding and slow.

The lack of a clear understanding of what integrated education means according to curriculum and pedagogy also impinges on the initiatives development. Especially in conflict-ridden societies where, for long, the denial of alterity has reigned, there is no experience with weaving different group historical narratives into one curriculum. The professional staff has no experience in managing educational activities that need to account for, at times, decades-long conflicts. Overcoming the impositions and traps of wider sociopolitical contexts that structurally position languages, historical narratives, and cultural expressions in an unbalanced hierarchical order makes the integrated education work tricky and problematic.

In spite of these intricacies, which at times might seem insurmountable, the authors of the chapters in this part are hopeful and point to multiple issues that need to be accounted for and strategies that need to be implemented to secure the creation and sustainability of integrated education. At the macro level, developing integrated education requires careful strategic planning and the creation of strong coalitions even with those who, at first sight, might not be considered natural partners. It implies recognizing the power of individuals and communities, even in areas where these seem to be subdued by powerful, ideological, and belligerent groups. At a more micro level integration requires a wide range of policies, practices, and pedagogies. The most important seems to be a strong belief that the creation of relationships of trust among stakeholders is of essence to confront difficult and sensitive issues. Understanding that each step forward in integrated education is accompanied by many steps back is of essence too—progress is not unidirectional, and without thorough planning progress cannot become rooted and accepted. Recruiting the right kind of staff and caring, constantly, for their training while understanding that the skills needed are various and include educational and ideological attributes and attitudes, not just goodwill, is also very significant. Last, and of no less significance, is the understanding that though ideology and vision are of importance in themselves, they will not do for they compete in a wide educational arena where education is a cherished commodity that, if not supplied, will fail the initiative.

2

STARTING INTEGRATED SCHOOLS AND TRANSFORMATION OF EXISTING SCHOOLS IN CONFLICTED SOCIETIES

INTRODUCTION TO PART 2

Zvi Bekerman

The second part of this book brings together authors form Northern Ireland, Macedonia, and Cyprus, the first two hopefully moving away from conflict, a move that is never easy, and the third somewhat in a stalemate the outcome of which is not clear. What connects these stories is that the authors of the five chapters that compose this second part are all involved in educational efforts geared toward alleviating conflict while emphasizing the need to reduce stereotypes, support tolerance and recognition, and labor toward coexistence. As all others, this part too asks us to pay attention not to scholars in universities but to humans at work, working through the hardships of a "real" life. It is not that scholarly work is not relevant, yet what the part intends is to present the realities as perceived by the main actors in educational scenes, educators, so as to allow us all, scholars and educators, to enter the only dialogue that can benefit both research and practice. This part is also an invitation to those who care about these issues in education to learn from the stories being told and reflect on what can be done in their own conflictual settings when considering the experiences related by these outstanding educators.

This second part includes five chapters; chapter 6 by Kevin Lambe from Northern Ireland, a development officer with the Northern Ireland Council for Integrated Education and also a principal at one of the integrated colleges in Northern Ireland, tells about his personal and professional experiences as these shape his understandings of integrated education. Kevin tell his story as a Catholic child in a family of seven in Belfast in the fifties, in an almost fully segregated environment, and the frictions, at times violent, that he and his family experience as times are changing (for the worst) in the surroundings. A series of events are woven into his story, some which emphasize moments when religious differences are easily erased and other moments when they are (un)proportionally augmented. The second part of Kevin's chapter is dedicated to his professional life and to what he has learned while being involved, over 25 years now, in integrative educational efforts. In this part he approaches in detail some of the institutional constraints that impede the development of integrated efforts, and some of the human qualities needed to support them. The chapter ends by emphasizing the importance of a wide understanding of integrated education as an all-ability approach.

Maria Asvesta, a teacher and senior leader of the English School in Cyprus (Greek Cyprus), writes the second chapter of this part. Maria's chapter can be easily contrasted with Kevin's chapter. Cyprus, as yet a divided society (between Cypriot Greeks and Turks), is described as not easily agreeable to integrated educational efforts. Maria describes the difficulties encountered in an elitist, mostly Cypriot Greek–populated school that the Cypriot Greek government encourages (because of its own political agenda) to accept a small percentage of Cypriot Turkish students. She underlines the need to strengthen teachers' multicultural training and the impossibility of developing integrated education without the strong support of parents. Yet, even in difficult political settings, she affirms, the dedication of teachers in their efforts to develop safe and managed spaces where students are given the opportunity to work together in mixed groups and build trust offers opportunities for positive change. The journey toward making education valuable in society's search for coexistence might be full of obstacles but, in Maria's eyes, it is well worth pursuing.

Chapter 8, written by Peter McCreadie, approaches one of the developmentsthat took place in Northern Ireland following the evolution of the integrated schools in the eighties and nineties. Peter tells his story from the perspective of someone involved in a transformed integrated college. Transformed schools, which in essence are segregated schools that for a variety of reasons choose to become integrated, are a rather new development in Northern Ireland that can be initiated either by parents or school governors. Peter's story is about a school that needs to overcome the public perception that 'transformation' is more than just a cynical attempt by governors to raise the profile of a school so as to gain additional governmental funding. Peter describes some of the strategies adopted when trying to develop the confidence of the minority students attending school, the curricular changes that needed to be undertaken, and the efforts that needed to be invested in gaining parental support. Peter believes transformed schools are a worthwhile option that hold promise for a better future and sees integration efforts always as "a work in progress."

The experience of integrated education in the Republic of Macedonia is reflected in chapter 9 where Vilma Venkovska Milcev presents the model developed by the Mozaik preschool group. Vilma underlines the importance of starting integrative efforts at an early age when children are free from prejudices toward and stereotypes of their peers. Since 1998 children, three to five years old, from different ethnic communities in Macedonia attend this new innovative educational setting called Mozaik that is based on the principles of tolerance and respect for cultural diversity. Vilma, like the others in this part, emphasizes the importance of governmental support for peace educational initiatives as it frees parents of worries regarding having their children join educational initiatives whose future is not secured; similarly, governmental support is important for the teachers' body to be much more dedicated to such initiatives knowing their pay is not dependent on the good intentions of donors but is instead officially funded by the government. Vilma also reflects on the positive model of collaboration between children as reflected in the preschool's activities and in the challenges the model has faced when encountering the official educational system in Macedonia.

In their chapter, 10, Biljana Krstevska-Papic and Veton Zekolli present the current situation and efforts that are being undertaken in the Republic of Macedonia toward the development of integrated education. In particular, the chapter focuses on the challenges that teachers face when the development of integrated education is just starting to take shape; Biljana and Veton discuss the role of teacher competencies in the process of planning and implementation of this form of education. Based on their experiences of working with the Nansen Dialogue Centre Skopje, Biljana and Veton discuss the difficulty in convincing parents and local officials to buy into the model of integrated education. They show how securing political support also proves to be an important component in this process and can enable or disable any future prospects for integrated education. They emphasize the importance of taking initiatives at different levels, especially at the level of supporting the teachers' pedagogical role and training in integrated education.

All in all, the second part allows the reader to be impressed by the trials and obstacles the initiators of integrated education in different parts of the world encountered. Perusing the chapters leaves us with a sense of achievement and optimism for the possible future of the integration model, yet it becomes clear that this future is dependent on the remarkable efforts individuals (parents, educators, and students) need to make to reach the goal.

6

ALL-ABILITY EDUCATION IN NORTHERN IRELAND

A PRINCIPAL'S PERSPECTIVE

Kevin Lambe

1.

My understanding of integrated education has of course been shaped both by my personal and my professional experience. The movement toward integration was begun by individuals coming together, trying initially to persuade the powers that be to take the initiative and, when that proved fruitless, moving forward despite those powers whose resistance to change proved immutable. When the first parents decided that they wanted their children to be educated together in a divided society, schools were either Protestant or Catholic and therefore either Unionist or Nationalist, governed by the state or by the Catholic Church. What became the integrated education movement began with one person placing an advertisement in a newspaper seeking like-minded persons to come forward. The fact that the movement grew not from government initiative but from people power was to prove its strength. In a society where government was seen by some as part of the problem and whose very existence was seen as controversial, any top-down initiative would have been distrusted by many if not most of the citizens of Northern Ireland. So the stories of the individuals who led the movement, who shaped it and established it, are the very building blocks of integration.

My own story is hardly uncommon, having grown up in a monocultural working class environment. Up to this day the working classes in Northern Ireland live predominantly in what could fairly be termed "ghettoes" and my particular ghetto was the Lower Falls, which gained notoriety through the Troubles for history-changing events like the burnings of Bombay Street and the infamous curfew of July 3–5, 1970 that entrenched the enmity between the official and the fledgling Provisional IRAs. Like many Northern Irish Catholic boys my education was entrusted to the Christian Brothers, strict disciplinarians determined to imbue in us the virtues of the Gaelic Athletic Association (GAA), the Irish language, nationalism, and the Catholic Church. So successful were they in their task that many of the leaders of the Provisional IRA were educated at my all-Catholic West Belfast Grammar School. Strange then that, on attending a formal reunion at my alma mater, when the Troubles were at their height, the guest speaker was a prominent Catholic high court judge. My peers and I reached our own conclusions.

The youngest of seven children, five boys and two girls, I was raised in a terraced house where the front room was a shop where we were the assistants and the unspoken but unfailing understanding always was that education was the only way to advance. The 1947 Education Act and its effect on the Catholic working classes enabled them to produce the judges, the professionals, the civil rights activists, the revolutionaries, and paramilitaries. Its effects on my Protestant peers living on either side of me, on the Shankill Road and Sandy Row, were unknown to me at the time, as were those peers themselves, yet the effects on them must have been just as significant and influential in what was to come.

All five of us boys were sent to the nearest Christian Brothers' primary school which was some 20 minutes walk away, and to attend that school we had to pass right by the local parish school, staffed by "lay," that is, non-clerical staff. The Brothers' school, in addition to being renowned for its strict discipline, was famous also for getting large numbers of Lower Falls Catholic working class boys successfully through the 11+ examination, and thereby on to grammar school. My sisters, on the other hand, attended the local parish school, a school out of which a friend of mine claims he was carried shoulder high by his fellow students, so rare was his feat of passing the 11+ examination. Thus, it seemed, our fates were sealed, and along gender lines, with my sisters now statistically likely to fail to gain entry to grammar school with all the advantages and opportunities that route offered, and the boys looking forward to academic and professional challenge and success.

And so it was to prove, more or less, as self-fulfilling prophecies usually do. It was only years later that I learned, to my relief, that my father had tried just as hard to ensure academic success for my sisters as he had for us boys. It seems he had repeatedly attempted to persuade the nuns at the convent primary school a mile and a half up the road to accept the girls. His attempts proved unsuccessful and my father harbored a suspicion thereafter, rightly or wrongly, that there was some class prejudice at work. Then, as now, the choice of school was crucial for children's life chances but at that time there were no such places as integrated, all-ability schools. With depressing inevitability the boys progressed to the Christian Brothers' grammar school, while the girls progressed to a secretarial school for girls, on the other side of town, that had been researched and investigated by my parents as an alternative to the local secondary school, in which they had little confidence. Then, as now, children were defined by their perceived success or failure in tackling an examination that has proved neither to be an accurate gauge nor a predictor of ability. Schools were perceived as good or bad depending on whether they catered for the perceived successes or failures. None of these perceptions was a particularly accurate indicator of the good and less-than-good teaching and learning that must have taken place in all schools, but the perceptions of what is to be aspired to in education, that is, selective grammar school education, persist until this day and, I would contend, continue to adversely affect our young citizens and our society.

Growing up in Belfast, the birthplace of integrated education, in the fifties and sixties was not so much a case of "us and them" as a case of "us." They, that is, Protestants or Unionists, rarely impinged on our daily lives. There was a Presbyterian church on the corner of the next block up from our block and it lay silent and locked for six days of the week, coming alive only on Sundays when a single service was held, attended by men in somber suits and women in hats, who travelled in and out of our exclusively Catholic area by car. This somewhat anachronistic weekly event ended when, due to dwindling attendances, the church closed, its passing to be marked only but memorably by a letter, read out at Sunday mass by the parish priest, in which the presbytery thanked us local Catholics, for the respectful, friendly, and welcoming way they had been received and treated over the years of their tenure of Albert Street Presbyterian Church. As a small child and neighbor, I felt proud and grateful that they should take the trouble to write, and I felt sad that their otherness would no longer brighten my Sundays. I was gratified when, during a subsequent riot that I observed and listened to as a young and frightened child from my room, I heard a rioter shouting, "Watch the church" when others were hurling stones and petrol bombs.

Less provident, and less welcome, were the only other interactions I had with my Protestant/Unionist fellow citizens, which happened every other Saturday for about three months of one particular Irish League football season when I was seven or eight years old. Our street was a major thoroughfare, linking the Catholic Falls Road and the Protestant Shankill Road, although few denizens of either community ever actually availed of the totality of that transport facility. On the rare occasions when they did and they had to pass through the "other" place, they normally kept their heads down and mouths clamped firmly shut, hoping that their otherness would not be spotted before it became safe to alight. However, it was not so on every second Saturday of the three-month period that particular year. Out of the blue, appropriately given that the onslaught was from Linfield supporters whose colors were predominantly blue, lightened with the red and white of the Union Jack, every second Saturday at around 5:15 pm, the double-decker buses would pass by, filled with (Protestant) Linfield football club fans, chanting sectarian abuse en route to their home on Shankill. While their abuse and taunting remained mobile it just about remained tolerable to the locals but when they took to passing on foot each match day, still chanting and taunting, it became harder for the locals to tolerate. On one particular Saturday this uneasy standoff boiled over into our lives when some four or five Linfield supporters entered our little shop and proceeded to physically assault and abuse my father, then in his late sixties. Two weeks later the same people returned, presumably with the intention of inflicting a repeat dose of insult and injury on my rheumatoid arthritis–inflicted father. Their intent was clear and they were on the point of repeating their assault on my father, when my three elder brothers emerged, by some prearrangement of which I was unaware, from the inside door of the shop to confront and chase them, and, I was subsequently told, to inflict some physical revenge on them. I witnessed these events as a child and, as a child, thought that what these people had done to my father horribly wrong and what my brothers had done to them to protect my father understandable and, from my childish perspective, admirable. The biweekly abuse ceased soon after when members of my local community reacted to the repeated intimidation by stoning one of the double-decker buses and confronting those within. That too I witnessed as a child and was horrified, but I was glad that the confrontations stopped soon thereafter. These two contrasting experiences of the "other" community pale into insignificance when compared to my one and only ongoing interaction with a person of the "other" community as a child. That person was a confectionery wholesaler who visited weekly to deliver his delicious goods and take our order for the coming week. Jimmy was, without doubt, one of the most interesting, different, gentle, and intelligent human beings who impinged on and affected my young life. Once a week he would arrive with his calorific treasure and once a week he brought with him a welcome sense of another world and another experience. He was creative and artistic and, fascinatingly for me, totally committed to visual as well as verbal communication. He was the first ever real person who I knew could draw so freely and beautifully. He could draw cartoons, still lifes, portraits, and, with all that talent and gentle ways, he was a hero to the five-year-old me. What is more, he indulged me, as when I would interrupt to ask him to draw Mickey Mouse and he would instantly indulge me with the most perfect representation of that now most odious rodent, and what's more he would then show me how to make an almost equally perfect representation of that creature myself, which exercise would maintain me until his next visit when I would implore him to teach me more, which of course he would, with grace and enthusiasm. With his indulgence and his talent, he was undoubtedly the person outside my family I admired most in my early life.

Jimmy went on to film the most important rites of passage of all my older siblings with his early 8 mm tapes of their weddings, editing the footage he would take of us and later adding headings like "The Lambe Family" in impressive typeface. It was like having Alfred Hitchcock or, these days, Martin Scorsese, as a family friend. He and his family attended our most important family events and he recorded those events beautifully. I came to expect Jimmy to be present at important family occasions and his presence made those occasions all the more special. What I did not expect was to return from school one day to find my parents discussing the fact that the parish priest had told my father that he should not attend Jimmy's daughter's wedding. The fact that my father had even discussed this matter with the priest amazed me of itself but the priest's reported response just made me angry. I must have been all of ten years old and I had stumbled upon an adult discussion about someone and something about which I cared deeply. Jimmy was one of our best family friends and here were my parents actually debating this matter. I shouldn't have spoken up but I really couldn't help myself. It was my opinion that they had to go to Jimmy's daughter's wedding. They did, and they didn't tell me off for my precocious and unsolicited advice.

Two other incidents stand out in terms of early experiences that influenced my later educational and pedagogical decisions. The first occurred soon after I had progressed to my Christian Brothers' Grammar School and it was to be the first face-to-face encounter I was to have with raw, unreconstructed sectarianism. Returning home from my new school in my new uniform, of which I was inordinately proud, one of my sisters, who spoiled me, "the child," terribly, asked me if I would accompany her to Reid's Shoe Shop, to buy a new pair of shoes for work. Of course I would. I loved my sisters and going shopping with one was a treat, and what's more I could proudly wear my new uniform. Reid's, a famous Belfast shoe shop, was housed on Sandy Row, our neighboring community which in 11 years I had never visited and which was completely and exclusively Protestant, just as our neighborhood was completely and exclusively Catholic. I gave no thought whatever to these matters as I set off with my sister. Why would I indeed, given that I was more or less oblivious to such concerns, cocooned as I was in my safe monoculture and more or less oblivious to others? I did of course know that others did not find their areas adorned with Vatican flags on significant religious feasts or on the occasion of visits from archbishops, that others did not share the euphoria experienced in my community when the final whistle sounded on May 25, 1967, and thousands of people, huddled around black and white televisions for the previous 90 minutes, burst out onto the late spring streets to celebrate en masse the victory of a team of Scottish heroes, most with Irish Catholic heritage, led by a Scottish Protestant manager, who had just won the greatest prize in European football, becoming the first "British" side to do so. Not that any of those celebrating on our streets that evening would have considered the word British in relation to that Celtic team. The clue was in the name: they, like us, were Celts, or so we liked to believe. We learned a Celtic language in our schools, which we were encouraged to consider our own, despite the obvious fact that our mother tongue was English and we lived in streets with names culled from imperial history, with names like Sevastopol, Raglan, Belgrade, and, of course, Albert. We didn't have passports as we didn't go abroad, but if we had had them then they would have been Irish of course, as was our entitlement and birthright. Our shops and parks and pubs didn't open on Sundays, by decree of our majority rule Protestant government, but Sundays were when we played our gaelic games and celebrated our culture in parks owned by the GAA, an organization formed in Thurles, County Tipperary, on November 1, 1884, as the Gaelic Athletic Association for the Preservation and Cultivation of National Pastimes. For many years the GAA played a central role in the promotion of Irish games and culture, banning the attendance at or playing of "foreign" games by its members. "Foreign" in reality meant English games like football, cricket, and rugby, and this prohibition, under the GAA's "Rule 27," was not rescinded until 1971. It was not until 2001 that the GAA revoked its overtly political Rule 21 that barred members of the British security forces and the Northern Ireland police force from becoming members of the GAA. Nationality was reinforced at school, at play, in church, and at home.

In any case, that sunny September weekday when I was a proudly uniformed eleven year old on a shopping mission with my beloved older sister, we walked, holding hands and chatting incessantly, toward our shoe-filled destination. As we neared the shop a young man, no more that five or six years older than myself, passed us, walking in the opposite direction, on the edge of the pavement. Just as he drew level he muttered three words, loud enough for us to hear and bring our happy conversation to an abrupt end. The words were addressed at my sister, spoken over my head, but clearly prompted by the sight of my uniform that placed me clearly in a particular religious and cultural camp, as did all school uniforms at that time and most still do. His words shocked me then and continue to do so: "Fucking Fenian bitch" he spat. I did subsequently, on many occasions, try to analyze why this total stranger, unprovoked, should decide to launch this hate-filled invective at my beloved sister who, to my knowledge, had never done a bad thing to anyone. I had arrived unwittingly in a new world, a world where my family and I were regarded not for what we were but for how we were perceived by people who did not know us. It was the fate of all of us who, by force of the system and structures that shaped us and that we inhabited, lived with impressions, shadows, and ciphers of the "other" rather than having any actual experience, understanding, and knowledge of them.

The second experience happened some six years later when, elected by my peers and driven by the desire to institute a formal dance and concerts (where I might also play guitar and sing), I found myself as head prefect of my school, a very proud school that in my final year won the All Ireland Gaelic Football Schools' Cup, the Hogan Cup. When asked in later years if I had played I always replied that of course I had, adding that I had played guitar, on the bus. Our achievement was huge and, as representative of the boys, I wanted to celebrate our achievement and even enhance our renown. I arranged to meet our principal, a huge and fairly intimidating Christian Brother, to suggest that we take our success to another level. My suggestion was that we, as All Ireland Champions, might challenge the Northern Ireland Schools' Cup rugby champions to a game first of rugby, perceived to be a Protestant game, and subsequently to a game of Gaelic football, the Catholic game. I proposed this idea having first consulted our champion players and they, of course, were up for it. The GAA rescinded Rule 27 at its Annual Congress in April 1971, so what better way to celebrate than by a meeting of the best young exponents of the two sports? The principal was not rude, just blunt. The games would not happen; there was no question of such an event taking place. I went on to organize the formal dance and the concerts, appearing second on the bill to the Boys of the Lough as it happens, but there was something missing for all of us in those troubled times. We rarely if ever met our fellow students who were "other," until there emerged a cross-community student group called Contact that began to suggest missing interaction and to organize shared events. I was very committed to my music in those days and joined with two of my school friends to form Eternity, a poorly disguised and pretentiously named rip-off of the Incredible String Band, with Donal's and my poetry providing the lyrics and Tony's mandolin and my guitar the rhythm. We performed in front of our friends and "others" in the Protestant Schools' Cup–winning grammar school, in what was a first and impressive cross-community school event. On the face of things nothing earth shattering nor society changing happened through Contact's efforts, yet we enjoyed a few opportunities to meet each other, we made many acquaintances and some friends, and, crucially, we young people engineered these opportunities ourselves, in spite of, rather than because of, the powers that were.

2.

My whole life since 1976 seems to have been dedicated to all-ability education and, since 1987, to all-ability integrated education. From 1990 to 1994, as the first development officer with the newly founded Northern Ireland Council for Integrated Education, I had the privilege of working with 13 groups of parents who decided they wanted to establish integrated schools. Of those just two were second-level schools. Primary schools were more straightforward, if such a description can be used in relation to the frenzied activity and total commitment required by all concerned to set up any school from scratch. Even during the height of the Troubles, opinion polls repeatedly indicated that a majority of our populace favored our children being educated together. However, when it came to postprimary education, even some parents who had been fervent advocates and supporters of integration at primary level seemed to lose their nerve.

Proponents of integrated schools largely succeeded in convincing parents that integrated primary schools were not only acceptable but desirable, should one be set up nearby, but my experience of parents' attitudes to postprimary education is that most continue to aspire to the selective ideal and, by that, they mean, of course, grammar schools, ignoring the "non-grammars" and those left to attend them. However, those parents I worked with to set up postprimary schools were unanimous: we set up schools that all of our children can attend. Why on earth would they not? If parents rather than governments or religious institutions are given the opportunity to set up schools, why on earth would they chose to create a school where all of their children might not be educated together and, even worse, be made to feel like failures if they could not gain entry to that particular school?

I have worked to set up schools with people with PhDs who still feel like failures themselves. The pernicious effects of the selection test continue to be disputed. For those who have "passed" that test, success usually means a grammar school education and inevitably that education, premised as it is on the concept of success and failure, brings with it a sense of satisfaction and entitlement, neither of which, I would contend, is good for our society. If as a society we can educate our children together and see them achieve their full potential together, then I contend that is what we must do so. While I and my contemporaries were growing up in what was not a shared society, with the very existence of the state seriously in dispute, and with scant regard for diversity and minority culture, a case could well be made for separate education by both sides. However, in a post-conflict society, where former enemies share power and the concept of a shared future is enshrined in statute, segregated education is a luxury too far and selective education is morally indefensible. That our society is scarred by selective education goes mostly unnoticed, but scarred it is. Why is it, for example, that whenever grammar schools make the headlines, for whatever reasons, they are described as "top" grammar schools, even when the reason for those headlines may well be drugs or violence or any of those other vicissitudes that affect the entire society? The implication is that such failings and weaknesses should not affect those among us who have passed an arbitrary and flawed test at age 11. How on earth have we arrived at this delusion?

All-ability education is not confined to integrated schools, nor is it confined to schools that are not grammar schools. I will refuse from this point to refer to schools that are not grammar schools as "non-grammar" schools, as is the media and departmental custom, in the same way that I refuse to call fellow human beings non-Catholics, as if Catholicism or grammar status were the norm or the ideal that should be aspired to. Grammar schools now admit children who sit transfer tests and achieve Cs and below, as many such schools have previously admitted children whose parents simply had the money to gain entry for them, but the reality that they are de facto all-ability schools goes unacknowledged, and the teaching methods and self-promotion continue to propagate the illusion that the product and outcome are somehow superior and exclusive.

It feels crass to cite my students who have excelled. Of course they have excelled. Students from our integrated, all-ability school have gone to Cambridge and Oxford, to Queen's and Durham, and many of the other esteemed universities and institutions. They also have gone on to work as engineers, plumbers, hairdressers, and artists. All of our students have been expected to study two foreign languages, English literature, music and drama, science, history, and geography, and sit a minimum of nine GCSEs. All of our students have been given the privilege of access to the totality of education as is their right and should be the right of all children. In 2012 a parent reported to me that her sister-in-law, on hearing of her niece's straight A*s and As from Shimna Integrated College, really did say that of course they sit different examinations in Shimna. This anecdote alone goes some way to proving that our selective education system constitutes an abuse of our people.

I offer a cautionary tale. I sat once in an admissions appeals tribunal where a parent, accompanied by his solicitor, contested our decision not to admit his son to Shimna. His son was a twin and our criteria stated that all eligible children in any family should have elected to attend an integrated school, a criterion devised to ensure that parents would chose our school for all their children rather than cherry-pick our school for those offspring unfortunate enough to sit the transfer test and not gain admission to a grammar school. This particular child's twin sister, who had gained a higher grade in the transfer test than her brother, had been sent to a grammar school while he, having "failed" the transfer test, had been put forward by his parents to attend Shimna Integrated College. The parent won the appeal on the grounds that his son was the eldest child, by virtue of being born one minute before his sister. That is how badly our selective system perverts perceptions and sensibilities. We subsequently changed the admissions criteria so that no other twins or multiple birth children would suffer similar indignity at the hands of their parents. The good news was that our fortunate elder twin seriously outperformed his sister who attended the grammar school. The bad news is that, as in all such cases, we must begin postprimary education by convincing such victims of this iniquitous system that they are most definitely not failures.

We can, of course, debate how we organize ourselves inside an all-ability system. I advocate all-ability teaching in all-ability settings and I am proud to have instituted and taught in that system myself. I believe that my teachers would revolt if they were told that we were to stream, band, or stratify our students in any other way than that which we now embrace. I once told a teacher who advocated streaming that, yes, I would permit her to stream children based on whatever test she decided to employ but that she would have to teach the bottom stream forever. She said that that would be totally unfair. I agreed and she never again made the suggestion.

In Northern Ireland we now have the opportunity to change our society; first, because we have the Good Friday agreement and a Stormont government that is working in partnership and, second, because we have no money and the school budget is seriously contracting. Grammar schools fill up with all those who apply while still claiming elitism yet still not realizing the potential of all their children. I have to question why grammar schools can continue to claim to be "top" schools when many such schools still do not teach English literature to all their students and when they let so many of their students leave when they fail to achieve at age 16, despite having selected them on their performance at age 11.

I personally would never teach in a school where children are selected at age 11 on the basis of a single test that is discredited and that has been proven to be useless either as a gauge of intelligence or as a predictor of achievement. My daughter recently sat her GCSEs, examinations undertaken at age 16 and the precursor to A Levels, the pre-university examinations. She was ill at the time and the examinations were therefore even more stressful than usual. She achieved ten A* and she attended Lagan College, the first integrated all-ability college in Northern Ireland.

If we can achieve academic excellence for all in one school then I contend that we must. I am a great believer in structures. They protect us and shape our reality and perceptions. The way we structure our education shapes our reality and our future. If we can achieve excellence, inclusion, and acceptance of diversity then I truly believe that that it is our duty to do so. I have to admit to being a bit of a zealot, albeit a bit of a liberal one. I was able to send my children to an integrated primary that I had helped parents to establish in 1991. I assisted the parents to set up the school when my first child was just one year old and it was a joy to be able to send him and, later, my daughter to that same school. I used to tell them that I knitted their school for them. When it came to transfer time I allowed my son to choose whether he would do the transfer test or not. He wanted to take the test and, thank goodness, he achieved an A grade. Liberal to the end, I took him around to all the schools, knowing that if he chose a grammar school I would just have to resign from my post as principal of Shimna Integrated College, founded in 1994 with me as the first principal. We visited our nearest grammar, a large voluntary grammar that has a mixed intake and a reputation as a high-achieving, "top" grammar school. On the evening of the Open Night the school band was on display and it was in truth fabulous and I feared it might sway my music-loving, clarinet-playing son. When we returned from our visit I explained that the school was a selective school and I talked about what that meant. We later went on to visit another local grammar school and afterward I explained that it too was selective but also that it was a school exclusively for Catholics. My then ten-year-old son turned to me and said, incredulously, "Are you serious?" Ultimately he chose Lagan College, the first integrated all-ability school in Northern Ireland. He and his sister who, naturally, followed him, were straight A students and that school was their natural first choice.

The truth is that all-ability education works and there is international evidence of the most robust kind to prove it. Finland is the example most often cited and it suits the profile of Northern Ireland beautifully. In essence children go to their local school; teachers are drawn from the highest academic background and encouraged in the highest standard of classroom practice. Schools are of human scale, five hundred being ideal, and focus on learning and formative assessment rather than high-stakes tests. Teachers, parents, and students have high expectations of each other and provide support and encouragement. Finland has rejected the evaluation-driven model that we have been shoehorned into and shaped by, and yet they consistently finish at the top in assessments of educational excellence.

All parents want the very best for their children and no parent wants to sacrifice their children on the altar of their idealism, be it integration or all-ability education. Shimna Integrated College finished top of the league tables the last time the Department of Education published such tables, and the percentage of A*–Cs has risen ever since. In Shimna we teach all-ability classes right through the age range, and our 18 years' experience has been that children rise to meet our expectations and nobody acts as if they are in the bottom set because there isn't one, and every child knows both that we have high expectations of them and that we will support them in achieving them. All-ability schools vary in the pattern of organizing their classes, and we must respect each other's way. The overriding principle must be that all our children are entitled to be under the same roof and to walk through the same door and know for certain that they are equally valued. I trust that the definition of integration will never be compromised by selection, and that we never attempt to solve one dimension of segregation through settling for another.

Our schools are integrated, academically excellent, all ability, child centered, and parent focused. We must hope and work toward a time when that definition will describe all our schools. John Steinbeck wrote that "socialism never took root in America because the poor see themselves not as an exploited proletariat, but as temporarily embarrassed millionaires." In a similar way we have succumbed, in Northern Ireland, to an aspiration for perceived excellence for a few rather that actual excellence for all. If we can change society then we must, and our education system is its most basic building block. Every society should look to its schools as the fulcrum of its worth and all-ability integrated education should be the ambition and validation of us all.

7

Two Steps Forward and One Step Back

A Journey to Creating an Integrated School in Cyprus

Maria Asvesta

In this chapter I will reflect on some of my experiences as a teacher and senior leader of the English School in Cyprus that began its journey to becoming an integrated school in September 2003.

Introduction

I was born and raised in London and feel very fortunate to have attended schools that were both diverse and multicultural in composition with some very supportive teaching staff. I chose to become a teacher because I acknowledged the great potential teachers had in making a positive difference to the lives of children who might be disadvantaged or at "high risk" of not fulfilling their potential at school.

Having begun my teaching career in London, I moved to Cyprus in 1989 as I was offered a job in an international school. In 1992, I joined the English School where I have been teaching Economics and Business for the last 19 years and have been a senior leader for the last four. During 2010–2012 I have also had the opportunity to teach Citizenship Education.

The English School is a prestigious, selective, co-educational private school with an unusual status. Its Board of Directors is appointed by the government and it receives a state subsidy although the largest bulk of its income comes from school fees. The school has always had a British head teacher and it follows the UK curriculum, the medium of instruction being English. It is well known for its high academic successes and is the premium choice school for the Cypriot elite. It was established by Reverend Canon Newham in 1900 to serve all the communities of Cyprus and was set up as a nondenominational school, though according to English School law it is "Christian in character."

In September 2003 the school re-admitted Turkish-Cypriot (TC) students on its roll after almost 30 years of segregation (following the Turkish invasion of 1974). This was a government decision and was part of a peace-building process emerging directly from the opening up of some of the border crossings in early 2003. In September 2003, six TC students crossed the borders to attend the school. The numbers gradually increased and today there are about 130 students enrolled in the school (about 14 percent of the school population).

MY UNDERSTANDING OF INTEGRATED EDUCATION

Very soon after the re-admission of the TC students to the school, it became apparent that a mixed intercultural school was not the same as an "integrated school." We did not teach our students to live together, and their educational experiences from the state primary schools had taught them very much the opposite (Spyrou, 2006). We are constantly reminded of our failure to create an integrated school community by the segregation of students by ethnic group in the school yard, witnessed on a daily basis, and the frequent occurrence of racist incidents. Indeed one telling research study on our school made the pertinent statement that our students were experiencing "parallel coexistence" rather than "reconciliation" (Zembylas, 2010b).

Integrated education means much more than placing students from different backgrounds, including post-conflict communities, in the same educational institution. It requires a whole range of policies, practices, and pedagogies to teach the students to learn to live together as well as reach their full potential. It involves building skills, values, and attitudes for the twenty-first century. It requires a school ethos that is rights respecting, where students have the opportunity to understand each other, learn about human rights and respect each other's human rights, appreciate those who differ from them, and recognize what they have in common as well as their differences. They should learn to use democratic and nonviolent methods to resolve any tensions or conflicts they may experience or feel and be able to take part in controversial discussions and deliberate.

My understanding of integrated education, however, is not that which is shared by the majority of educators in Cyprus, including a number of my colleagues, whose understanding of intercultural education pertains to the additive or assimilation model of multiculturalism, often regarded as tokenistic (Papamichael, 2008). Although the Cyprus Ministry of Education introduced the Reform Act (2004) in an attempt to promote intercultural and democratic education within Cypriot schools, it has not been sufficiently determined in promoting the type of intercultural education that will lead to fundamental changes in schools so as to address issues of inequality and social justice. It has adopted a minimalistic approach that supports the assimilation model of intercultural education rather than the critical model that questions the inequality and power dimension of multiculturalism and that promotes the appropriate pedagogy required for reconciliation (Zembylas, 2010a).

The Commission for Educational Reform (2004) and the European Commission against Racism and Intolerance (Papamichael, 2008) suggest that the efforts in the field of intercultural education in Cyprus need to be emphasized and strengthened (Papamichael, 2008). It seems that the Ministry of Education is working in this direction though the progress appears to be slow.

The rather conservative and minimalistic understanding of intercultural education in Cyprus has been an obstacle for the management of the English School, whose efforts to develop an integrated school have been perceived to be experimentations by some people. The English School has been a pioneer in some of its initiatives in relation to other schools in Cyprus, as it seeks to uphold the principles of inclusion and equality of opportunity. As a result of its commitment, it has faced severe criticism by some powerful and influential persons who perceive its policies to be driven by leftist political agendas. If the English School is to be able to move ahead with integrated education it will require greater support, both direct and indirect, from the Ministry of Education, something that has been missing until now due to the sensitive sociopolitical situation in Cyprus.

The Journey Begins: Steps and Impediments in Our Journey

I would like to focus on a just few of the many challenges that we have been confronted with on our journey to becoming an integrated school. I have chosen three areas of interest as I believe that they have been of particular significance. I hope that they may offer some insight and assistance to other educational practitioners who may be experiencing similar challenges on their own road to integration and peace.

Staff Training

Soon after the TC students were readmitted to the school in September 2003, the senior teacher Staff Development, Antonis Antoniou, arranged a number of training seminars on issues pertaining to European Union (EU) laws and anti-discriminatory practices as well as pedagogical methods to enable staff to create a safe classroom environment and break down prejudices. It is important to note that in 2004 Cyprus became a full-fledged member of the EU so there was now a legal obligation on us to follow EU anti-discrimination laws. University scholars and other experts in the field were invited to deliver these seminars between 2004 and 2007. However, these sessions, although valuable, were sparse and infrequent as they could not be fitted into the relatively short school calendar year. They were met with mixed responses from the staff, some of whom thought they were too many and unnecessary. Indeed a vocal minority of staff had made the following remarks on more than one occasion: "We don't need this kind of training"; "There is no racism here at the English School!" Certainly this was not consistent with the findings of two separate and independent research studies conducted in our school (Johnson, 2006, 2007; Zembylas, 2010b, 2010c) or what many teachers were witnessing in their classrooms and corridors.

It became increasingly apparent that the training sessions were too few to equip teachers with the skills and competencies to deal confidently with the possible scenarios that they might be confronted with and to enable them to help create an environment where everyone felt safe to learn and could reach their potential. As a result, the senior teacher in charge of staff development arranged a more intensive series of seminars for teachers, this time on a voluntary basis. This was a recommendation made by Johnson (2007). The first cohort of teachers (12 in all) who completed a series of training workshops in 2007–2008 had the opportunity to visit integrated schools in Northern Ireland at the end of their training to observe how the theory reconciled with the practice of integrated schooling. I was one of the teachers who completed the training and had the opportunity to visit Belfast in May 2008. I also had the opportunity, while in Belfast, to visit the Northern Ireland Council for Integrated Education , and to meet Professor McGlynn of Queens University Belfast. Our visit to Northern Ireland was a real awakening and I made the following overriding observations.

Although we were a so-called multicultural school in a post-conflict environment we could not call ourselves an "integrated" school, like those we had visited in Northern Ireland. Our students had not learned to respect one another, treat each other with dignity and equality, and acknowledge the great benefits in making the effort to get to know each other and each other's culture, religion, and histories. Our teachers were not equipped to challenge racism and bigotry and avoided having controversial discussions. We did not have the policies, pedagogical methods, curriculum, or ethos necessary to achieve a truly integrated educational environment.

It was indeed possible to reconcile the theory of antiracist education / intercultural education that we had learned from our training, and the practice, as evidenced by the many successful integrated schools that we visited in Northern Ireland. These schools could exist and did exist. Students from Protestant and Catholic backgrounds were living and learning together in a respectful and peaceful environment. Friendships flourished while racist incidents were negligible. Students sat side by side and told us, with pride, that their differences and turbulent past did not create barriers to their friendships.

We had a long journey in front of us and a number of serious constraints that were likely to impede us on our journey. One of the factors that had made integrated schools so successful in Northern Ireland was the fact that the schools were set up initially through a parent-backed initiative. Everyone was apparently "on board" and valued the aims and mission of integrated schooling. Parents who sent their children to these schools were not averse to seeing old divisions crumble and the creation of peaceful coexistence between the two communities as a key element and goal of their children's schooling. This meant that the children and teachers applying to attend and work in such schools were very likely to share this common vision and everyone was singing from the same hymn book.

Unfortunately this was far from the situation at the English School. The English School Parents Association (ESPA) has been at times vehemently opposed to the school taking initiatives, including training, that promoted greater integration and equality between the different communities. They viewed this as an infringement of their own (Greek) cultural heritage, identity, and values. For example, they were especially opposed to the removal of the orthodox icons from the classrooms in 2003, which had been placed on the walls after the war of 1974, and the school's decision to have two holidays for the Moslem Bayram.

Soon after the teachers returned from their trip to Northern Ireland
a number of them became the targets of a modern-day witch hunt. A
parent group, calling themselves "The Parents Initiative," set up a website in January 2009 where they publicly intimidated some of the teachers who had undertaken intercultural training and visited Northern
Ireland. They invited students and parents on their website to act
as a watchdog committee—to post "personal opinions about teachers, as well as any unacceptable incidents which take place within the
school"—in an attempt to demonstrate that teachers had been involved
in political indoctrination. Teachers were ruthlessly named and criticized without substance or remorse. Their only crime had been to follow school policy and the teachings of their training that advocated
that they challenge racism and bigotry whenever they saw it, encourage
critical thinking, and create a space for children to have controversial
discussions in a safe and managed environment. These teachers were
human-rights defenders and yet their own rights were violated.

During this period, parents also used the media to spread
unfounded rumors about the school and its teachers. This included
mistruths such as that the school had forbidden the wearing of the
cross, banned the national anthem, and that its teachers actively discriminated against the Greek-Cypriot (GC) children. This created
hysteria in the community regarding what was happening at the
school and had the effect of stifling the efforts of the school to create an integrated and safe school environment. It also had the effect
of silencing any teacher who was willing to stand up for equality,
diversity, and human rights, at least temporarily, and it led to further
tension in an environment that was already festering.

The outcome of this smear campaign was that the named teachers
were informally investigated by the head teacher and the deputy head.
The allegations made against them were found to be unwarranted
and thus the matter was deemed to be closed. The teachers' union
made a statement requesting that the offensive website be removed
otherwise they would be forced to consider industrial action. Soon
after this the website was removed but the damage to the good name
of the school was severe and the teachers had to endure tremendous
personal cost to their reputation and health. For some time after these
events, teachers were less inclined to challenge racism in their classes
as robustly as they had done in the past and refrained from engaging
in any type of controversial discussion unless it pertained to the subject they were teaching.

However despite this terrible experience and setback, the training
in intercultural education was imperative as it created a strong base

for future progress and change. There were now a significant number of teachers in the school who had the knowledge and skills required to help support policies, initiatives, and pedagogies conducive to integrated education even though they now needed to tread more cautiously regarding how they practiced, implemented, and advocated them.

The School's First Multicultural Week (May 2009)

One initiative in my first year as senior teacher in charge of intercultural education was to arrange a multicultural week that would include a number of events and an afternoon festival where parents / students/ community would be invited. After intensive planning with a team of volunteer teachers called the Hearts and Minds Group, the multicultural week was finally arranged.

During the week guest speakers from various nongovernmental organizations and government offices were invited to the school to lead assemblies and workshops on the theme of "Diversity and Anti-Racism." A number of impressive displays were prepared by a variety of departments and extracurricular societies. A book exhibition was organized and was unveiled by the local mayor. The Active Citizenship Society, an extracurricular club for students, organized a number of events in the afternoons including the screening of international movies promoting antiracism and human rights. They also produced an impressive short video called *Exploring the Multiple Identities at the English School* that involved interviewing a diverse number of students in the school demonstrating that our identities are multiple, flexible, and evolving.

The festival on Wednesday afternoon began with a short play by the Modern Languages department that acknowledged that there are over 40 different cultures and languages represented at the school. The play was followed by presentations on the Cypriot communities and cultures. Students from each minority group were invited to make a presentation about their culture, music, religion, and history, and to present their music and dances.

The minority groups that were initially invited to make presentations were the Armenians, Maronites, TC, and Latinos since these are the visible and traditional minorities of Cyprus. The Latinos, who were only a handful of students, chose not to present. The reason they gave for not wishing to present was that they did not feel comfortable distinguishing themselves from their peers. Although their decision was respected, it was one that is worthy of further analysis as it illustrates the complexities of issues of identity, privacy, and the curriculum (Chan, 2007). Teachers from the same background as the minority group volunteered to assist the students in preparing their presentations, and I was responsible for the final product.

Soon after announcing that we would be organizing a multicultural event, I was approached by a student in year six called Nicholas who felt that it was important that the GC culture and religion were presented alongside the other minority cultures. Although this was not my understanding of a multicultural event, I acknowledged that that the student had the right to express this request which, in retrospect, was not unreasonable. Both the ESPA and the English School Old Boys and Girls Association had articulated in the recent past their fear that the school was attempting to "dehellenise" its students. Given these allegations and the recent experience with the website, I thought it best to tread carefully and to allow the majority culture to be heard, as long as it did not dominate the other presentations. I believe that the decision was correct in this context and had the added potential bonus of providing an opportunity for greater interaction among the diverse groups of students.

The multicultural event could be seen to have been a success, and not merely a token event, for the following reasons: First and foremost it actually created the space and opportunity for interaction between many students from diverse backgrounds who had never previously collaborated. Over one hundred students were involved in the event. They were working for a common goal and this may have given them the opportunity to identify with each other and clear some of the misconceptions they held. This was especially the case with the play produced by the Spanish Department, and the short video, produced by the Active Citizenship Society, since in these activities students from different backgrounds collaborated over a period of time and produced an excellent outcome. This is consistent with Allports's Contact Theory (1958) according to which common goals and regular contact can help to break down stereotypes between groups.

A second reason why the multicultural event could be deemed successful was that it was very rich in terms of quality—the student presentations on the minority cultures were very interesting and were presented confidently and with pride The play, music, video, and dances were amazing and gave everyone the opportunity to see how talented some of our students were in areas we had not previously recognized—the boys dancing to Armenian music were especially impressive. The different foods were appealing to the eye and the taste buds, and the parents at the stalls seemed to be having a great time socializing with one another. Third, the festival involved a great number of teacher, student, and parent volunteers and was a wonderful sight of intercultural and inter-generational collaboration. Finally, it gave students, parents, and teachers a chance to learn things about each other's culture and language that they did not know before and to discover that there were many similarities as well as differences between them. This was especially evident in the case of the GC and TC presentations where it was observed that they shared similar food, music, values, traditions, and even common words in their dialects.

However the multicultural event did create some tensions between the students making presentations on their own cultures and history. The GC presenters felt that it was important to emphasize in their presentation that the Greeks were in Cyprus first and had been in Cyprus longer! There was disagreement regarding how close to the present time the history should be presented. The TC students stated that if the GC students insisted in presenting up to and including the 1974 invasion (or "occupation") they would present the intercommunal strife of the 1960s. I informed the students that we should avoid the recent history since it was too controversial for a multicultural event; this needed to be discussed in the context of a history class where multiple perspectives could be safely dealt with. The purpose of the multicultural event was to build bridges and not to destroy them.

I learned from this experience that if we were to organize a similar event again, we should do some things differently. First and foremost, students would not be requested to include history in their presentations, not because the issue of history should not be discussed but because it stirred up a great deal of commotion between some of the groups that could not be resolved easily in the time frame and confines of a multicultural festival. I understood very clearly from this event that history needed to be discussed, that students wanted to discuss it, and that students' different perspectives of history needed to be heard, but this had to take place in the parameters of a history class with trained history teachers who were confident and able to allow controversial discussions in a safe and managed space. I felt neither qualified nor confident to hold these debates, especially since I was not a history specialist.

In addition we learned that although it was necessary to discuss the controversial issues that were close to home, it might be more appropriate to discuss these issues after communication and collaboration of less emotive issues had commenced first. Students needed to have the opportunity to build relationships and understand what they had in common before discussing the more controversial issues that divided communities. They needed to build trust and friendship by working on projects that were less emotive, at least to begin with.

The Armenian Cypriots felt that it was necessary to include in their presentation a reference to the Armenian genocide since it was the event that caused their ancestors to flee to Cyprus for asylum. Some of the TC students found this offensive and wanted to pull out of the event. They felt that reference to the genocide would be linking them to the "evil" Ottoman Turks and give the GCs further justification to resent them. They already felt marginalized at school and had experienced exclusion and racism frequently, hence their fears were understandable. The teachers responsible spent a great deal of time and effort trying to resolve this conflict. We attempted to explain to the TC students that the Armenian presentation was not meant to be offensive to them but was directly relevant to their history and to their arrival in Cyprus. To my great relief, the TC students, after having deliberated among themselves, finally decided not to withdraw from the event.

The GC students felt offended that the trial presentation of the TC students showed images of attractions in the "occupied" areas, referring to them as being in "Northern Cyprus." I tried to explain to the GC students that it was not realistic to expect the TC students to refer to their homes as being in the "occupied areas" or "pseudo-state" especially since these terms are not used on the other side. At the same time I asked the TC students, rightly or wrongly, to consider refraining from the use of the term "Northern Cyprus" since it had caused offence due to its association with the Turkish Republic of Northern Cyprus and to consider using the term "North Cyprus," which appeared to be more acceptable as it was a geographic term rather than a political term.

One controversy followed another and at one point I felt we were never going to see it through. However it was a learning experience for us all. Although the justifications made for those decisions may not have been the right ones for everyone, the main success in dealing with these controversial issues was that it led to students considering perspectives that they had never had to take into account before, and understanding that matters were more complicated than they had previously thought and perhaps sometimes what was needed was a compromise.

However, a major weakness in the resolution of these conflicts was that they were not resolved through deliberation among the students. The students preferred to voice their concerns and disapproval of the other group's presentation to me in private and not directly to the students of the other group. However, given the great sensitivity and tension that existed, perhaps this was the most appropriate manner to proceed at the time, even though it was not the ideal. It was necessary for relationships to be built before these discussions could take place.

CURRICULUM CHANGES AND STRONG LEADERSHIP

In September 2009 a new head teacher called Deborah Duncan joined the school. She had experience from the UK public sector and was keen to take the school forward into the twenty-first century. She had an agenda for change and saw it as essential that the school introduce modern educational initiatives and innovations to enhance teaching and learning. Due to her drive, knowledge, and skills of diplomacy, she succeeded in winning over all the parents regardless of their political affiliation and outlook.

After consulting with staff, students, and parents, the Senior Leadership Team drafted a new mission statement and a five year strategic plan, which were approved by the board of management. The consultations that took place were a great opportunity to advocate for curriculum changes, including the introduction of Citizenship and Religious Education (RE). Such changes were crucial in creating a more integrated school ethos. The head teacher supported the introduction of Citizenship Education and the introduction of RE (alongside Religious Instruction) as she strongly believed that these courses would help to break down barriers and cultivate greater respect between the different religions and cultures. Teachers who had visited integrated schools in Northern Ireland also advocated for these curriculum changes since they had learned from their visit that subjects like Citizenship, history, and RE were imperative in giving students the opportunity to collaborate, learn about each other, as well as have the controversial discussions that they needed to have in a safe and managed space.

I was absolutely thrilled that so soon after Professor Johnson's recommendations, the introduction of Citizenship Education and RE was to become a reality, especially since there had been stark resistance to these curriculum changes expressed in the staffroom only a year earlier.

However today at the English School, Citizenship Education is a compulsory subject in years one–three and students now have the chance to learn about children's rights, human rights, identity and diversity, the media, peace, and conflict in a rights-respecting and child-centered environment. This will allow them the opportunity to get to know each other, understand and respect one another, and slowly learn to live together, by breaking down the barriers and prejudices of the past.

CONCLUSION

It is clear that integrated education is a journey with its own joys and tribulations. There will be periods of progress followed by inevitable obstacles and setbacks. There is no magic formula for creating an inclusive integrated school, and some schools will have to face greater constraints than others as a result of the school and country context. Mistakes will inevitably be made along the way as it is a learning process for all involved, and the level of calculated risk that is to be taken should be weighed carefully.

For integrated education to be truly successful in any school context it requires a holistic approach but it may not be possible to achieve this in the short term due to limited resources, lack of funding, and lack of sufficient support from influential stakeholder groups. In the case of the English School it seemed appropriate for us to focus on some key areas of priority such as staff training and policy making (the school has recently devised an Anti- Bullying Policy and an Equal Opportunities Policy). However, at the same time, we were fortunate that we were able to embrace opportunities that arose, as a result of other school initiatives and innovations, concerned with improving the standard of teaching and learning, for example, project-based learning, child-centered pedagogy, and personalized and inclusive learning, which also complemented the development of a more integrated school.

Staff training and the advice of experts was and continues to be absolutely imperative in the case of the English School, which has had to deal with a number of stakeholder groups that are openly hostile to the tenets of integrated education. This has been particularly important due to the fact that the school is a pioneer in establishing integrated education in a hostile environment without overt support from the Ministry of Education.

The significance of a strong and committed leadership has also proved to be a significant factor in bringing some changes more swiftly and demanding their universal acceptance.

The experience of the multicultural event implies that it is imperative that educators create safe and managed spaces where students are given the opportunity to work together in mixed groups on projects that will allow them to build trust, break down barriers, and develop friendships. It may be more appropriate to work on projects in class, in the formal curriculum, and begin with project themes that are less emotive, to allow students to break down stereotypes and barriers, and form trust and build friendships, before gradually introducing more controversial themes and issues.

There have been various times along our journey when the obstacles and constraints have been unbearable and have made some of us consider giving up the struggle for the sake of an easier and less stressful existence. However it is my strong belief that schools and educators have a duty to persevere with the journey as it is the right thing to do, the professional course of action to take, and consistent with the aims of education as specified in the United Nations Convention on the Rights of the Child (1989). We have a long journey ahead of us and there is no doubt that the ride will not be easy, but it is one that is clearly well worth pursuing.

REFERENCES

Allport, G. (1954). *The nature of prejudice.* Reading, MA: Addison-Wesley.

Chan, E. (2007). Student experiences of a culturally-sensitive curriculum: Ethnic identity development amid conflicting stories to live by. *Journal of Curriculum Studies, 39*, 177–194.

Commission for Educational Reform. (2004). Democratic and humanistic education in the Euro-Cypriot state [in Greek]. Nicosia, Cyprus.

Johnson, L. (2006). *The English School summary report of findings: School climate survey.* Unpublished manuscript.

Johnson, L. (2007). *Consultation report on the English School: Findings and recommendations.* Unpublished manuscript.

Papamichael, Elena. (2008). Greek-Cypriot teacher's understandings of intercultural education in an increasingly diverse society. *The Cyprus Review, 20*(2), 51–78.

Spyrou, S. (2006). Constructing "the Turk" as an enemy: The complexity of stereotypes in children's everyday worlds. *South European Society and Politics, 11*, 95–110.

Zembylas, M. (2010a). Critical discourse analysis of multiculturalism and intercultural education policies in the Republic of Cyprus. *The Cyprus Review, 22*(1), 39–59.

Zembylas, M. (2010b). Negotiating co-existence in divided societies: Teachers' and students' perspectives at a shared school in Cyprus. *Research Papers in Education, 25*(4), 433–455.

Zembylas, M. (2010c). Pedagogic struggles to enhance inclusion and reconciliation in a divided community. *Ethnography and Education, 5*(3), 277–292.

8

PRIORY INTEGRATED COLLEGE

A TRANSFORMED INTEGRATED COLLEGE—
A COLLEGE TRANSFORMED

Peter McCreadie

In this chapter I shall attempt to describe the transformation journey and the challenges faced by governors, staff, pupils, and parents as they sought to transform Holywood High School to become Priory Integrated College. Additionally I will endeavor to evaluate the impact becoming an integrated college had upon the school and wider community.

THE PROCESS OF TRANSFORMATION

Two routes can be taken in the founding of an integrated college in Northern Ireland. One, a group of founding parents can work together in a particular geographical area to establish a grant-maintained integrated primary school or postprimary college. This is an extremely demanding and costly process. Grant-maintained schools are initially founded without the financial support of the Department of Education and funding is not made available until the school meets rigorous criteria set down by the department. Founding parents and governors must seek funding to purchase land, construct school buildings, and recruit staff and pupils, and resource the new school. This process enabled the majority of integrated primary schools and postprimary colleges to be established. Their establishment would not have been possible without the huge commitment and total dedication of all those involved.

A second route to establishing an integrated school or college is the process of transformation. This route is open to already established schools housing a minimum of ten percent of what is defined as the minority religious population in a particular area. Governors wishing to transform their school must engage in a process of consultation with parents, staff, and pupils before a vote is taken that allows the school or college to be designated as integrated. This is a much less costly route to integration particularly because it does not involve the purchase of land and erection of new buildings. However the transformation process is exactly that, a process, and it is a process that makes huge demands upon all those involved: governors, staff, pupils, parents, and the local community. Transformation is not simply the renaming and re-branding of an existing school.

Transformation presents many challenges. The most obvious challenge for the newly transformed integrated college is to attract greater numbers of the minority community to attend the college while, at the same time, not alienating members of the majority community already in attendance. The Department of Education sets transformed integrated colleges a target of attaining a 70 percent–30 percent religious balance within five years (70 percent representing what is defined as the majority faith in the college catchment area). It seems that the Department of Education believes that attaining a particular religious mix makes a school integrated. However, the process of transformation demonstrates that being integrated is about much more than religious balance.

A fundamental challenge for newly transformed colleges, and one that may not be immediately obvious, is to understand what it means to be an integrated college, to understand how being an integrated college should impact upon ethos, curriculum, and pedagogy. A key question must be what makes an integrated school or college different from schools in other sectors for staff and students.

The transformed college also faces cynicism from many in the wider community. Individuals and community groups may be at best cynical or at worst hostile toward the idea of their local school explicitly stating it will strive to create a more mixed religious community where all beliefs are explored and valued. Experience has also demonstrated that many of those connected with new built, grant-maintained integrated schools and colleges view transformed schools with suspicion and even hostility.

THE TRANSFORMATION OF HOLYWOOD HIGH SCHOOL

I joined Priory Integrated College as vice principal in September 2000. I was excited and proud to be entering a sector that I understood was committed to making a positive difference to our community by educating together young people from different religious and cultural backgrounds. My instinct told me that this type of environment would help young people understand, respect, and embrace difference but never ever having worked in an integrated school I had no clear understanding of how all this happened. My previous experience helping found Northern Ireland's first community college cultivated my belief that a child-centered, community-focused college could make a really transformational impact upon students and the wider community.

However when I joined Priory College ("integrated" was not a part of the school name then) I had no clear understanding of the integrated movement in general and integrated colleges in particular. I looked forward to learning how my educational philosophy would impact upon, and be influenced by, an integrated environment.

I needed to understand how being integrated impacted upon my new school. I was surprised to discover that many working in the college were also struggling with the same question. It was at this point that I began to understand that I had not joined an integrated college; I had joined a transforming integrated college.

The former Holywood High School had transformed to become Priory Integrated College two years previously, and staff and governors were trying to understand how this transformation should impact upon the ethos and life of the college.

In the first year in the life of a transformed college only the first year intake and their parents have chosen to attend an integrated school. While the majority of parents and staff had voted in favor of the school becoming integrated, many had limited understanding of the impact this would have upon the school and a significant minority of parents and pupils and some staff were not in favor of becoming integrated.

In the year 2000 there was no clear understanding of what being integrated really meant even for those who voted in favor of transformation. This was not the result of lethargy or a lack of desire to grapple with the issue. Rather there was no experience of integration in the college, and governors and staff were "groping in the dark." At the time of transformation governors had the choice to transform either as a controlled integrated college, under the management of the South Eastern Education and Library Board (SEELB), or as a grant-maintained integrated college supported by the Northern Ireland Council for Integrated Education (NICIE). Governors opted to transform as a controlled integrated college. This may have resulted in a degree of separation from the NICIE. When I joined the college in September 2000 the process of integration seemed to have become becalmed. The SEELB was unable to support the transformation because they had no experience of integrated colleges and the NICIE was not involved with the college because the organization did not want to encroach upon SEELB responsibility.

In attempting to understand the impact being integrated should make upon the college it became clear that I needed to understand why the school had transformed from Holywood High School to become Priory Integrated College.

Holywood High School had been a failing school in the late 1980s with a school population of less than 160 pupils. However in 1989 a new principal was appointed and with the support of key staff and governors he led the school through an improvement process that had increased the student population to over 360 pupils at the time of transformation. At this time local demographics resulted in Holywood High School housing a mixed faith student body with a little over ten percent of the student population coming from the minority Catholic community. Governors examined the idea of transformation and concluded it was the next logical step in creating a school that would better meet the needs of pupils and the wider community. The process of transformation is lengthy and involves extensive consultation with all school stakeholders before a vote is taken. In the final ballot taken in 1997 72 percent of all those eligible voted in favor of transformation, the largest majority ever recorded by a school participating in this process.

This was encouraging but what had parents and staff voted for? My discussions with governors, staff, and parents suggested that they voted to establish a college that educated Catholics and Protestants together to help break down the religious and cultural barriers so evident across the country. There was an understanding that the college would change to accommodate pupils and staff from a wider range of faith and cultural backgrounds though the central part that being an integrated college would play in all aspects of the life of the college was not yet recognized. This was something that would become apparent throughout the transformation process.

Priory Integrated College is situated in North Down where the Catholic population sits at around 15 percent. The Catholic population of Holywood in particular remains stable at around 12.5 percent. Neighboring East Belfast has a similar religious demography. Therefore the college faced, and continues to face, a real challenge to meet the religious balance targets (70 percent–30 percent) set by the Department of Education for transformed integrated colleges. The college houses a significant majority of pupils from the Protestant tradition. At this early stage in the transformation of the college the focus was upon creating a neutral environment to ensure that members of the minority community would not feel intimidated by symbols or overt displays of loyalty to the majority tradition in the area.

Governors invited staff to apply to become part of an Integration Committee with the aim of developing the school as an integrated college. The committee took steps to create an ethos and environment that would not be threatening to members of the minority community. National and club sports tops were banned from physical education as were badges and insignia with political connotations. The school discipline policy was amended to prohibit writing sectarian graffiti and stop pupils from engaging in overt displays of behavior that reflected a particular cultural tradition.

These first steps were small steps in a very long journey that would ultimately transform the school but even these small steps were difficult and contentious for many. Shortly after I arrived at the college I remember having a discussion with a senior pupil who could see nothing wrong with whistling a Protestant marching tune in the playground. When I reminded him that he attended an integrated college he forcefully stated he had not chosen to join one. This was not an isolated incident and many resented the enforcement of new rules. I had conversations with a number of pupils, parents, and staff who were suspicious of these attempts to create a neutral environment, which they viewed as attacks upon their cultural heritage. Several years later I knew things were changing when I invited a different Year 12 pupil into my office to discuss why he felt it necessary to whistle the same marching tune as he walked along the school corridor. He initially replied, "I am just celebrating my culture." This was heartening for two reasons. First because this suggested that something was happening in the college that enabled the pupil to overtly connect cultural values to behaviour, and second because the pupil engaged in a very interesting and genuine discussion about how students who identified with the "other" culture might view this behavior.

What had happened in-between times that enabled a member of staff and a pupil to engage in a conversation that objectively examined cultural values in both communities and resulted in an agreed solution? (His form tutor facilitated a whole class exploration of marching and music culture within both traditions.)

In the early 2000s the integration committee concluded that a whole school exploration of what it means to be an integrated college was essential and that this would involve building relationships with other integrated colleges and seeking support from the NICIE. The former was to provide further challenges.

In March 2007, Dr. James Whitehead submitted a thesis to the University of Birmingham for the degree of Doctor of Philosophy. His research included a case study of Priory Integrated College. In the abstract to his thesis dissertation Dr. Whitehead suggested that the view held by many committed to the integrated movement was that "transformed (integrated) schools are based on a narrow conception of integration and consequently pose a threat to the credibility of the integrated movement."

I quickly came to understand the low esteem in which transformed integrated schools and colleges were held by many connected to grant-maintained or new built integrated schools. I discovered that many connected to these "founder schools" thought the transformation from the "failing" Holywood High School to Priory College was a cynical attempt by governors to raise the profile of the school in the local community and to access additional funding from the Department of Education.

In the early days I was viewed with, at best, suspicion by many when I attended meetings organized by the Association of Principal Teachers in Integrated Schools. I felt in some way "unclean" and eventually made this point at one particular meeting. The principal of a grant-maintained post-primary school agreed that transformed schools lacked credibility for many in the grant-maintained sector and explained that this lack of credibility was based upon a view that schools transformed to increase enrollment and access additional Department of Education funding rather than to nurture pupils in a genuinely integrated environment. This openness was welcome and invigorating and enabled conversations to take place and relationships and collaborations to develop that significantly impacted upon the transformation of Priory College.

Seeking support from the NICIE proved to be hugely significant in the college's transformation journey. Two individuals working for NICIE, Mr. Terry McMackin and Mrs. Nichola Lynagh, were assigned to support the college, and regularly met senior management and the Integration Committee. Initially they helped staff develop their understanding by sharing their knowledge of the ethos and practices of other integrated colleges. Slowly they helped change the focus upon integration. Rather than being just being a part of the college, they helped senior management and members of the Integration Committee understand that integration should be at the center of the college and should be the foundation upon which the ethos and practice of the college was built. It was becoming clear that being integrated should not be a "bolt on" accessory.

In February 2001 governors and all members of the teaching and nonteaching staff were taken off-site for an in-service training day designed and delivered by Mr. McMackin, Mrs. Lynagh, Integration Committee members, and external facilitators from the Mediation Network. A series of workshops challenged participants to explore four areas. These were:

1. What is our vision for integration in Priory College?
2. How can we translate this vision into practice in the school environment, in classes, in the delivery of the curriculum?
3. How can we develop a system that encourages the value of the individual in terms of self-respect and respect for others?
4. What are the college's relationships with the wider community?

This was an exciting and challenging day that invigorated all attendees. It fostered an understanding and acceptance by the majority of participants that they were at the start of a journey that was going to fundamentally change relationships within the college and with the wider community. There was strong agreement that an integrated college must be a child-centered environment and that the students should be closely involved in the journey to become an integrated. There was recognition that the transformation of the college was viewed with skepticism by many in the wider community and that negative perceptions had to be challenged if transformation was to be successful.

The in-service day raised awareness that an integrated school environment and ethos was different and that it was something staff genuinely aspired to creating. There was acknowledgement that becoming integrated would impact upon every area of college life and understanding that this journey would be long and challenging.

It was agreed that community perceptions had to be addressed. The college was rebranded Priory Integrated College on all literature and stationery and the word "integrated" was discussed in class and at year and whole school assemblies. The school motto "Thorough" on the blazer badge became "Together" and this was also extensively discussed. Staff committed to using the word "community" when talking to pupils about school-based issues such as vandalism or bullying and to exploring the idea of community at every opportunity, in class and in year group and whole school assemblies.

An evaluation of relationships within the college resulted in the senior management team being extended from four to seven members and becoming the senior leadership team. In-service training was sourced from the Regional Training Unit to move the focus of the team from management to leadership. Members were developed to become effective leaders and given particular areas of the college development plan to lead. Senior leaders replicated their training with middle management and again the emphasis moved from managing to leading. Acceptance of new responsibilities was difficult for a number of members of staff. However real consultation and extensive support in the precise setting, monitoring, and evaluating of targets that were an integral part of the college development plan helped empower and develop all staff.

It was agreed that pupils must play a key role in the transformation of the college. They had to be given opportunities to consider what it meant to be a pupil at an integrated college, to contribute to the development of the school community, and to celebrate integration. They had to be given opportunities to make a positive difference to their school community.

The large percentage of Protestant pupils attending the college presented a challenge. There was a danger that students from the minority Catholic community would lack confidence to celebrate their faith and culture in such an environment. It was becoming clear that pupils and staff must feel confident to discuss their beliefs and values in order for respect and understanding of others to grow. An initial strategy to develop the confidence of pupils from minority communities was to link with a grant-maintained integrated school that had a majority of Catholic pupils. This allowed pupils and staff from both colleges to participate in a variety of activities that promoted an understanding of culture and celebrated difference. Pupils and staff from Priory and from Oakgrove Integrated College, (London)Derry, visited each other's schools, shared ideas, and established friendships that remain strong even today.

Both colleges also developed an important relationship, through NICIE, with Questions of Difference (QOD), a London based strategic business consulting company that specializes in organizational development and cultural change in organizations. QOD were interested in using their affirmative questioning techniques with young people in Northern Ireland to promote positive community change. QOD's work with members of staff and pupils in both colleges challenged perceptions about the nature of relationships in an integrated community. Initially, at Priory, they worked with a group of 40 pupils and six members of staff. At the end of the first year this "Pacesetter" group delivered a two-hour whole-school interactive program to vertical groups of 20, with each group housing a cross section of the whole school community. Pacesetters facilitated conversations that allowed every participant to celebrate in words and pictures something positive about the college. This was captured on a "Wall of Greatness" that is still on display at the center of the college. Pacesetters were the start of pupils becoming involved in making a positive difference to their college community. Today students participate in a range of focus groups including the Student Council, the Eco Warriors, Pacesetters, and the Charity Committee. Membership of these groups is open to all students and recruitment and organization model the democratic process.

Perhaps the most important outcome of the Pacesetter process was that it started pupils and staff really thinking about, and celebrating, difference. Up to this point difference was viewed in almost exclusively religious terms; now the wide range of differences found within any community—gender, sexuality, race, ability, size and shape, interest group, social background, and so on—was being recognized and celebrated. Understanding was growing that an integrated environment is about much more than simply teaching Catholics and Protestants in the same building.

It was becoming clear that talking about respect for others and self was pointless unless staff and students experienced being valued. Pupils needed opportunities to actively learn about each other and be able to agree and disagree without the fear of humiliation or retribution. In-service training enhanced teachers' skills in leading small group work in the classroom that would develop pupil self-confidence and communication skills.

Governors and members of staff were beginning to understand how low levels of self-esteem contributed to divisive behavior and sought to create the conditions that would improve pupils' sense of self-worth. Pupils needed opportunities to regularly succeed and have this success recognized. A Student Council was founded and facilitators from the SEELB trained recruits. The council worked with staff to create a merit system that rewarded all pupils on a daily basis for positive contributions to the school community. Additionally they designed a positive classroom management plan that was adopted by parents, staff, and governors, and applied consistently across the school.

The next step was to understand how the curriculum could promote our objectives as an integrated college. Departments undertook an audit of opportunities offered by their syllabi to promote integration. Many subjects offered obvious opportunities for pupils and staff to explore contentious issues centered on, for example, faith or

culture. History, geography, Religious Education, and English literature offered obvious opportunities but others wondered how they
could meaningfully contribute when content did not seem relevant.
However many were resourceful. For example, the Mathematics
Department used national flags to discuss symmetry and used this
as a stimulus to debate the wider notion of flags and what flags
represent.

It was becoming clear that the way the curriculum was delivered
was closely linked to the ethos of integration. An integrated college
must be fully inclusive; therefore the curriculum must be delivered in
a way that included and engaged all students in learning. The NICIE
facilitated and funded a volunteer group of teachers to explore how
children learn. They focused upon Accelerated Learning techniques,
which recognize that students favor one of three particular learning styles: visual, auditory, and kinesthetic. They came to understand
how teaching targeting one particular style could exclude many students from learning. This group of teachers had to bring their conclusions to the staff body, convince them that Accelerated Learning
was the way forward, and plan and roll out a five-year program to
implement Accelerated Learning throughout the school. The manner
in which staff committed to this new way of working with students
demonstrated their commitment to child-centered education. In
effect staff had to retrain "on the job" to deliver Accelerated Learning
lessons. Dramatically improved examination results at Key Stage 3,
taken upon completion of Year 10; General Certificate of Secondary
Education, taken upon completion of Year 12; and General Certificate
of Education Advanced Level, taken upon completion of Year 14,
confirmed their faith in this individualized learning. In March 2012,
the *Belfast Telegraph* carried out a survey of General Certificate of
Education Advanced Level results in 2011 in 168 postprimary schools
in Northern Ireland. Priory Integrated College was in the thirty-eighth
place, outperforming 33 selective (grammar) schools with 78 percent
of its students attaining three Advanced Level passes at grades C and
above. The significance of this statistic becomes clear when compared
to pupil outcomes at the time of transformation when the college did
not offer General Certificate of Education Advanced Level examination and not a single pupil attained five or more General Certificate
of Secondary Education passes at grades A–C (the minimum target
set for all postprimary schools by the Department of Education).

A whole-school and departmental evaluation of how student work
was marked and how results and progress were reported to parents
accompanied the implementation of Accelerated Learning. Marking

became marking for improvement that was designed to motivate students to achieve their potential and reports were redesigned to allow teachers to write very specifically about individual students' strengths and areas for improvement.

New curricular opportunities were offered to pupils who, for a variety of reasons, were excluded from the traditional range of General Certificate of Secondary Education subjects. This sometimes involved forming links with other educational providers, for example, accessing very vocational Key Stage 4 (Years 11 and 12) programs of study at South Eastern Regional College and North Down Training Ltd. Pupils attended these providers for a portion of the school week to gain appropriate vocational qualifications in areas such as construction and catering. An additional benefit was that they worked in classes with pupils from schools in the maintained and controlled sectors, thus widening their experience of others.

Following an approach by SEELB, governors and staff had no hesitation in establishing a base within the school for students diagnosed with Autistic Spectrum Disorder (ASD). This was founded on the explicit understanding that the base would not be a separate unit housed within the college. It would be a resource designed to develop and support the needs of these young people so that they could spend as much time as possible in mainstream classes. This development alone offers so much to mainstream and ASD pupils as they learn from and about each other.

Until 2006 Priory educated children up to the General Certificate of Secondary Education level. It became clear that many pupils wanted to remain at the college for two further years to study for the General Certificate of Education Advanced Level qualifications. Departments were surveyed and teachers were keen to take up the challenge. A small suite of Advanced Level subjects was offered initially. This has grown annually and now a full range of general and applied Advanced Level subjects are offered by the college with partner providers in North Down and Ards Learning Community. Priory hosts the largest collaboration between any schools in Northern Ireland with 70 sixth formers from the local selective (grammar) school attending Priory to study one applied Advanced Level subject (Applied Business). This collaboration has broken down social barriers that previously existed between the majorities of pupils from both school communities. An annual audit of pupils participating in the collaboration asks pupils from both schools whether participation has changed their perceptions of the other. Unfailingly pupils from both schools answer, "I used to think that Priory/Sullivan pupils were ..."

Parents have played a huge part in the transformation of the college. A parent teacher association was in existence at the time of
transformation. The chief remit of this group was to raise funds for
the college. As the school transformed this group became "Parents
for Priory." They continued to seek ways to financially support the
school but as they moved along their own integration journey they
realized that their relationship with the school should be mutual.
Senior college leaders joined the group and they explored ways the
college and parents could support each other. The Parents for Priory
group now meets every month. In addition to hosting regular fundraising events to support the school they facilitate seminars to support
parents on topics such as "Parent Teen Coaching," "Understanding
How Children Learn," and "Internet Safety." These parents are the
college's most enthusiastic advocates and several members are also
parent governors. Their work has been hugely important in changing
community perceptions about the college and members are proud
that the school is now consistently oversubscribed.

The college is an active member of the Holywood Shared Services
and Spaces Initiative. Community groups are encouraged to make
use of college facilities at a nominal cost, for example, the Northern
Ireland Festival Irish Dance Championships hosted by the college
annually. The college has also supported the loyalist Recon group
in its community work with local young people. During and after
school, pupils visit and work with groups seeking to improve the local
community, for example, Holywood Transition Town.

Close links have been formed with the local nursery school and
primary schools. All nursery pupils, staff, and parents annually visit
the college to participate in a day of science-based activities. Pupils
from local primary schools in all sectors regularly participate with
Priory pupils in dance, drama, and musical activities. These links
bring a diverse range of parents to the college and let them taste the
integrated experience.

Becoming integrated has transformed Priory Integrated College
in every sense. The transformation journey was challenging. Several
members of staff resigned, unable to commit to the developing integrated, child-centered ethos. Parents and pupils and members of
staff often needed support, reassurance, and challenge. There was no
eureka moment that demonstrated integration was now at the center of the college. Progress was incremental and founded upon the
transformational nature and success of each initiative. Relationships
between pupils, staff, and parents became more positive and mutual
as they connected to the developing ethos of the college. School

attainment and public examination results improved as the integrated ethos embedded. Relationships with the wider community slowly became extensive and positive. Progress in every area of college life was, and is, celebrated in the classroom, in college assemblies, and the local press.

Currently 77 percent of the student body and 70 percent members of staff follow the Protestant tradition. This is unlikely to change significantly given the religious demographic of the catchment area. The challenge will always be to monitor and evaluate all practices to ensure that every member of the school community, regardless of faith, race, social, academic, or other backgrounds, experiences an integrated education that will enable him or her to participate positively in the diverse society found inside and outside school.

Fourteen years of experience and reflection demonstrates that transformation is a journey. As the process developed it became clear to school leaders that it is a journey without a destination. The key questions identified at the in-service training in 2000 are always relevant and provide the stimulus for regular reflection and evaluation by all those connected with the college community. Being integrated is always a work in progress.

REFERENCE

Whitehead, J. R. (2007). *What's in a name? Insights into what it means for a school in Northern Ireland to become integrated.* Unpublished dissertation thesis, University of Birmingham.

9

Building Bridges at the Earliest Age through the Mozaik Model for Multicultural Preschool Education in Macedonia

Vilma Venkovska Milcev

> In a preschool group, a little girl named Aleksandra, using wooden blocks, is building a church and a mosque next to each other. She invites everyone in the group to give ideas for how the mosque and the church should be best positioned within close proximity to one another. Her wish, as she explains to the group, is that when she and her classmate Ensar grow up and marry each other, they will remain close even when she will go to the church and he to the mosque.

This is just one example of the "Mozaik" preschool groups in Macedonia where children aged 3–6 years are socialized for a multicultural society, regardless of their ethnic background and language. Starting at an early age, when they are free from prejudices toward and stereotypes of their peers, children from different ethnic communities in Macedonia are emerging in an environment called "Mozaik" that teaches the children to see "the other" with respect and appreciation. This new and innovative educational approach is based on the principles of tolerance and respect for cultural diversity.

Since 1998, when the project started with three pilot groups in the public (state) kindergartens, Mozaik has developed and expanded to thirteen preschool groups in nine multiethnic municipalities that today are integrated in the formal educational system in Macedonia. Mozaik teachers are on the payroll of the Macedonian government, ensuring the continuity of the program. Now that children and parents need no longer concern themselves with the immediate continuity of the program, I am proud to say that Mozaik as a project has reached the ultimate goal of many international and local education initiatives—to become a sustainable program that is not only embraced by, but also institutionalized in the formal education system in Macedonia.

In this chapter, I will reflect on the positive model of collaboration between children in a multicultural society embodied in the Mozaik educational model, and on the challenges we have faced with its institutionalization in the educational system in Macedonia.

SOME BIOGRAPHICAL AND CONTEXTUAL NOTES

Macedonia's recent history is marked by conflicts between the country's Macedonian majority and its large Albanian minority. Although interethnic communal tensions have existed for some time, they never exploded into full civil strife as they did in Kosovo. Macedonia was on the verge of a civil war in early 2001, when the ethnic Albanian National Liberation Army clashed with Macedonian security forces. Stability was restored by a timely international intervention that resulted in the signing of the Ohrid Framework Agreement, yet several threats to sustainable peace still exist. Macedonia is still highly divided and lacks the socio-political mechanisms to build lasting trust and sustainable, positive relations between the ethnic communities.

I grew up in a family where ethnic and religious differences were much appreciated; my father is an Orthodox and my mother is a Protestant Christian, a minority and marginalized community in the country despite the fact that the Protestant Church has been officially recognized in the Macedonian Constitution since 2001. I decided at an early age to become a doctor, and qualified at the Medical Faculty in Skopje. As a general practitioner, I was very happy to work in a multicultural and ethnically mixed environment, learning many Albanian phrases in order to communicate with my young patients. It was not an easy task at that time to work in an environment full of stereotypes and prejudices about learning and speaking in the language of the Albanian minority.

Aside from my medical practice, I become very interested in international peacebuilding interventions and in 1994 I joined Search for Common Ground (SFCG), one of the leading conflict transformation and peacebuilding organizations in the world. Macedonia was their first field office. Through my work at SFCG I had the opportunity to meet and work with colleagues from different ethnic and religious backgrounds, which enriched my experience and deepened my knowledge and skills in creating peacebuilding initiatives. I learned that people often tend to have stereotypes and prejudices about each other when there is no communication and regular interaction. In addition, I noticed how segregation leads to mistrust and violence and that often people allowed their differences to escalate into dangerous conflicts.

I was moved by the approach that we were using in designing our peacebuilding projects: to bring people from different ethnic, religious, and gender backgrounds to work together on issues of common concern; to learn to appreciate each other's differences; and to act on their commonalities. It is a very powerful approach, and indeed, not only have other civil society organizations adopted a similar approach, but also donors. I learned that many cultures struggle with how best to resolve differences and conflicts in a mutually beneficial way. I consider conflict transformation is lifelong skill, a skill that lies at the heart of each one of us as an individual and as communities. I made a life-changing decision to work on the creation and implementation of educational peace interventions for building integrated, multicultural societies.

Understanding Integrated Education

I believe that every society has to "fight" for an education that is free of discrimination and that ensures equal access for and treatment of all students. There is a strong link between education and peacebuilding, so it is crucial for a country to recognize that one of the its security issues is an educational system that incorporates models that fosters integration of the society.

Education is a powerful tool that can alleviate intergroup conflicts whether they are international, interethnic, or interracial. "Education offers the chance to shape minds, hearts and behaviors of succeeding generations. If we can educate young people to respect others, to understand the cost of group hatreds, to avoid stereotypes, to develop tools for resolving disputes, to choose to stand up to demagogues and to be peacemakers we might hope to prevent the future" (Minow, 2002, p. 2). Indeed, education plays an essential role in fostering interethnic communication, and can break down stereotypes, explain the value of diversity, and broaden understanding of universal human rights and values. However, an education system that reinforces social differences, stereotypes, and prejudices can exacerbate tensions and even promote conflict. The role of education in promoting the identity of individuals and allowing the expression of identity within cultural groups is particularly important in building stable multiethnic societies because it allows persons belonging to the national minorities to pass on their culture to future generations, preserving and developing their minority characteristics.

Education provides children with the means to develop their capabilities as well as personalities in order to become full members of the society. In many respects, education is a prerequisite for the fulfillment of other rights and freedoms—such as the right to participate, to associate, and the freedom of express—that are instrumental for the democratic stability and economic prosperity of the country. Schools not only provide children with educational attainment but also promote social cohesion by enhancing a shared sense of belonging among individuals of different backgrounds.

The basic principle of integrated education is to bring students from different backgrounds together in a shared learning environment so that they can learn to understand, respect, and accept different cultures, traditions, and languages. Integrated education does not assimilate or segregate students, but rather tries to combine the two aspects—societal cohesion and the right of the children to preserve and develop their own culture and identity—by providing a safe space for children to interact and learn from each other.

An essential element of integrated education is *language*, which can be used as a tool for social cohesion or as a tool for exacerbation of conflict. Multiethnic societies should provide opportunities for ethnic communities to learn and receive instructions in their mother tongue. This right however needs to be combined with appropriate tuition in the state language in order for all to be able to fully participate in society.

Aside from language, other efficient tools for fostering integration are *curriculum development* and *textbooks*, especially the teaching of history, culture, and traditions of the different ethnic communities in the country. This way, students will be given the opportunity to learn more about other's history and culture and to respect differences.

Another key element of integrated education is to ensure the *engagement of all stakeholders*, from the central government level to the local government. Policies of integrated education should also strive to ensure that decisions are made at a level that is as close as possible to the parents and those receiving education. In the process of developing curricula and teaching materials the participation of representatives of the various ethnic communities should be ensured. Equally important is the need to consult representatives of the ethnic communities to ensure the curriculum is accurate. This will enable those directly affected to be heard and to have their views taken into account.

The importance of *finding a balance* between the two aspects of integrated education—promoting minority rights and policies of integration—should also be emphasized. That is, it is important that members of the national minorities have the right to education in their mother tongue, but at the same time they should take on the responsibility to integrate in the wider society by acquiring sufficient knowledge of the state and its official language. If such a balance is not achieved, polarization between the different communities may arise and become a source of considerable tension. Therefore, it is vital for every culturally divided country to ensure integration through education in its efforts to build a peaceful and democratic society (OSCE HCNM, 2011).

BUILDING BRIDGES BY LAUNCHING AND IMPLEMENTING THE MOZAIK MODEL

Education in Macedonia is highly segregated based on ethno-linguistic criteria. In public institutions, children from the country's various communities commonly attend separate classrooms and study in their own languages. This continues right through to the university level. The majority of children rarely come into contact with peers from other ethnic communities, and when they do, these encounters are often negative. Through such isolation, children absorb stereotypes about "the other" from the adults and wider community in their lives and perpetuate negative social attitudes in their own adulthoods.

Preschool education is also marginalized and neglected although it is a crucial part of education for every individual. Indeed, the main attitudes and characteristics of a person are formed before they are six years old, as the learning process of a child starts long before its first day of school. According to the United Nations Economic and Social Council, preschool education is "one of the critical long term answers to the problem of violence in the society, since patterns of violence and aggressive behaviour in adolescents and adults can be traced to behavioural and social problems in early childhood" (United Nations Economic and Social Council, 2009). Hence the importance of increased access to and quality of preschool education cannot be overstated. In addition, the existing preschool educational programs in Macedonia lack activities that promote the resolution of interethnic and intercultural differences, tolerance, and understanding. On the other hand preschool teachers are not given continuous/systematic training to equip them with the skills and awareness needed for fostering interethnic and intercultural tolerance and understanding, and students are not encouraged to engage in intercultural activities.

As a multicultural country, Macedonia has made efforts to achieve these two aspects of integrated education both with the constitutional changes in 2001 and the Government Strategy on Integrated Education as a follow-up measure on the recommendations given by the Organization for Security and Co-operation in Europe High Commissioner on National Minorities in January 2008. According to the constitutional changes each community residing in the country has the right to "instruction in their language in primary and secondary education" (Art. 48, §4). As a result, instruction in the Macedonian, Albanian, Turkish, and Serbian languages has been extended to the full curriculum in primary and secondary education, while instruction in the languages of smaller ethnic communities has been encouraged and some progress has been made in this area. There are non-compulsory classes in the language and culture of the other minorities in Macedonia such as the Bosniaks, Romani, and Vlach in a number of primary schools. Two institutions of higher education have also been established with Albanian as the main language. These institutions, together with the Pedagogical Faculty of Skopje University, are the primary source of teachers trained in their own language (Schenker, 2010).

Overall, it may look as though the education situation in the country is quite satisfactory in terms of providing students with the right to education in their mother tongue, but there's greater opportunities for one ethnic community hugely impacted the other ethnic communities in the country and their interactions. It seems that increased access to minority languages has not affected negatively the level of knowledge of the Macedonian language as an official language of the country.

According to the government strategy "Steps towards Integrated Education in the Education System of the Republic of Macedonia" (Ministry of Education and Science, 2010) adopted in October 2010, the "aim is to bring about a tangible and considerable change in the general approach within the education system in accordance with the multi-ethnic reality of the country and so contribute to achieving the country's strategic targets, for which stability and inter-nal cohesion are just as key as good interethnic relations" (Ministry of Education and Science, 2010). The policy measures are divided into five thematic strands, each one representing a separate, complex issue. The strands touch upon questions of democratic school gover-nance in a decentralized environment, the issues of joint curricular and extracurricular activities, language acquisition, the complexity of curricula, textbooks and teacher training, complemented by a set of guiding principles to avoid ethnic separation in new schools. The fourth thematic strand, in particular, addresses the importance of integration of preschool education as one of the crucial elements in achieving the overall goal of the strategy.

I truly believe that the interventions for an interethnic integrated education based on the principles of tolerance and respect for cultural diversity should start at the preschool level when students are free from prejudices toward and stereotypes of their peers. In addition, accord-ing to the current trends within the European Union (Edelenbos, Johnstone, & Kubanek, 2006) it is desirable that language acquisition begins at the preschool level. Only such an approach can lay the foun-dation for a thorough reform of the education system, which should aim at overcoming the widening gap between children with different ethnic and linguistic backgrounds.

In 1998, SFCG launched the Mozaik project, a model for mul-ticultural, preschool education in Macedonia, a unique model of a bilingual, child-centered pedagogical approach designed to support educational institutions in bridging the gap created by preschool ethnic, cultural, and linguistic segregation in public kindergartens in Macedonia. Mozaik was based on an analysis of the conflict in Macedonia and the role that education can play in escalating intereth-nic divisions. Structural segregation of the Macedonian educational system by ethnicity and language was a huge obstacle in providing regular communication among students from different ethnic groups, and contributed to prejudice, mistrust, and conflict. Through struc-tured contact among young children from different ethnic groups, they would learn about the identities, cultures, and languages of the other groups and would gain the skills necessary to behave with respect for the diversity and multiculturalism in the country. The pilot project that started with three Mozaik Macedonian-Albanian groups has grown to thirteen groups in nine multicultural munici-palities in five cities and four local languages (Macedonian, Albanian, Turkish, and Serbian).

THE MOZAIK MODEL

The Mozaik model set out to change personal attitudes and behavior, and induce changes in the preschool education system. It has been developed with two primary aims:

- To introduce and implement the approach of bilingual and multi-cultural education at the preschool level
- To develop and implement a child-centered pedagogical approach, including conflict-resolution skills

The Bilingual, Multicultural Approach

The bilingual, multicultural approach encourages understanding of other cultures and appreciation of languages other than one's mother tongue. It ensures that languages are not perceived as barriers, but as communication tools that can contribute to a better understanding between persons with different ethnic and linguistic backgrounds. Mozaik promotes the *equality of cultures and languages* by engaging two teachers from the two different ethnic communities, by having a proportional number of children from the different ethnic communities, and by the proportional usage of the two languages. Mozaik groups are the only example of bilingual preschool education using local languages in Macedonia. This refers to the understanding that integrated education does not assimilate or segregate students, but combines the societal cohesion and the right of the children to preserve and develop their own culture and identity. It is therefore of major importance that the educational programs use the languages of the local communities in the municipalities in which they function. The main goal of the bilingual approach is not for children to learn fully the other language, but to be exposed and sensitized to the other language and culture as well as learn words and phrases and other elements from the non-mother tongue.

In the beginning, the bilingual model of Neve Shalom/Wahat al-Salam Kindergarten and Primary School in Israel was an important source in the developing of the Macedonian bilingual Mozaik model (Mark, 1999). In 2002, a group of Mozaik teachers, and representatives from the Ministry of Labour and Social Policy and the Ministry of Education went on a study visit to Switzerland, and experiences from both private and state Swiss educational systems were incorporated to some extent in the Mozaik model as good practices for education in multicultural environments.

The bilingual technique works through paraphrasing, and not translation. Mozaik teachers speak to the children exclusively in their mother tongue (Macedonian and Albanian/Turkish/Serbian) so that children have the most solid model for forming their own languages and for an introduction to the other languages. Mozaik children are allowed to express themselves and to communicate with others in the language they are familiar with. Paraphrasing is one of the key elements of the bilingual approach, unique to the Mozaik model. When giving instructions for daily activities or when telling stories, the Mozaik teacher always paraphrases what the other Mozaik teacher said before continuing. This way they do not lose time in translation. At an individual level the teachers often engage children who speak the other language. A prerequisite for such communication is for both Mozaik teachers to learn and become fluent in both languages that are used in their Mozaik group. This paraphrasing technique has been used to train other teachers who work in bilingual classes in the Mozaik approach—for example, in the schools in Jegunovce, Tetovo, where, on request, Mozaik teachers trained teachers from the Nansen-Dialogue Centre in Macedonia who implement the project in this community.

The Child-Centered Pedagogical Approach Including Skills for Conflict Resolution

The pedagogical approach is child-centered, encouraging children's self-esteem and self-confidence and the development of a positive and realistic self-concept (self-image). The pedagogical-didactical approach of the Mozaik model is based on three elements.

First, considering the preschool educational curriculum, the Mozaik model acknowledges the requirements of the official (state) program for kindergartens in Macedonia, particularly for the inclusion of required elementary educational themes and contents.

Second, it strengthens the traditional curriculum emphasizing the social-emotional and multicultural goals of children's socialization process, incorporating internationally appreciated theories of social learning by role modeling. The following theories are incorporated in the Mozaik-model (Takasmanova-Sokolovska, 2002): (a) Piaget's theory about assimilation and cognitive conflict, (b) *Vygotsky*'s theory about the "zone of proximal development," and (c) Bruner's theory on the role of language in cognitive development and the process of thinking. Therefore, children in the Mozaik groups are mixed by age and learn through playing, discovering, and working in small groups, while Mozaik teachers are educated to serve as role models and to work individually with the children. The third important element of the pedagogical Mozaik model is conflict resolution. This is based on the collaborative negotiation and mediation model developed by Ellen Raider and Susan Coleman from the International Center for Cooperation and Conflict Resolution, Columbia University, New York. The same model was adjusted by Petroska-Beska (1997), from the Department of Psychology in Skopje, to fit teachers' approaches to resolving conflicts with children, offering them an opportunity to acquire conflict-resolution skills through experience. Mozaik teachers were trained in conflict-resolution skills so that they can act as mediators/facilitators in resolving conflicts among children, thus empowering children to come to a joint solution by themselves. Also Mozaik teachers were trained to use collaborative negotiation when in conflict with a child and to use group problem-solving strategies (based on brainstorming and consensus building) whenever needed to arrive at a group solution.

TURNING THEORY TO PRACTICE

Using the theories described above, Mozaik groups are formed mixing children by age, gender, and ethnicity. The children are between 3–6 years old and from different ethnic communities, while their language of communication can be one of the local languages (Macedonian, Albanian, Turkish, or Serbian). In the pilot phase the Mozaik groups contained children from two ethnic communities (Macedonian and Albanian) as the Mozaik model was first established only with the children from these two communities. However, very soon, when it was proven that this model was very successful in the socialization of children, we expanded Mozaik model by establishing Macedonian-Turkish and Macedonian-Serbian preschool groups. Also, the criteria for enrollment in the Mozaik groups were modified—from ethnicity to the language in which children communicate. For example, we had a Romany child who spoke Macedonian, and also children whose parents came from the international community and wanted their children to be socialized in the mixed environment, as well as children of parents with mixed marriages (a Bosnian family with children speaking both Albanian and Macedonian). Such children were very important to have in the Mozaik groups for both creating a positive group dynamic and learning to appreciate multiculturalism in the country.

There are many advantages to having mixed age groups of children: younger children learn from the older ones, while, at the same time, the older ones develop their character, social and emotional skills, and improve their cognitive skills through their contact with the younger children. Mixed ages also stimulate children's independence, self-confidence, and democratic behavior. In practice, the older children spontaneously help the younger ones, and by doing so, they expand their own knowledge and skills. Explanations offered by the older children to the younger ones serve to confirm the abilities and skills they have already learned, and help to make the older children become more self-assured, showing a higher degree of self-confidence and self-respect. They also mature in reasoning when their assistance is needed (Rood, 2000).

So far, all Mozaik children have shown great interest in attending Mozaik groups. They have always been ready when their parents bring them to the kindergartens in contrast to the children going to the conventional kindergartens. They often ask their parents why Mozaik kindergartens are closed on Saturdays!

The following anecdote reflects the great interest of the children attending Mozaik groups. A girl named Jana explained to other children in the Mozaik group the meaning of the word "nostalgia." She said: "Nostalgia is when we are at home and we miss and want to be at the Mozaik group!"

Beside the children, parents are an equally important target group, as they participate with their children in several events and activities, both inside and outside the classroom. Whereas in the early days of the program parents were under severe pressure from local communities to withdraw their children from Mozaik, today an ever-increasing number of parents place their children on waiting lists for the program. They regard Mozaik as a crucial element in the development of their children and the future of Macedonia's ethnically diverse society.

The support and success of Mozaik is recognized by educational authorities in Macedonia as a pedagogical model for all preschool teachers. For example, in Struga, in contrast to the increased interethnic tensions caused by conflicts between high school students, Mozaik preschool groups are highly appreciated. Based on the parents' and community demands expressed at local strategic meetings that we organized in each of the communities where Mozaik groups were established, we opened a second Mozaik Macedonian-Albanian group in Struga in 2006. Since then the two Mozaik groups have functioned so well that the mayor of the Struga municipality and the educational counselor are willing to transform all kindergartens into the Mozaik model. This way, we hope that very soon, a whole Mozaik model preschool institution will be established in one of the most conflict-sensitive multicultural communities in Macedonia.

INSTITUTIONALIZATION OF THE MOZAIK MODEL

In January 2012 Mozaik was institutionalized—a crucial element for the model's sustainability. Policy developments at the national and local levels were an important factor in institutionalization and sustainability. The Law for Protection of Children was adopted and formally recognized the introduction of pilot preschool programmes based on new pedagogical principles, thus providing a legal basis for Mozaik's sustainability. The Mozaik model was recognized and incorporated in the revised National Program for Preschool Education.

Since its inception, the Mozaik project has been designed to work at three *levels of society* (the Lederach Triangle): grassroots (children and their parents); mid-level (kindergartens, preschool directors, teachers, and professional staff); and structural (Macedonian educational authorities, government representatives at central and local levels). Through *engaging key actors*, Mozaik has been instrumental in getting a legal basis that recognizes bilingual, preschool education and the handover of Mozaik teachers to the ministry payroll and, with that, achieving Mozaik institutional integration.

However, the institutionalization process took place gradually as the project faced various challenges and obstacles during its implementation. One of the most serious challenges was that it touched upon politically sensitive issues. The project was initially set up as separate from the "mainstream" kindergarten, so there was strong resistance from "classical" teachers, lack of ownership on the part of some school directors, difficulty in integrating the Mozaik groups in the kindergartens, and a general perception of Mozaik as a foreign project.

Therefore in 2002 we developed the Mozaik institutionalization strategy, as a step toward the sustainability of the model and at the same time we made several essential modifications to ease the way for Mozaik's integration. We formed a professional advisory board consisting of representatives of all the project's stakeholders, which was responsible for institutional support of the Mozaik approach. We revised the original four-teacher Mozaik model to the two-teacher model that maintained the same qualitative goals. We expanded the Mozaik approach, as a successful practice, to new ethno-linguistic communities so that other minority groups in Macedonia can be exposed to this multicultural model; and we disseminate the Mozaik principles through numerous seminars to non-Mozaik teachers throughout the public preschool institutional structures in Macedonia as well as in the local communities.

Other limiting factors were beyond the project's control: political instability; frequent changes among the key representatives in the ministries; the slow process of defining a national policy for preschool education; and the lack of donor coordination. Over my12 years of implementing Mozaik, 15 different people at the Ministry of Labour and Social Policy have been assigned to this project. Each of them was totally unfamiliar with our work and had to be educated and convinced of the Mozaik's value from scratch.

The next step was to move the institutionalization strategy to a higher level—from a strategy focused on the "educational community" to a strategy that had to reach out to a broader "public opinion" and policy makers, especially at the decentralized level. Our team's continuous efforts over the years in advocating for Mozaik's institutionalization, at the central and the local level on the one hand, and the regular monitoring and evaluation of the implementation of Mozaik on the other hand were critical in achieving our ultimate goal—integration of the Mozaik model into the preschool educational system and Mozaik teachers to be on the payroll of the Ministry of Labor and Social Policy. The Macedonian government integrated the Mozaik project across the country in October 2010, at the same time as the Government Strategy on Integrated Education was adopted. A year later, when the teachers' salaries were assumed by the ministry, the government decision became fully functional.

CONCLUDING REMARKS

Although in theory integrated education can be easily understood and its merits recognized, achieving integrated education *in practice* is a complex task that can take time and needs action and interventions at all levels of society. A good model of an integrated educational system ensures the engagement of all stakeholders from the central to the local government level. Also, policies of integrated education should create the necessary conditions to involve stakeholders at all levels of the government, and at the level of those receiving education. At the same time, these policies must be continuously evaluated and adjusted, as necessary, in order to take into account changing social requirements. Finally, policies should incorporate existing good practices as the key element for developing functional integrated educational approaches that will fit the country's multicultural context.

I believe that by implementing such an innovative, multicultural educational model in Macedonia, we are contributing to building a new generation of Macedonia's society. Mozaik is raising children freed from the limitations and confinement of their own community, enriching them with new social values. These values will help them respect and accept cultural differences in their country and will enable these children to gain new skills so that, as adults, they are able to live together in peace and mutual understanding, both with people living next to them, as well as with people in the rest of the world.

REFERENCES

Edelenbos, P., Johnstone, R., & Kubanek, A. (2006). *The main pedagogical principles underlying the teaching of languages to very young learner.* European Commision, Education and Culture, Culture and Communication, Multilingualism Policy (http://ec.europa.eu/education/languages/pdf/doc425_en.pdf)

Mark, B. (1999). NS/WAS assisting bilingual education project in Macedonia (former Yugoslavia). Accessed online at http://www.nswas.com/school/updates/macadoni.htm

Ministry of Education and Science. (2010). *Steps towards integrated education in the education system of the Republic of Macedonia.* Skopje, Macedonia.

Minow, M. (2002). Education for co-existence. *Arizona Law Review, 44,* 1–29.

OSCE High Commissioner on National Minorities. (2011). Creating vision and standards—the Role of Higher Education in Fostering Inter-cultural Dialogue and Understanding in a Multiethnic Society, conference, Skopje, Macedonia.

Petroska-Beska, V. (1997). *Conflicts, what they are and how to resolve them.* Unpublished manuscript. Faculty of Philosophy, Skopje, Macedonia.

Rood, R. (2000). *Evaluation of Mozaik kindergartens in FYR Macedonia.* Unpublished manuscript.

Schenker, H. (2010). *Final evaluation on Mozaik bilingual kindergarten.* Unpublished manuscript.

Takasmanova-Sokolovska, T. (2002). *Mozaik-approach in the education of the preschool children.* Skopje: Prosvetno Delo.

UN Economic and Social Council Annual Ministerial Review. (July 2009). *National report on Millennium Development Goal.* Geneva: ECOSOC.

10

INTEGRATED EDUCATION IN THE REPUBLIC OF MACEDONIA

CHALLENGES FOR TEACHERS

Biljana Krstevska-Papic and Veton Zekolli

INTRODUCTION

The Republic of Macedonia is a multiethnic, multicultural society: 64.18 percent of the population is Macedonian, 25.17 percent Albanian, 3.85 percent Turkish, 2.66 percent Roma, 1.78 percent Serbian, 0.84 percent Bosnian, 0.48 percent Vlach, and 1.04 percent belong to other ethnic communities (Census of Population, Households and Dwellings in the Republic of Macedonia, 2002, p. 591). The ethnically heterogeneous structure of the population in the Republic of Macedonia suggests that there is a need for integrated education to act as a means to promote mutual cooperation and communication among the different ethnic communities. However, the Macedonian educational system is facing a major challenge to build integrated education that will meet the needs of the Macedonian social context, where several ethnic communities coexist and have developed multidimensional cultural relations.

The purpose of this chapter is to present the current situation and efforts that are being undertaken in the Republic of Macedonia for the development of integrated education, as well as the importance and the role of several teacher competencies in the process of planning and implementation of this form of education. The focus, then, will be on the challenges for teachers to develop and implement integrated education.

THE REPUBLIC OF MACEDONIA AFTER
THE ARMED CONFLICT IN 2001

The Republic of Macedonia is confronted by a huge challenge—to develop integrated education according to the determination of the country to promote integration through children's upbringing and educational process. It is interesting to take a look at the current situation in the Macedonian educational system, as well as the challenges that integrated education is facing. After 2001 and the armed conflict, the Macedonian society has faced strong segregation processes, especially in the area of education, where there is an intensive and continuous physical, even territorial segregation of the students on an ethnic basis; this situation has produced ethnically segregated schools and the gradual extinguishment of ethnically mixed schools, which have been the best reflection of a heterogeneous social community. After the armed conflict in 2001, the Framework Agreement (August 13, 2001) was signed; its main goal was the promotion of peaceful and harmonious social development, respecting the ethnical identity and interests of all Macedonian citizens. The plan was that teaching in the primary and secondary education would be carried out in the mother tongue of the students, according to unified curricula for all Macedonia.

Precisely under these provisions within the overall educational system, from primary to university education, two parallel systems of education have developed, one in Macedonian, the other in Albanian language, that is, there has been institutionalized segregation at all educational levels. This type of institutionalized segregation soon had a negative impact in the other spheres of social life and found a fertile soil in the educational system for further support and deepening of the division in Macedonian society.

Not surprisingly, segregation at all educational levels in the Republic of Macedonia seems to further mistrust, mutual ignorance, disrespect, intolerance, and lack of cooperation between the students who belong to different ethnicities. Also, these conditions have a negative effect on cooperation among educators from different ethnic communities as well as among parents of students from different languages and cultural origins. All these indications of extremely poor interethnic relations in the Macedonian education system have created the need to develop the idea of integrated education, with clear principles and objectives on which the subject structure of this complex model of education will be based.

Our Understanding of Integrated Education

Integrated education can be defined as education for unity, solidarity, respect, mutual tolerance, help, friendship, empathy, honesty, trust, and other values of a subtle nature. It is also education that enables the promotion of diversity. Integrated education transforms the educational system from being rigid, divided, closed, and adjusted to the interests of the ethnic groups into one that is open to support dialogue between different ethnicities, that is, into a system that skillfully incorporates diversity in its subject component that then enriches itself in a qualitative manner and overcomes the danger of favoring cultural exclusivity; it is this exclusivity that is often a source of physical and emotional distance between young generations, generating intolerance and violence.

Integrated education is education based on mutual understanding, an important life skill, that is, an education not limited only to the adoption of knowledge on a cognitive level, but one that also primarily promotes the upbringing component as the foundation for developing, nurturing, and improving the life skills necessary for quality coexistence in the Macedonian society.

We have analyzed the basis for developing the concept of integrated education through a review of official documents, as well as by analyzing the current legal framework in the Republic of Macedonia that defines the contours of the educational system. In the Law on Primary Education (2008) of the Republic of Macedonia, the importance of developing mutual tolerance, cooperation, respect for diversity, basic human freedom and rights is stressed in the goal (Article 3) of primary upbringing and education; this goal also mentions the development of awareness among the students about belonging to the Republic of Macedonia and nurturing their national and cultural identity. According to Article 9 the upbringing of and educational work for members of different nationalities should be conducted in their respective language and alphabet in parallel with learning the Macedonian language. In addition, the National Program for Educational Development 2005–2015 emphasizes the role of ethnic and cultural cooperation in the educational process, which should constantly promote integration across all educational levels, starting from preschool, for strengthening cohesion, tolerance, mutual respect, and trust.

In 2010, the first document on integrated education was prepared focusing on the idea of integrated education as a necessity for the Macedonian society. In this document entitled "Steps toward

Integrated Education in the Educational System of the Republic of Macedonia," prepared by the Ministry of Education and Science and the OSCE High Commission on National Minorities (2010), the need for overcoming ethnic alienation and encouraging interaction between all stakeholders in the upbringing and educational process has been emphasized.

The measures provided for in this document are divided into five thematic groups, that is, they anticipate that integration will be encouraged and developed at different levels through: (1) organizing joint curricular and extracurricular activities at multiple levels (school, municipal, or statewide); (2) increasing the mutual knowledge of languages of the members of different ethnic communities; (3) adjusting the curriculum, the program, and the textbooks; (4) improving the competences of the teachers for integration in education; and (5) "de-politicizing" the educational system through the involvement of all stakeholders in leading and managing the schools in a decentralized context.

Despite the envisaged measures, the strategy for integrated education is still blocked and boycotted owing to the Macedonian government's January 2010 decision of mandatory inclusion and learning of the Macedonian language in all schools where teaching is being carried out in other languages (Albanian, Turkish, and Serbian).

THE NANSEN MODEL OF INTEGRATED EDUCATION

The Nansen Dialogue Centre (NDC) Skopje is a nongovernmental organization that has been working devotedly for several years for the promotion of the concept of integrated primary and secondary education in the Republic of Macedonia. In 2008, NDC Skopje opened the first integrated primary school in the Republic of Macedonia, in the post-conflict municipality of Jegunovce (village Preljubiste), as a result of several years of implementation of the program "Dialogue and Reconciliation"; this program has been a platform for the reestablishment of trust, mutual respect, and tolerance between the Macedonian and Albanian ethnic communities, whose relations and communication were seriously damaged after the armed conflict in 2001. The strongest negative influence of the conflict was the complete physical, territorial division of the students on an ethnic basis; at the same time, this development has signaled the necessity of creating an integrated school in cooperation with the local municipal authorities, relevant educational institutions, and of course, with parents, as main partners, supporters, and promoters of the idea of integrated schooling. The opening of the first integrated school in the Republic of Macedonia was a complex task in many ways including creating a multifunctional, modern school space; creating an original program for integrated activities whose contents will be closely correlated with the official national curriculum; developing sense among parents about the importance of their active participation in the school activities, as well as promoting the importance of quality parenting; and creating homogeneous, compact student groups in a positive emotional environment.

The development of the Nansen model of integrated education has continued over the past few years. In 2009, another generation of students was enrolled in the integrated primary school; in 2010, the first integrated secondary school was opened in the same municipality, and at the end of 2010, the project was started in Strumica municipality also, where, for the first time, students from the Turkish community have been involved in the integrated activities. The year 2011 was marked by the reception of another generation of students in the secondary integrated school, as well as with expansion of the Nansen model of integrated education in another two multiethnic municipalities—Vasilevo and Cair.

Certainly, one of the most sensitive and multilevel tasks in the development of the Nansen model of integrated education has been the selection and preparation of teachers who can deal with the challenges of integrated education, that is, those who possess the skills, background knowledge, and motivating spirit as a prerequisite for the successful implementation of the main goals of the program on which the model for integrated education promoted by NDC Skopje is being based.

NDC Skopje faced many challenges and difficulties while implementing the Nansen model for integrated education. The first challenge was to gain the confidence of parents from different ethnic backgrounds for their active participation in the project activities that were established in a bilingual environment. An important aspect of the Nansen model for integrated education is its presence in the rural and symbolically small communities where the ethnic division between the two biggest communities is much more apparent. The decision of parents to include their children in this kind of education in the beginning was marked as a betrayal toward their ethnic community; these parents were often considered strangers in their own villages and they received many threats.

During the first few months the parents were not sure whether they had made the right decision; they were afraid that if the model was not successful it would become very hard for their families to continue living in the same village. The parents were afraid that politics would get involved and their children would not get accepted in any other school if integrated education was not successful; these parents were already marked because they were assimilating their children and allowing them to study and cooperate with the "enemy." It is worth mentioning here about the influence of the religious communities in this rural municipality that most of the time pressurized parents not to register their daughters in the school or at least not let them continue studying in the higher grades.

Another challenge was securing political support from the four biggest political parties that are most powerful in the local and central government. NDC Skopje approached each party and presented to them a model of integrated education that would improve the interethnic relations as well as the quality of the educational system in Macedonia. This process is ongoing and the communication with political leaders is important in order to inform them properly about the vision of integrated education. In general, all of these difficulties were the stepping stones on which the Nansen model for integrated education was permanently built; these challenges optimized and upgraded the model.

THE TEACHER'S PEDAGOGICAL ROLE AND TRAINING IN INTEGRATED EDUCATION

In general the vision of the Nansen model of integrated education is creating a quality upbringing and educational model that will be an appropriate example for the education of all ethnic communities in multicultural environments and a mirror for future modern upbringing and educational system in the Republic of Macedonia. The mission of integrated schools is facilitating a modern, successful, multiethnic upbringing and building educational institutions that will provide quality bilingual integrated educational activities closely correlated with the contents of the regular teaching process. That is why the integrated schools that operate according to the Nansen model for integrated education believe in cooperation and dialogue as a tool for problem resolution and bringing people together, but also as a precondition for mutual respect and creating a society where everybody is equally important and respected.

The main objectives of the Nansen model for integrated education are to deepen the constructive collaborative relations between children from different ethnic communities as well as to develop a sense among them about respecting the mutual differences and overcoming stereotypes and prejudices related to their ethnic and cultural backgrounds. Also, the students under this model are being trained for constructive resolution of conflict situations, as well as for developing a positive emotional climate in their groups. It is also foreseen to strengthen the team and tandem cooperation, as well as a spontaneous learning of terms and phrases from the non-native language. One of the goals of the model is also to support children's curiosity, originality, and creative potential, as well as develop their critical thinking.

An array of extracurricular activities as a basis for integration is conducted daily throughout the academic year. The programs for extracurricular activities are based on many sections (Art, Ecology, Film, Young Explorers, Math, Drama, Young Constructors, Education for Peace and Tolerance, Me and the Others, Sports, and so on), that offer an abundance of interesting, encouraging program situations through which the bilingual approach is promoted as a link between the two languages (the prerequisite here is that both teachers speak both languages equally well).

The program structure of the Nansen model of integrated education has imposed a series of requirements and expectations from the people who will implement it. According to the key objectives of the Nansen model, the team for education, training, and development at NDC Skopje has prepared a list of competencies that every teacher involved in planning, organizing, and implementing the material should have. These competencies—values, knowledge, skills, and abilities—aim to support the processes of integration and interaction in heterogeneous groups of students. For example, these competencies include the ability for tandem and team cooperation with colleagues, as well as for constructive cooperation with students and parents, and the active role of students, that is, developing their talents, abilities, and skills through an individualized approach. Certainly, it is expected that teachers will be trained for a constructive approach when solving conflict situations in the group, as well as for overcoming the stereotypes and prejudices among students toward diversity. It is equally important for teachers to have bilingual skills for carrying out integrated extracurricular activities, as well as for encouraging and building a positive emotional climate in the group with a heterogeneous ethnic structure. Also, it is expected that teachers show readiness for constant cooperation with the school management, the expert team of NDC Skopje, the local municipal authorities, the experts active in the school, and the other subjects involved in the realization of the project; and participate in developing models for self-evaluation.

Each of these components is a prerequisite for creating innovative, interesting, integrated activities for students of different ethnic origins. Certainly, they impose high standards on and expectations from the teachers, who, unfortunately, during their university education in the Republic of Macedonia (although it is declared as a multiethnic social community), did not have the opportunity to acquire the competencies that are a prerequisite for working in integrated schools.

This complex problem has also come up during the implementation of integrated extracurricular activities in primary schools, where the annual programs for integrated bilingual extracurricular activities first started. The priority was to establish tandem cooperation between the teachers from different ethnic groups, from different language origins, as a prerequisite for establishment of a bilingual communication in a group with mixed ethnic composition. Although most teachers (previously within other projects and trainings) have attended several trainings for tandem cooperation and communication, most of them carry out the regular teaching process individually, which allows them to have an independent role as creators, performers, and evaluators of the process. The participation in integrated extracurricular activities has imposed the need for mutual agreement and joint planning, facilitating, and evaluation of the outcome—that has had a subtle influence on the perception of the teachers about their role and position in the process of realization.

The teachers' concerns focused on whether this kind of content and approach would reduce their authority in the regular teaching process, that is, whether their role as promoters, strategists, and guides would threaten their role as teachers, coaches, and evaluators. The initial feeling among most teachers was that working in tandem is more complicated, because they will need greater mutual balance, adjustments, arrangements, and negotiations, which can make the entire process more difficult. The teachers felt the need to keep their status as authoritative performers of the regular teaching process, which is, very often in our schools, being carried out in a routine and formal manner. Most teachers have initially experienced the involvement in the extracurricular integrated activities as an innovation that will reduce their authority and will endanger their position in front of parents, students, and other teachers, because the implementation of the programs for extracurricular integrated activities has imposed the need for nurturing a continuous, open, flexible cooperation and communication with all key stakeholders in the teaching process.

The second problem that most performers of integrated extracurricular activities were faced with was the completely different didactic and methodical approach when carrying them out, unlike the dominant approach in the mandatory teaching process. While in the regular teaching process, the frontal type of work is still a dominating one, complemented by the method of oral presentation or lecture, the integrated extracurricular activities are promoting the game approach, enriched with team and tandem work, as well as an individualized approach toward each student, according to his abilities, skills, knowledge, and potential. The gamelike nature of the activities has caused teachers to wonder if it would affect the behavior of the students, which would have an indirect influence on the quality of their knowledge and success within the mandatory education process. The problem has been also deepened by the teachers' fear that the game approach would impose on them a role of "entertainers," which will mar their professionalism and expertise. The teachers have been discouraged by the thought that this type of working will diminish their reputation among parents, students, other colleagues, and school administrators, a feeling that was particularly obvious among the teachers from the integrated vocational school, where most employees are electrical and mechanical engineers and are teaching vocational subjects.

The request for applying the "paraphrasing technique," as a bridge between two languages has further complicated the process of realization. Paraphrasing enables equal representation and treatment of both languages even if it is the language spoken by the majority population in the Republic of Macedonia or if it is one of the languages of the ethnic communities. The proportional representation and the parallel use of both languages was one of the basic reasons why parents have supported the implementation of the Nansen model for integrated education in several schools across the country. It was a big challenge for the teachers to overcome the paraphrasing technique, for which the basic prerequisite is to have good cooperation between the performers of the extracurricular activities with detailed, precise joint planning, as well as tandem realization.

The paraphrasing technique also means having the skill for active listening, and flexible and fluent expression in a bilingual environment. Paraphrasing has proved to be a great challenge because the majority of teachers from the Macedonian ethnic community have very little (or no) knowledge of the nonnative language (Albanian or Turkish). On the other hand, the teachers who belong to the other ethnic communities have a slight advantage, because most of them have a solid knowledge of the Macedonian language, which has significantly facilitated the realization of their bilingual activities.

Certainly, many other skills are also necessary for the successful implementation of integrated extracurricular activities, such as implementing constructive conflict resolution; overcoming stereotypes and prejudices; creating and maintaining a positive emotional climate in the group; implementing an individualized approach tailored to the needs of each student, and so on. In order to gain, and successfully and actively implement those skills, the team of NDC Skopje has developed special training programs for teachers, and they have been structured to include the following topics: the characteristics of integrated education; forms, methods, and techniques for work in integrated groups; ways of planning and creating integrated extracurricular activities; the integration of the teaching and extracurricular material; the role of the bilingual approach in the implementation of the extracurricular activities; types of communication in integrated classes; the role of the parents as active partners and supporters of the Nansen model for integrated education; the role of the team and tandem cooperation; and overcoming stereotypes and prejudices in ethnically mixed groups. Training sessions are organized regularly for all teachers who participate actively in the implementation of the integrated extracurricular activities and lend it constant support, to strengthen their competencies and skills, to upgrade their knowledge, and to improve their abilities.

CONCLUSION

So far, we are pleased with the fact that the external evaluations since 2008, conducted by several evaluators (e.g., D. Galovic, Dr. P., Dutkiewicz, and Dr. Z. Velkovski), have indicated the following, very subtle point: the teachers involved in the implementation of the Nansen model of integrated education are characterized with strong motivation, commitment, and readiness for change (Velkovski, 2011). The additional training that NDC Skopje is conducting for teachers has shown some positive results, mainly in the area of understanding the ethos of the program, the organization of the activities, and the approach toward students. The current evaluations also have emphasized that the cooperation between teachers is an excellent example for students about how members of different ethnic groups can work with each other. This point is very important and should be enhanced, because it is one of the pillars on which the success of the program rests.

The Nansen model for integrated education has been evaluated as an educational model that has quality and produces positive effects on the students, as well as on the teachers and the schools. Current evaluations confirm that the model is original for the environment in which it is being implemented and represents an initiative that is fully in accord with the national priorities in the education. This model offers numerous opportunities for the development of social skills and competencies among teachers (but also among students and their parents), and for tolerance, mutual constructive cooperation, and assistance, which is the basis of quality coexistence in a community that bears the hallmark of heterogeneity. We believe that despite its challenges and weaknesses, this educational model could be a good example for integrated education in all 48 municipalities of the Republic of Macedonia.

REFERENCES

Census of Population, Households and Dwellings in the Republic Macedonia, 2002. Republic of Macedonia State Statistical Office.

Republic of Macedonia. (2008). Elementary Education Law. Official Gazette of R.M., no.103 (Закон за основно образование, Службен весник на Р.М., Скопје, 2008, бр.103).

Velkovski, Z. (2011). *Periodical evaluation report*. Nansen Dialogue Centre— Integrated and bilingual education in Macedonia. Accessed online at http://www.mon.gov.mk/images/stories/dokumenti/integrirano_obrazovanie/policy_paper_adopted_mk.pdf

Conclusion to Part 2

Zvi Bekerman

While reading through the chapters in this part, the reader is not allowed to relate to integrated, peaceful, and coexistent educational efforts as separate from other more regular and general educational concerns. This might sound redundant but it's not. Many times academic compartmentalizing needs, for the sake of creating specializations, to draw some unnatural divisions between areas that allow an understanding of their complexity only when considered in their overlap. The authors in this part, all involved in the practice of integrated education and committed to its development, will not allow for such divisions to simplify the scene.

At other times it is romantic approaches and the idealization of human efforts that blind us to the complexities of using education as a leverage to alleviate conflict. Again the chapters in this part do not allow for this. The authors refuse to idealize their struggles; they emphasize that it was only through a pragmatic approach, one that accounts for both individual and group interests, that they have managed to make progress.

We are told how individual initiatives were the ones that allowed for first steps to be taken for contact in a sociopolitical context in which elders and betters might oppose them; yet these efforts, we are told, could have stayed inconsequential without a political parallel struggle geared toward changing power relations.

We are informed about how in a rather post-conflict context such as that of Northern Ireland, the costs of maintaining separate school systems for Protestants and Catholics might actually encourage further development of the integrated initiative. Within this same context we are informed that even when communities and parents might be easily convinced of the benefits of integrated education for lower grades, when approaching secondary education, given the existing selective schools systems, these same parents might hesitate for they will not find it easy to surrender to "peaceful ideologies" their dreams for the social success of their children in a society where mobility might not be easy.

These tensions, outside the wider social context, are reflected in the functioning of integrated settings for they need to push multiple educational agendas—tolerance, recognition, and academic achievements too—so as to keep being relevant to families that care about their children's futures. Needless to say these need not be, necessarily, contradicting goals and yet, not few are the times that an academic achievements agenda based on individual skills and competitive attitudes can shape educational strategies and pedagogies that in some ways counter efforts toward tolerance and recognition.

Integrated schools struggle with these questions and have in a way become not only the precursors of education for peace in conflict-ridden societies but also pioneers of an all-ability education that champions equality and excellence for all.

It becomes clear that reaching this goal will not be easy. The schools, even the older ones working in Northern Ireland, realize that the path is full of obstacles. There is not really an educational tradition to be followed; education for the most part has been approached and implemented as a homogenizing effort when guided by nation-states. Developing an actual, not a theoretical, tradition for strategies and pedagogies of inclusive education implies taking calculated risks and being constantly involved in a process of learning. We are told such an education implies adopting a holistic approach that cannot be delimited by disciplinary borders. Integrated education, to succeed, needs to be reflected in all aspects of the educational process and in the practices affected by all stakeholders involved; it cannot truly be achieved in a short period nor can it evolve with limited human and material resources.

Though trying to overcome the human and material limitations of educational systems might be a worthwhile undertaking, a more realistic one might request us to think about a variety of options not considered at first by integrative efforts. Again here, Northern Ireland, the area of conflict with the longest tradition of integrated education, is experimenting with new options that are described in this part. Transformed schools, those that implement partial integration of populations but adopt an integrated educational ethos and "shared educational" initiatives, those that bring religiously segregated schools to share resources and while doing this encourage contact, are practical attempts at overcoming hard structural realities. Though, at times, criticized for not being examples of an integrated ethos, these attempts need to be considered when realizing that socio-political conflict and post-conflict contexts cannot be approached with any one-size-fits-all solution.

I think that it is worthwhile, in the last part of these conclusions, to emphasize that, though we have pointed out the importance of considering all stakeholders involved in and with the educational integrated settings, it is the educators who need our greatest support. Teachers are at the forefront of the potential success of these initiatives. They are the ones who meet the students the most and it's their training that might help achieve the goal. They (and our children) are the ones directly exposed to the complexities of our conflicted societies and it is they (and our children) who inhabit the classrooms in which conflict reigns even before the beginning of any academic year. Overcoming the presence/absence of a conflict that imprisons us all, well before classes start, needs ongoing work of reflection and a dedicated effort toward self and social criticism that can be gained only if we account for these in regular educational activities. This implies the need to secure the resources for an ongoing and thorough pre- and in-service training effort, one that is guided by perspectives that seriously take into account the best in educational practice as well as the rich and often troubled trajectories and experiences of the educators themselves.

3

CURRICULUM AND PEDAGOGY ISSUES
IN INTEGRATED SCHOOLS

INTRODUCTION TO PART 3

Michalinos Zembylas

The third part will investigate curriculum and pedagogy issues that have been raised in integrated schools to respond to student diversity and to historical divisions. It will consider the challenges of planning appropriate curricula for integrated education initiatives. This part will explore how difficult topics can be approached in integrated school classrooms and it will also consider the training needs of teachers. Authors in this part will reflect on the possibilities that are created for curriculum development in three societies in which integrated schooling exists: Israel, Croatia, and Northern Ireland. As noted in the previous parts of this collection, it is important to keep in mind that attempts to develop and implement curricula and pedagogies in these societies take place at different stages. In Croatia, for example, the effort to develop and implement curricula and pedagogies for integrated schools is at a rather rudimentary level, whereas in Israel and Northern Ireland there is already considerable experience. Despite the differences, however, there are also important similarities when it comes to the challenges and opportunities in efforts to develop "appropriate" curricula and pedagogies for integrated education. But let's start with a brief summary of each chapter; in the conclusion of this part, we will identify a few common themes that permeate all chapters and deserve our attention.

Julia Schlam Salman reflects on her experiences as an English language teacher and researcher in one integrated, bilingual school in Israel. Specifically, Julia examines three overarching curricular ideologies that, over the years, have made her feel confused, frustrated, and concerned. These are the identity-based curriculum, bilingual curriculum, and ideology as curriculum. The identity-based curriculum is grounded in highlighting identity and the formation of strong ethnic identification; bilingual curriculum pays attention, in variable degrees depending on the bilingual model, to students' first and second language and aims to produce students who are bilingual and who possess a certain level of multicultural awareness; finally, the issue of ideology as curriculum emphasizes the ways in which "ideological" schooling accompanies each and every educational initiative. These three curriculum issues have important consequences in an integrated school in Israel, as Julia argues, and so she highlights some potential ways to address these repercussions, suggesting that proactive and preventative measures may ultimately have an important role in the school's socialization processes and educational outcomes.

The chapter by Bob Mark, again from Israel, narrates his efforts to delve deeper into the culture created through the Jewish-Arab encounter by following routine classroom experiences of a single child (Khalil) in the school. Bob provides us with an in-depth case study that shows how identity politics influence the work of teachers and the school culture in bilingual, integrated schools. Bob's analysis shows that the needs of students in integrated schools should be constantly revisited, because our ideological assumptions interfere with initiatives to respond to these needs. "Discovering Khalil and learning about ourselves through Khalil," writes Bob, requires hard work, "because the banality of the discursive practices that reflect our social reality makes it hard to pay any attention to them." Bilingual, integrated schools have many success stories but they also show that teachers in these schools need critical pedagogies that disrupt the social reproduction of segregation practices.

Marinko Uremović and Ivana Milas take us to another post-conflict region, Vukovar, Croatia, and examine the problem of segregated schooling in the city after the war in former Yugoslavia. Marinko and Ivana try to explain the reasons why and how such schooling came to be, and how the main stakeholders in Vukovar (i.e., the Croatian majority and the Serbian minority) resist efforts to develop integrated schools. Despite the challenges, though, the authors describe their involvement with an initiative undertaken by the Nansen Dialogue Centre to promote peace and school integration. In particular, Marinko and Ivana analyze two different approaches taken by the Nansen Dialogue Centre: the New School project, an initiative to open an integrated school in Vukovar; and the implementation of the intercultural subject entitled "Cultural and Spiritual Heritage of the Region," that has been introduced in the curriculum of segregated schools. The authors discuss the lessons learnt from their work, by presenting both the achievements and the obstacles they have encountered in their journey to promote integrated schooling in Vukovar.

The remaining two chapters in this part are related to Northern Ireland, though they are written from different perspectives. In the chapter written by Helen Killick and Sharon Verwoerd, two chaplains at a secondary integrated school, the focus is on the chaplaincy's efforts to respond to conflict and segregation by facing controversial issues together as they arise, rather than hiding from or avoiding them. Helen and Sharon explain how an issue becomes controversial in school and the curriculum and explore two examples of controversy among staff and students in their school. One is a specific response to the event of the funeral of Pope John Paul II, navigating a way forward through a process of consensus building. The second example is about how the chaplaincy engages with issues related to violent conflict in and about Northern Ireland and specifically the visits of ex-prisoners to the school, which challenges the staff and students to face their own prejudices and to grow in understanding. Both examples, explain Helen and Sharon, show that controversial issues in the curriculum can be opportunities to explore differences positively and strengthen relationships.

Finally, Paula McIlwaine, a staff member at Northern Ireland Council for Integrated Education, describes her experiences of training teachers to consider their roles in implementing an anti-bias approach in integrated schools. Paula explains that anti-bias training is designed to be highly interactive, including both participatory tasks focused on assumption making (and the relationship between assumptions, bias, prejudice, and discrimination) and an analysis of the development of anti-bias in a local and global context. Paula also discusses teachers' responses at the end of the course; some of the teachers' comments show increased awareness and understanding of their own bias, while others reveal the challenges and discomforting feelings that teachers experience. The author emphasizes that her experience suggests that teachers need to be guided through a careful and well-designed process of examining their own attitudes to difference and be facilitated to discover their own biases. It is argued that despite teachers' discomfort and the challenges that arise, an antibias approach provides a valuable curriculum framework for professional development in integrated schools.

11

A PRACTITIONER'S REFLECTIONS ON SCHOOLING IN BILINGUAL INTEGRATED CONTEXTS

Julia Schlam Salman

I have worked as a teacher and a researcher in integrated bilingual education for the past eight years. My roles and responsibilities have waxed and waned—depending on the positions I have assumed and/ or been awarded. Most notably, I am an English teacher and responsible for facilitating English language acquisition and proficiency among L1 Arabic- and L1 Hebrew-speaking students. There are many advantages to my field of expertise—both on a symbolic and a practical level. At the most obvious level, English language education is one step removed from many of the still salient and jarring conflicts that continue to divide Jewish and Palestinian Israelis. These issues are inherent in civics or a history lesson. In an English class, we can examine injustices and incongruities from alternative vantage points—drawing on examples from other cultures and societies and later returning to our own circumstances. This is not to say that these sometimes highly palpable issues get ignored. But they are framed against a more global perspective, one that seeks to educate students about other and additional conflicts as well as examples of resolution and justice.

At the same time, and much of the time, an English class is *just* an English class. Students practice their reading comprehension skills, build their vocabulary, learn to write well in English, and develop critical thinking skills. As a self-declared critical pedagogist and social constructivist, I know that something else is also always transpiring, getting constructed and co-constructed. However, in order to ensure that my students are well schooled in a language linked to power and social mobility (Shohamy, 2007) I tend to focus on helping them to achieve their highest level of proficiency possible in English. I am inclined to leave ideologies to the wayside except that they are ever present and unavoidable. They inform curricular goals as well as the general educational models supporting integrated bilingual education in Israel.

This chapter is first and foremost a reflection of my experiences as an English language teacher in one integrated, bilingual school in Israel. More specifically, I have opted to examine and further investigate three overarching curricular ideologies which, over the years, have stirred in me confusion, frustration, concern, even doubt. These include identity-based curriculum, bilingual curriculum, and ideology as curriculum. These conceptualizations, I will subsequently argue, inform, to varying degrees, the overarching integrated bilingual educational model employed at the school. Through anecdotes and reflections, I discuss these curricular premises both in a general way and within the context of English as a foreign language classroom. While ethnographic and drawn from my experiences as a teacher in one integrated, bilingual school, the considerations I address are not meant to serve as a substitute to formal qualitative or quantitative investigation. They constitute solely my firsthand experiences and subjective opinions and perspective.

IDENTITY-BASED CURRICULUM

"He is a Jew," states one of the Arab-Muslim teachers, as we discuss several "problematic" students during one of the quarterly student evaluation meetings. "He is not a Jew," I think to myself, knowing that the student and his parents define themselves as Christian. The discussion continues. "He is not ethnically Arab," the teacher goes on to explain, "so he gets counted as a Jew." I refrain from responding but am reminded of the over 200 million non-Arab Christians who reside in the United States, my place of birth and country of residence before moving to Israel a decade ago. I am struck by the irony that here in this contextual setting a Christian American is so much of a minority that he gets marked as a Jew for lack of a better or more appropriate classification. "I mean clearly, he's not Arab," concludes the teacher, and the issue of the student's ethno-religious identity appears to be settled. Nobody seems particularly bothered by the limited identity discourse at our disposal or the fact that we are so wedded to two reified categorizations—Jew or Arab— that we do not have the language to articulate anything else.

Identity and the formation of strong and particularistic ethnic identifications stand at the forefront of the integrated bilingual model of education (*from Hebrew*, Amara, 2005). Over the years, the school staff members have invested significant time and resources in building an "identity based curriculum" to be implemented by homeroom teachers in the first through sixth grades. A central component of this pedagogical initiative remains the "unspoken rule" that each group must preserve its identity, avoiding tendencies toward acculturation or assimilation. According to Bekerman (2003a), the schools have "created an educational environment that purposely, from the start and throughout, categorized people not by constructing them but by preventing even the most minute attempt to dismantle even the tiniest brick of their identity…a Jew is a Jew and a Palestinian is a Palestinian" (p. 143). As was exemplified in the anecdote about the non-Arab Christian, there is little acknowledgment or support for identities outside of the Jewish-Arab binary.

The political, cultural, and theoretical rationale for emphasizing two, separate identities is not entirely transparent to me. Generally speaking, I recognize that the underpinnings of the integrated bilingual schools are rooted—among other theories—in intergroup contact theory. Sometimes referred to as the contact hypothesis (for further discussion see Allport, 1954 and Pettigrew, 1988) such theoretical perspectives focus on bringing together people who are in conflict with the assumption that by understanding each other and working together, conflict will subside. Allport specified four conditions for intergroup conflict: equal group status, common goals, intergroup cooperation, and the support of authorities (Pettigrew, 1988, p. 66).

Bringing Jewish Israelis and Palestinian Israelis together under the common goal of schooling would appear to be an optimal circumstance for fostering successful, long-term intergroup cooperation. To a great extent, students function in remarkable harmony. Moreover, to a certain extent, this intergroup encounter results in a recategorization (Pettigrew, 1988) in which all members (students, teachers, parents, and personnel) adopt the identity of individuals committed to integrated bilingual education between Jews and Palestinians. On the other hand, we are predefined—as Jew or Palestinian, with little freedom to dismantle or construct or to prioritize any other identity markers.

English language usage and its function as an identity marker somewhat complicates this binary. "What are you?" the students often ask me. "Are you a Christian or a Jew?" The month is December.

A holiday cheer fills the school with the onset of the winter celebra-tions—Hanukah for the Jewish students, Christmas for the Christian students, and Eid Al-Adha for the Muslim students. Decorations are hung, songs are sung, and candies and gifts are shared. The stu-dents discuss their various celebrations and ask me how I will cel-ebrate Christmas. I hesitate for a moment, considering the identity I have erroneously been awarded. "Actually, I am Jewish," I explain to my students. For an instant, I have complicated the binary that encompasses this educational initiative sometimes referred to as a "Jewish-Arab school" where the Jews speak Hebrew and the Arabs speak Arabic and anybody who could or would be something other or in between eventually becomes an Arab or a Jew. But as some-one associated with English, I seemed to my students—if only for a moment—to be something else.

Indeed, I am something else. I am a teacher, an educator, a mother, a woman, a runner, a musician, and have many other identities. But as with my students, these identifications are drowned out by the force of politically salient categorizations. The perpetuation of two, solidi-fied, binary identifications, I would argue, paralyzes individual iden-tity negotiation processes allowing for the saliency of solely politically delineated categorizations. Identity is perpetuated as a reified entity whose boundaries are fixed and predetermined. Such a tendency tends to serve the status quo and recreate the very divisions and con-flicts the school seeks to ameliorate. Students are not free to undergo identity-negotiation processes common to adolescence, maturity, and general self-determination.

I bring up the notion of identity-based curriculum in order to raise the question as to whether such a pedagogical perspective suc-cessfully advances the goals of intergroup encounters in general and the integrated bilingual school in particular. Students are ultimately heavily schooled in recognizing and solidifying their own identity as Jew or Palestinian. But whether they remain open to other and additional identities as well as the junctures where the two ethnic groups may overlap—as soccer players and Lady Gaga lovers—remains unclear.

Bilingual Curriculum

"I can't understand," whines one of my Hebrew-speaking students, as several Arabic-speaking students discuss a concept I have just described in English. "Translate," she says in Hebrew to no one in particular. "It's not fair." I am momentarily dumbfounded by her audacity but none of the students appear especially concerned. The Arabic-speaking students repeat themselves in Hebrew and everyone seems clear that we are discussing how to conjugate irregular verbs in the past tense in English. I suddenly realize that though my classroom has only three L1 Hebrew speakers, as representatives of the majority language, they are not used to *not* understanding. In fact, my L1 Arabic-speaking colleagues tell me that they literally say everything twice—once in Arabic and once in Hebrew. When Arabic usage dominates in any way, as in one year when it was suggested that the science books be in Arabic, outrage burgeoned from L1 Hebrew-speaking students and parents alike.

To a degree, in English we are able to bypass issues related to Arabic-Hebrew bilingualism. In general, the English staff teaches in English. Moreover, Ministry of Education–approved English language textbooks contains translation to both Arabic and Hebrew. On occasion, as in the example provided, issues arise. However, for the most part, students accept the fact that in English class they are surrounded by English. They achieve high levels of proficiency and demonstrate linguistic competency in a variety of English-dominant domains.

In addition to promoting English language acquisition, the integrated bilingual school advocates a bilingual curriculum emphasizing Arabic-Hebrew bilingualism. Ostensibly, the school has adopted what can be defined as a strong additive bilingual approach that focuses on symmetry between Arabic and Hebrew in all aspects of instruction (Bekerman, 2005).

In additive bilingual educational models, students attend school using their first language (L1) and a second language (L2) is added to their repertoire of knowledge. The aim is to produce students who are bilingual and who possess a certain level of bicultural/multicultural awareness. Additive bilingual programs typically view the acquisition of a second language as advantageous and contributing to students' cognitive, social, and psychological development (Garcia, 1997, pp. 408–409).

There are several types of additive bilingual models. The integrated bilingual model appears to exemplify an integration of two types—two-way dual language programs and maintenance bilingual programs (Garcia, 1997). Two-way dual language programs include students representing both the majority language and minority language. Both languages are used as languages of instruction and allow all children to acquire a second language while maintaining and developing skills in their mother tongue (Fitts, 2006).

Maintenance bilingual programs also use both minority and majority languages. According to Garcia (1997) maintenance programs aim

> to promote the maintenance and development of the minority language and the increased knowledge of the minority history and culture, as well as the full development of the majority language and knowledge of its history and culture. Maintenance programs thus provide the enrichment that language minorities need and the pluralistic perspective needed by the majority society. (pp. 414–415)

While the bilingual-integrated schools do not overtly declare themselves as following a particular bilingual program, their approach contains many of the elements characterizing both dual language programs and maintenance programs.

The premises behind the school's bilingual curriculum support the major aims of both two-way dual language programs and maintenance bilingual programs. These include pluralism, biliteracy, and linguistic/cultural enrichment for both majority and minority speakers (Roberts, 1995). Skutnabb-Kangas and Garcia (1995) further argue that the three main advantages of an effective bilingual program include (1) a high level of multilingualism; (2) equal opportunity for academic achievement; and (3) a strong, positive multilingual and multicultural identity including positive attitudes toward self and others. These elements are evident in both the declarative aims and the curricula of the umbrella organization overseeing bilingual integrated education in Israel (for further information see http://www.handinhandk12.org).

In theory, these objectives are ideologically admirable and pedagogically sound. In practice, the contextual reality surrounding the integrated bilingual school contains sociolinguistic factors that complicate and hinder proficiency in both languages. These include language status, usage, and power. Despite concerted efforts to promote Arabic-Hebrew bilingualism, for the most part, this aim has not been achieved. Rather, the lingua franca of the school is Hebrew (*from Hebrew*, Amara, 2005, p. 42). Moreover, Palestinian-Israeli children quickly demonstrate fluency in Hebrew whereas Jewish-Israeli children generally do not acquire high levels of proficiency in Arabic.

As a language teacher and a researcher interested in the production and reproduction of power through language (Bourdieu, 1991), I am concerned with the lack of critical discourse surrounding the absence of Arabic language acquisition. One way the school has dealt with the lack of Arabic acquisition among Jewish students is by changing the focus of its mission from bilingualism to simply bicultural/multicultural education in general and Jewish-Arab education in particular. This focus shift is encapsulated by the name change of the organization overseeing integrated bilingual education in Israel. Originally, the organization was called the Center for Bilingual Education. Today, this same organization is called the Center for Jewish-Arab Education. While language learning remains an objective of the school and the educational model, other ideological measures associated with successful integration and coexistence have been privileged.

I would argue that acknowledging and dealing with factors affecting Arabic acquisition and the lack of acquisition among Jewish students is critical for the long-term success of the bilingual integrated school. Many additive bilingual models simultaneously address linguistic issues and issues related to power and inequality. According to Fitts, "No program can be a panacea and any bilingual program that attempts to address linguistic issues without also addressing issues of status and power will not fully succeed in its mission" (2006, p. 340). Rather than examine some of the contextual factors playing a role in Jewish students' "failure" to learn Arabic, the school has simply changed the focus of its curriculum. This curricular realignment, along with an absence of critical discourse within the school, means that the integrated-bilingual model ultimately perpetuates the Hebrew-Arabic language hierarchy the initiative strives to dismantle.

In the end, what concerns me is not the lack of bilingualism per se but rather the absence of critical discourse regarding this lack of bilingualism. The school's "failure" to achieve Hebrew-Arabic bilingualism is hardly the fault of the school. Yet broader sociopolitical and sociolinguistic factors are overlooked and issues regarding language status and the relationship between language and power are largely ignored. Within the current sociopolitical/linguistic climate in Israel, Arabic carries less symbolic power than Hebrew or English (Shohamy, 2007). Fluency in Hebrew, to use Bourdieu's term, carries more "cultural capital" (1991) in the linguistic marketplace than Arabic. To date, the school does not appear to have addressed these issues of power and inequality and Hebrew usage dominates most arenas.

Ultimately, in all language classrooms, multiple factors are at play and recognition of these factors—be they oppressive or liberating—I contend, is imperative for equality to prevail. Even in the most well-intended initiatives, oppression and inequity triumph when hierarchies—linguistic or otherwise—are left unchecked.

IDEOLOGY AS CURRICULUM

A few days before Israel's Memorial Day, I pass by one of the teachers setting up a bulletin board in the courtyard of the school. Next to several poems and drawings is a large Israeli flag. She carefully removes the staples from the cloth, taking down the flag and replacing it with a smaller, less conspicuous one. "It's too big," she explains, and tacks up a rather dismal replacement. "The management is afraid someone will get upset," she goes on to explain.

A hesitancy to venerate nation-state symbols in a context striving to bridge one of the most intractable ethno-national conflicts in the world makes sense to me. On the other hand, I find the wishy-washy ideology that underpins many of the school's policies and practices frustrating and, at times, pedagogically erroneous. As a school, which ideologies and practices do we support? Which do we condemn? As educators, teachers, and participants in this community of practice, what are we agreeing to support either overtly or tacitly?

Having a policy of no flags because as an institution we do not support nation-state ideology is a clear stance. Not hanging up a large flag because "someone might get upset" sends an unclear message about who is in charge and avoids making a commitment to any stance. In fact, it seems that quite a few decisions at the integrated bilingual school are made in an attempt to appease one of the many stakeholders in this initiative or to avoid ruffling anyone's feathers. The problem with such a practice in a context infused with ideology is that ambiguity prevails and someone's feathers almost always get ruffled.

As in the example above, these issues of ideology and practice are particularly paramount in the spring months when Israeli national holidays are observed and the Palestinian *Nakba* is commemorated. I do not wish to focus my discussion of ideology as curriculum on these specific events. They have been well documented by others (see, for example, Bekerman, 2002, 2003b) and they are the most overt symbols of the challenges facing integrated bilingual education in Israel. I mention them solely to demonstrate that the school's approach to these historical/national symbols exemplifies a wider practice of avoiding unified ideological principles except on the broadest of levels (i.e., we support peace, coexistence, and equality between the Jews and Arabs of Israel). However, when a Palestinian student tells me that six million Jews did not really die in the Holocaust or a Jewish student tells me she feels guilty because her parents stole land from Palestinians, I feel ill-equipped from an organizational perspective.

On an individual level, I can respond as I deem appropriate. But as a teacher in a specific educational context, I sense that there is a lack of a clear institutional framework in which to anchor my responses.

The ideological "schooling" that accompanies any and every educational initiative lacks transparency in this particular context. Generally speaking, integrated bilingual education in Israel is informed by liberal ideologies such as pluralism, multiculturalism, and tolerance. However, in my opinion, teachers and parents taking part in integrated bilingual education have a right to a clearer picture of the schooling processes their children are undergoing or they are advancing as teachers and parents. The ideology remains murky. Moreover, its translation into an applicable school curriculum that can compete in the educational "market" has proven to be challenging.

At times, social/ideological agendas clash with more traditional academic objectives—with teachers, students, and parents needing to choose between, for example, a lesson involving a visitor from Amnesty International and a standard math lesson. Jewish parents tend to choose the former. They see the school as a means for advancing an ideological agenda and they have at their disposal countless educational options and facilities. Palestinian parents tend to choose the latter, understanding the school to be an avenue for educational excellence and wanting to equip their children with the tools necessary for socioeconomic advancement (Bekerman, 2005).

As a teacher, I see this divergence of expectations as one of the principal tensions accompanying ideology as curriculum. The integrated bilingual model seems to continuously vacillate between academic objectives and ideology, between ensuring student acquisition of the educational skills necessary for social mobility and seeking to satisfy all invested in the schools. Until now, ideology seems to have triumphed over academics. Jewish stakeholders tend to be more vocal about their wishes and concerns. Sometimes unknowingly, they comfortably assert the power and influence associated with the majority group. Sometimes this happens at the expense of the minority group.

Appeasing ideology at the cost of academics, I would argue, has potentially detrimental effects on all students. They may not sufficiently acquire the skills necessary to advance through the educational system. For Jewish students, they can go elsewhere or they learn from their parents—who are able to equip their children with the necessary "cultural capital" for succeeding in the Israeli milieu. For Palestinian students, they stay in the integrated bilingual system because they have few options available to them. Their parents—as minorities—may or may not have the time, money, and resources to equip their children with the mobility tools necessary for success and achievement. Either way, the Palestinian students are further disempowered. This is not the ideal result of an educational initiative devoted to equality. The aims of integrated bilingual education in Israel remain nebulous. The school and the broader umbrella organization for integrated bilingual education have fashioned themselves as an educational model and yet they are also attempting to be a force for ideological change. The question remains whether they can successfully bridge the current gaps between ideology and academic achievement, ensuring that equality ultimately reigns.

DISCUSSION AND RECOMMENDATIONS

In the previous sections, I have detailed some of the unintended ramifications of three curricular components employed in one integrated bilingual school in Israel. In the following section, I will highlight some potential ways to address these repercussions of schooling, suggesting that proactive and preventative measures may ultimately have an important role in the school's socialization processes and educational outcomes.

With respect to identity-based curriculum, there is a need to recognize and acknowledge the prevalence of binary discourse and to examine whether such an emphasis on Jew and Palestinian strengthens the general principles and goals of integrated bilingual education. Students, parents, teachers, and other stakeholders might be encouraged to take part in identity-building activities aimed at promoting the saliency of other and additional identities as well as the fostering of prejudice awareness and reduction. When individuals are predefined according to solely ethno-political categorizations, they remain associated with certain stereotypes and prejudices. Uncovering and constructing shared identifications where groups in conflict overlap are critical for prejudice reduction and coexistence. Equally important, in my opinion, is dispelling nation-state rhetoric that suggests that all Jewish Israelis and all Palestinian Israelis belong to singular and opposite ethno-political groups. The diversity within each side of this perpetuated binary warrants recognition and is key to re-categorization and reconciliation.

With respect to bilingual curriculum, more education and training may be warranted. To date, Hebrew and Arabic are presented as symmetrical languages—with little reference to the broader sociopolitical context. While the school may strive for linguistic symmetry, the local linguistic landscape is highly asymmetrical, with Hebrew constituting the local language of power, clout, and social mobility. Students' motivation, acquisition, and language-learning success are affected by this wider sociopolitical context that needs to be examined critically and taken into consideration when language curricula are being designed and implemented. In particular, teachers and school educators may benefit from additional trainings around issues related to language learning, language status, and power.

Additionally, the outstanding linguistic and sociolinguistic characteristics of Arabic need to be acknowledged, better understood, and taken into consideration when constructing and implementing an Arabic-Hebrew bilingual curriculum. In particular, this pertains to the diglossic nature of Arabic—that is, the fact that the language contains two markedly different linguistic varieties—one for spoken communication (colloquial variety) and one for written communication. Diglossia affects both L1 and L2 Arabic language learners and undoubtedly has an impact on language acquisition and fluency. Teachers aiming to promote Arabic-Hebrew bilingualism would benefit from further information concerning the roles and consequences of diglossia in language learning. Moreover, given that Hebrew is not a diglossic language, this may be an additional deliberation when considering symmetry between the languages.

Finally, with respect to ideology as curriculum, the parameters of the school's ideology need to be better fleshed out and clarified. Likewise, the objectives and goals of the umbrella organization advocating integrated bilingual education in Israel need to be clearer. Broad, all-encompassing, liberal principles are perhaps a good place to begin conversations about equality and coexistence. But educators in this educational initiative are ultimately responsible for transmitting a shared ideology that, in my opinion, lacks form and therefore longevity. This lack of clarity frequently translates to a lack of clear objectives regarding both ideological and academic goals. As an initiative designed to school, I contend that first and foremost we must educate students *well* and empower them with the skills they will need to navigate and flourish within an already constructed system. Alongside scholastic empowerment, we can begin constructing more specific notions of ideology regarding narratives, history, practices, and traditions. I would argue that this process of building a more concretized platform on which to stand is imperative for long-term sustainability. Without it, the educational experiment as a whole remains precarious.

CAVEATS AND CONCLUSIONS

In this chapter, I raise critical issues concerning *schooling* in integrated bilingual education in Israel. More specifically, I discussed three curricular components—identity-based curriculum, bilingual curriculum, and ideology as curriculum. My stance has been both critical and reflective, drawing on my experiences as a teacher in one integrated bilingual school. While I am deeply concerned with the repercussions of unexamined schooling processes stemming from these curricular components, I feel compelled to end on a note of tribute.

Integrated bilingual education in Israel remains revolutionary, incomprehensible within mainstream educational trajectories modeled on two, fully segregated systems—one for Jews and one for Arabs. Attempting to integrate different ethnicities, religions, and languages is not a simple endeavor. Attempting to bring together and equalize majority and minority groups in conflict is an even more challenging endeavor. Daring to propose change—to defy the status quo—is, in and of itself, a remarkable first step. However, if we are to bear witness to the crystallization of a long-term, sustainable educational model that can truly herald change, we must proceed in a more critical manner.

REFERENCES

Allport, G. W. (1954). *The nature of prejudice*. London: Addison-Wesley.

Amara, M. (2005). *Hand-in-Hand's model of bilingualism*. Jerusalem, Israel: Hand-in-Hand Center for Jewish-Arab Education in Israel (in Hebrew).

Bekerman, Z. (2002). Can education contribute to coexistence and reconciliation? Religious and national ceremonies in bilingual Palestinian-Jewish schools in Israel? *Journal of Peace Psychology, 8*(3), 259–276 .

Bekerman, Z. (2003a). Never free of suspicion. *Cultural Studies, Critical Methodologies, 3* (2), 136–147.

Bekerman, Z. (2003b). Reshaping conflict through school ceremonial events in Israeli Palestinian-Jewish co-education. *Anthropology & Education Quarterly, 34*(2), 205–224.

Bekerman, Z. (2005). Complex contexts and ideologies: Bilingual education in conflict-ridden areas. *Journal of Language, Identity, and Education, 4*(1), 1–20.

Bourdieu, P. (1991). *Language and symbolic power*. Cambridge: Harvard University Press.

Fitts, S. (2006). Reconstructing the status quo: Linguistic interaction in a dual-language school. *Bilingual Research Journal, 29* (2), 337–365.

Garcia, O. (1997). Bilingual education. In F. Coulmas (Ed.), *The handbook of sociolinguistics* (pp. 405–420). Oxford: Blackwell.

Pettigrew, T. (1988). Intergroup contact theory. *Annual Review of Psychology*, *49*, 65–85.

Roberts, C. (1995). Bilingual education program models: A framework for understanding. *The Bilingual Research Journal*, *19* (3–4), 369–378.

Shohamy, E. (2007). Reinterpreting globalization in multilingual contexts. *International Multilingual Research Journal*, *1*(2) 127–133.

Skutnabb-Kangas, T. & García, O. (1995). Multilingualism for all? General principles. In T. Skutnabb-Kangas (Ed.), *Multilingualism for all* (pp. 221–256). Lisse: Swets & Zeitlinger, Amsterdam, Series European Studies on Multilingualism.

12

KHALIL, KHALIL, AND KHALIL

Bob Mark

The Village School[1] is one of the five integrated Jewish-Arab schools in Israel that set out to advance understanding and equality through bilingual multicultural education. In Israeli social reality, creating opportunities for Jewish and Arab children to learn together and develop friendships at an early age is no small accomplishment. The Israeli school system is divided between Jewish and Arab schools and it is rare that Jewish and Arab children in the country find opportunities to develop relationships.

Research on multicultural issues in the integrated schools tends to focus on how the schools address different holidays, ceremonies, identities, and historical narratives. These questions are important in examining how teachers, parents, and state authorities negotiate the meaning of culture and shape school policy. As a teacher in the Village School for 23 years I have been more interested in looking at multiculturalism by examining the mundane classroom practices that shape our images and expectations of each other. This chapter is based on my attempt[2] to learn something about the culture created through the Jewish-Arab encounter by following routine classroom experiences of a single child in the school.

Identity politics and holidays often lead the Village School to separate the Jews and Arabs for study in "uninational" forums. For example the school's conviction that it is important to strengthen each group's national and cultural identities led it to separate the Jewish and Arab children for weekly study of holy books. The combination of uninational and binational forums provides us with opportunities to see how the same children respond to different classroom contexts. Naturally one of the important differences between these contexts is in the use of language. Despite the integrated schools' progress in creating a bilingual reality for the children, the Arabs' Hebrew remains incomparably stronger than the Jews' Arabic in all five schools (Amara et al. 2009; Bekerman, 2009; Nasser & Abu-Nimr, 2007). With Hebrew as the dominant language the Jewish children can always count on being able to communicate in their mother language regardless of the context. Only the Arab children find themselves in situations in which they have no choice but to function in their second language. For this reason I chose to focus on an Arab child, examining how his participation changes from one forum to the next. I call him "Khalil."

INTRODUCING KHALIL

The idea of examining the school by following a single student was inspired by Varenne and McDermott's (1998, 25) case study entitled "Adam, Adam, Adam and Adam: The Cultural Construction of a Learning Disability." Varenne and McDermott demonstrate how differently the same child can be perceived in different classroom contexts, often with far-reaching consequences. By observing the strategies that Adam employs to overcome the obstacles of various classroom settings, our attention is focused not on Adam but on the institutional structures that labeled him as learning disabled. Similarly, following Khalil from one classroom to the next was to provide me with an eye-opener at the institution that I helped to build.

Khalil was in the fourth grade. I did not normally teach his class but, as a Jewish teacher, I worked with the Jewish fourth graders on Arab holidays when the Arab children and teachers remained home. I often entered their classroom with my guitar and repertoire of songs in English, and the lessons were relaxed and enjoyable. As the Jewish children began to acquire more and more songs I decided to come on an Arab uninational day and teach the Arab children some of the songs as well. That was when I first met Khalil. The lesson was a nightmare. It seemed to me that if it were only ethical to keep Khalil gagged and tied to his chair I might have stood a chance at conducting a lesson with many of the other children. Khalil struck me as the ringleader of the troublemakers and I clearly did not have whatever it would take to win him over.

Several Arab teachers explained to me that the difficulty of working with the Arab children in the school is that they come from many different places. They came from four all-Arab towns and villages, from the two mixed Jewish-Arab towns of Ramla and Lod, and from well-off houses in a liberal Jewish-Arab community. Reviewing the school's history I found that the Jewish children actually came from four times as many different places as the Arab children. However this was never regarded as more than a problem of logistics. The middle class surroundings of the Jewish families were very similar to each other. When the Arab teachers spoke about different places they were referring to very different social realities.

Khalil came from one of the mixed Jewish-Arab towns. Mixed towns are predominantly Jewish towns with Arab minorities. Out of the 70,000 Palestinians in Ramla and Lod prior to the 1948 Arab-Israeli War, approximately 68,000 were evicted (Morris, 2004, pp. 425–437). The evicted residents were replaced by Jewish immigrants and by Palestinian internal refugees who were evicted from their villages but remained in Israel (Morris, 1994). In the 1960s Bedouin Arabs whose land in the northern Negev was expropriated were also relocated to Ramla and Lod and after the Palestinian uprising in 1987 Palestinian collaborators from the Occupied Territories were housed there by Israeli security authorities. The discrimination experienced by the Palestinian minority in Israel reaches extremes in the mixed towns. Whereas homogeneous Arab towns at least have representative municipal bodies, Arabs in mixed towns are at the mercy of Jewish municipal authorities who have a history of neglecting Arab residents' interests. Having been thrown together without much say in the matter, the Arab communities in these towns have been characterized by a lack of social cohesion and a lack of political channels to advance their interests. The overcrowded conditions and the discrimination in budget allocations characterizing the Arab neighborhoods are well documented in the Shatil organization's survey of Jaffa, Ramla, and Lod (Jabarin & Hamdan, 2002).

Khalil was from a Bedouin family. The more deprived neighborhoods of Ramla and Lod are largely Bedouin. From discussions with several Arab parents of children in the Village School, the Bedouin appear to be a stigmatized group. One of the Arab parents, who grew up in Lod, presented the influx of Bedouin as part of a scheme:

> It's apparently part of a policy, I think. It [the Arab community in Lod] was a healthy population and bringing in these people [the Bedouin] seriously hurt the original residents socially, economically and from every other aspect.

Several Arab parents echoed concern about working with such a great socioeconomic gap when bringing children from Bedouin neighborhoods into the school. Khalil originally appeared to justify their concern and I did not want to focus attention on anyone regarded as being particularly problematic. However as I watched the children I began to discover Khalil's sense of humor and I was captivated by the way he got through the day.

LIFE AT THE SCHOOL WITH KHALIL

Hebrew classes were opportunities to see how Khalil managed in lessons with one of the Jewish teachers. Shiri, the teacher, had prepared work corners with a large selection of tasks aimed at enabling children to work independently and progress at their own pace. The children worked in pairs and brought their completed tasks to her for correction. Tomer, an introverted Jewish boy who I often found alone on the playground, would have been an unlikely partner for Khalil under any other circumstance. Tomer began by working alone and Khalil joined him with a Hebrew task from the work corner. Khalil sat down with the task, looked around for several minutes, and then declared to no one in particular (in Hebrew), "I'm going to do this alone. I'm not retarded." He took out a piece of paper, slowly copied the instructions, threw the paper away, and spent the next five minutes watching Tomer work on the assignment. Finally Khalil decided that it was time to check in on his friends and disturb some of the other children in the class. He made his rounds and when Tomer finished the task Khalil joined him again in order to bring "their" work to Shiri for corrections. Shiri made her comments, Tomer made the corrections, and they moved on to the next task.

I later asked Shiri if she was aware of how little Khalil actually managed to do in the lesson. She was not surprised. She explained to me that everyone does what they can:

> A few weeks ago Khalil took work home and copied it on the computer. Some of it he understood. He's not like Daniel, David, Fatin or Nasrin. They're on a much higher level. Whatever Khalil absorbs, he absorbs, and I hope that by next year he'll progress a little more. He's slow, but he's making progress.

Shiri's conclusions about what Khalil is capable of doing were based solely on her interaction with him in Hebrew. In principle the Jewish teachers are expected to learn Arabic, or at the very least to learn some basic concepts connected to their subjects. The following exchange reflects Shiri's attitude toward the minimal language demands made of her. Aishe had approached Shiri's table with her completed Hebrew task. Shiri tried to explain something about the imperative but Aishe was not familiar with the word:

Shiri: (*raising her voice and looking over the class for help*) Ehhh … Fatin. How do you say "imperative" in Arabic?
Fatin: Amr.
Shiri: (*looking confused*) How?
Fatin: Amr.
Shiri: (*continues to look at Fatin for a second and then turns to Aishe*) Did you understand her? (*Aishe nods her head and Shiri continues with her explanation*)

Translated from Hebrew

As a language teacher, Shiri might have been expected to take this opportunity to demonstrate at least symbolic interest and make an attempt to acquire an important grammatical term such as "imperative" in Arabic. Instead she made it clear that translation is *Aishe's* problem. As far as Shiri was concerned the problem was solved as soon as Aishe confirmed that she understood the word. There was nothing exceptional about this interaction. In an art activity that I observed, a Jewish teacher introduced techniques of drawing a profile and a frontal view of a face. She explained the concept of profile and, to define the frontal view, she used the French "en face," shortening it and expressing it "fas." Unfortunately she was unaware that "fas" in the colloquial Arabic means "fart."

Teacher: Our goal is to draw a face both in profile and fas.
Child: What fas?
Children: Fas!
All of the Arab children and several of the Jewish children break up laughing.
Teacher: Fas is when they look at you straight on.
Children: (*one after another*) Fas? Fas! Fas!
Teacher: (*calmly*) Yes, that's fas.
Child: Fas is …
Teacher: Profile is when you only see one eye …
Child: Say fas!

Translated from Hebrew

What was noteworthy in the above cases was not the teachers' lack of understanding, but their lack of interest in acquiring essential Arabic vocabulary or in clarifying what was stirring up the classroom.

The Arab children are accustomed to speaking a language and coming from a world from which their Jewish teachers are disconnected. As I continued to observe Khalil I began to see exchanges like these as reflections of a much more fundamental problem.

The introduction of Arabic into the classroom opened the door to a very different kind of interaction with Khalil. Arwa, the Arab English teacher, jumped back and forth between Arabic and Hebrew, each time appearing to invite either the Arabs or the Jews to discussion. While transcribing the lesson, I came across a part in which Arwa explained the difference between "sorry" and "forgive me." This was followed by one of the boys breaking into a blues rendition of the text singing in an American accent, "I'm sorry, please forgive me!" I had no question that it was one of the Jewish boys who I taught on the uninational days but I could not identify which one. When Arwa heard the tape she laughed and told me without hesitation that it was Khalil and that it was typical of him. Khalil would have been my last guess. At another point Arwa searched for a way to explain a particular concept in English and Khalil provided her with a parallel expression in Arabic that captured what she was trying to say. These were the first of several exchanges in the data that were to illustrate Khalil's language skills. Later, during a Koran lesson, there were two points at which Khalil explained to the other children the implications of a word in the classical Arabic text as opposed to its more familiar usage in modern Arabic. In each of the two lessons that involved reading Arabic texts, the teachers turned first to Khalil to read in order to ensure that the children would hear a proper reading of the language.[3] As long as Khalil's Jewish teachers and classmates were restricted to speaking to him in Hebrew, they were not likely to notice or appreciate his language skills, nor were they likely to experience him as someone who contributes to the lessons.

There was an exceptional episode in one of the lessons in which the Jewish children, if they were paying attention, might have noticed a change in Khalil. An Arab teacher brought the children a very short and simple poem about friendship. It was written in both Hebrew and Arabic. She suggested a novel idea, asking the Arab children to read the Hebrew version and the Jewish children to read the Arabic. The Arab children had no trouble with the Hebrew. Several of the Jewish children read the Arabic better than I expected. However Hanna, a Jewish girl, read the Arabic with tremendous difficulty. For two full minutes she worked on three brief lines of the poem, one syllable at a time. The class was absolutely silent, giving her all of the time that she needed. The only other people occasionally heard from were the teacher and Khalil. Khalil sat on the edge of his seat enthralled by Hanna's efforts, helping her through words at times and once pointing out a missing vowel mark that made the reading difficult. Hanna's difficulty was not cause for embarrassment. She did not seem to think less of herself for struggling in public with her second language. This contrasted with Khalil's concern in Shiri's class that his difficulty with the Hebrew task might be construed as a sign that he was mentally challenged. The episode was a warm moment in which the Jewish children were hosted by the Arab children in Arabic. It stood out because of how rare it was that such conditions were created.

The differences between teacher-pupil interactions in Hebrew and in Arabic went beyond language. The Arab and Jewish uninational lessons were characterized by educational discourses that positioned the teachers and children very differently in each forum. Since Khalil was the focus of my work with the fourth-grade class, I accompanied the children primarily in the binational and Arab uninational forums. I only observed one lesson in the Jewish uninational forum in Khalil's class. It was a Bible lesson on the Ten Commandments. Bible lessons in the Village School, as in most secular schools in Israel, are conducted as literature lessons rather than as a source of moral teaching or of faith. Here the teacher opened by explaining that this Bible lesson was to be exceptional. They were going to read Deuteronomy because that's where the Ten Commandments are, "otherwise Deuteronomy wouldn't interest us because it's all about laws and laws interest the religious. They don't interest us." The children were seated behind tables set up in a horseshoe arrangement. The teacher facilitated the discussion and the children directed their comments at each other. Children analyzed the commandments identifying the distinction between those relating to one's relationship to God as opposed to those relating to people's relationships with each other. It was agreed that those regarding God were of less interest to them and they focused on commandments regarding people's relations with each other. They conducted lively discussion often opening their remarks with: "Well, I don't believe in God, but…" and they went on to analyze biblical law offering sociological explanations of rules that societies need in order to function.

The Koran lesson with the Arab children was very different not only in regard to religious belief but also in the very structure of the discussion. When speaking Hebrew the teachers are addressed by first name. However Arab children address Arab teachers by title: "ma'alme" for women and "ustaz" for men, each literally meaning "teacher" but used here as terms of respect. I translate the titles as ma'am and sir. The children were seated in rows facing the teacher. Most of the teacher's questions were closed questions inviting one-word responses. The children's responses were always directed at the teacher.

The structural differences between these two uninational lessons are consistent with patterns found in much more extensive data gathered six years later for my present research work on another class in the Village School. Social theory such as Cazden's (2001, p. 5) IRE (initiation—response—evaluation) versus discussion-based discourses and Bernstein's discussion of how the hierarchy and pedagogical relations within the classroom are "framed" (Bernstein, 2000, p. 12) to reflect and reproduce the larger social order outside of the classroom are helpful in examining these differences. However, they may also help us to lose sight of Khalil.

Just before one of the Arab uninational days, I asked Rawan, the teacher, if I would have a chance to observe a Koran lesson. Rawan told me that it was an excellent idea: "I don't like the way that some of the girls have been speaking to each other. This is a good time for a Koran lesson. Come tomorrow at 8:00." Gender distinctions in the Arab group and the introduction of God in the Koran lesson in particular added to the sense of hierarchy in the Arab classroom. The Koran was mobilized to address the children's behavior. The lesson the next day was on Surat al-Humazah, a chapter warning against mockery. The belief in God was taken for granted, reflected in Rawan's regular reference to "Rabna," our lord. To illustrate the problem of gossip and mockery, Rawan described the way that the people of Mecca initially made fun of Muhammad for praying to a God that he can't see. Khalil banged his fist on the table and asked how they could pray to statues that they themselves made. "*You* made *it*! How can you believe that *it* made *you*?!!" I never saw Khalil so engaged in a lesson and I was impressed by the eloquent case that he made against the pagans. Khalil was among the few in the Arab uninational forum who broke the pattern of one-word responses. Rawan went on to introduce the text:

> Rawan: The words that you will learn today—humazatin and lumaza-tin. 'Adada comes from the word? . . . 'adad, ya'id. Humazatin is one who always points out people's faults. *Khalil*, what does that mean, one who points out people's faults?
> Khalil: Like you.
> Rawan: (*looking surprised*) How? Tell me.
> Khalil: Like the way you speak about the girls who make problems and the boys who make problems . . .

Rawan: I meant…is this verse talking about me or is it referring to them?

Khalil: To them.

Rawan: It's referring to them, not about me. And what do I do?

Khalil: You embarrass them (btifdah'ihum).

Rawan: That's not a nice word, what do I do?

Khalil: You correct them.

Translated from Arabic

Khalil's suggestion that the Koran was warning against behavior such as Rawan's appeared to me to be an innocent misunderstanding. When Rawan heard the recording of this excerpt she smiled, shook her head and said, "That bastard." It was clear to Rawan that Khalil knew exactly what he was doing. As in the case of the English lesson I was surprised once again by how differently the Arab teachers experienced Khalil.

Rawan eventually addressed the agenda of her lesson by instructing the children to close their eyes and silently consider whether they too may have been guilty of the sin of mockery. As I watched them I thought of how inconceivable it would have been to use a Bible lesson with the Jewish children for such an exercise. I found it interesting that here the Arab children cooperated. However, after a short period of silence I noticed a low hum in the classroom and I turned to find Khalil sitting in lotus position with his eyes closed as he emitted a long and quiet "ommmmm."

McLaren (1999) describes the class clown as one who expresses resistance by trivializing instructional transactions and exposing the classroom cultural codes before all. Khalil may indeed have been working at exposing the classroom's cultural codes; however it was hardly "before all." Khalil's quiet satire of the moment of silence, his blues rendition of the English lesson, and the subtle way that he managed to turn the Koran against the teacher all required a considerable amount of work to notice. In fact Khalil's disappearance from the school also seemed to go unnoticed.

In November of the following school year I entered Khalil's class, now in fifth grade, and suddenly realized that I had not seen Khalil for a while. The children told me that after his misbehavior in the school van, the driver said that he was no longer prepared to drive that line as long as Khalil was on it. Khalil's family took him out of the school. The principal later confirmed the story and added that the family asked if they could return him to the Village School. Hearing this, a Jewish teacher sitting with us immediately responded with, "Oy vay!" (i.e., "oh no") followed by an Arab teacher who said, "That would be great."

I arranged a visit with Khalil's father, Jawad. Khalil was to meet me by the local grocery store and show me the way to their house. The rows of new and identical three-story apartment buildings on the way to the store were not how I imagined Khalil's neighborhood. Khalil met me on his bicycle and led me down one more road into a large lot. Behind long lines of laundry was an un-plastered cinder-block house that had obviously gone through various stages of development— one improvised extension added to another. Khalil's grandmother sat outside behind a table sifting through a pile of lentils, while around her seven or eight chickens searched for food among the pebbles. More three-story apartment buildings loomed over three sides of the lot and I had a sense of being watched from the rows of windows overlooking Khalil's home. Khalil was the youngest child in the family. His three sisters slept in one bedroom, three brothers slept in another, and Khalil slept on a couch, sharing the living room with his grandmother at night. Though agreeing to the interview, Jawad did not want to be recorded. His trust had to be earned. The turning point may have been when Jawad's brother joined us and we shared a series of laughs exchanging stories about Khalil's antics in the classroom and at home.

Jawad told me about his struggle to maintain a hold on their home. His lot was the last remnant of what was a Bedouin neighborhood. Their houses had been registered to a public housing company that provided homes for the Bedouin after their family's land in the Negev was taken from them decades earlier. The other Bedouin in the neighborhood succumbed to pressure to sell out and move again, this time to make room for the new apartment buildings built to accommodate the latest wave of Jewish Russian immigrants. Jawad told me that his new neighbors were assured that a shopping center would eventually replace his home as well. Money did not prevent Jawad from fixing up his house. The fact that he sent Khalil to the Village School indicated that he had money for the modest tuition fees that the school charged. However any attempt to renovate his house or even to repair his leaking ceiling without a permit would give the public housing inspector the excuse that the company was waiting for to evict the family on grounds of a breach of contract. Needless to say, receiving the required permit was out of the question.

So what happened to Khalil? The family did take him out of school after the incident in the van but a week later he wanted to return. They called the principal several times, leaving messages with the Village School secretary. They abandoned the idea when no one returned their calls. Knowing that the principal had received those messages I later asked him why he never returned Jawad's call. The principal told me that it was the family's choice to take Khalil out of school and that all they had to do was to bring him to the bus stop and send him back to the Village School again. The fact that this message did not reach Khalil's family indicated that the principal was not keen on seeing that actually happen.

The number of ways that Khalil could be treated as a troublesome interference is mind-boggling. Municipal authorities, neighbors, teachers, and a Village School bus driver seemed to be working hard to ignore Khalil and his family. While a discussion on the nature of culture exceeds the scope of this chapter, it is a key component in Varenne and McDermott's (1998, p. 4) discussion of Adam. "Inner city and suburb," they tell us, "do not belong to different worlds. They belong to the same differentiated world." Similarly any attempt to untangle and broach the forces acting on Khalil must include an examination of the differentiated world of Jews and Arabs—and in this case of Arabs and Arabs. It is not clear if or how the school's multicultural approach contributes to such an examination. A wealth of literature warns against the attempt of liberal multiculturalism to celebrate difference while overlooking power relations. McLaren (1997, p. 47) warns that "multiculturalism as liberal pluralism...always has an ideological center of gravity which rarely gets defined for what it is: liberal pluralism as the politics of white supremacist patriarchal capitalism."

Approaching culture as if it is a schedule of holidays and an anthology of texts and narratives allows the Village School to evade examination of how power and class relations position us and influence the value of each group's cultural capital (Bourdieu, 1977). It is an approach that obfuscates the way in which our culture is cocreated and the way in which our identities are shaped in dialogue with and in response to each other (Wexler, 1992).

I could and generally do speak about the Village School through its many success stories. This particular story is obviously not one of them. It is easy to criticize the Village School for adapting to the constraints of mainstream discourse just as it is easy to criticize Shiri, the Hebrew teacher, for her low expectations of Khalil. Yet when I first met Khalil I wanted him gagged. Discovering Khalil and learning about ourselves through Khalil requires hard work. The work is hard because, as Bekerman (2004) points out, the banality of the discursive practices that reflect our social reality makes it hard to pay any attention to them.

Many of the issues that surface in the Jewish-Arab schools will never be confronted in Israel's mainstream schools. That in itself is one of the Jewish-Arab schools' most important contributions. The Village School is a site where discursive practices sustaining the social order can be exposed and challenged. Putting the spotlight on Khalil—or better yet handing the spotlight over to him—may be the kind of Freirean (Freire, 1999) work that is needed to show us the way.

NOTES

1. "The Village School" and the names of all people in the chapter are pseudonyms.
2. The research was conducted for an MA thesis supervised by Dr. Zvi Bekerman.
3. This was confirmed by the teachers.

REFERENCES

Amara, M. H., Azaiza, F., Hertz-Lazarowitz, R., & Mor-Sommerfeld, A. (2009). A new bilingual education in the conflict-ridden Israeli reality: Language practices. *Language Education, 23* (1), 15–35.
Bekerman, Z. (2004). Potential and limitations of multicultural education in conflict-ridden areas: Bilingual Palestinian-Jewish schools in Israel. *Teachers College Record, 106* (3), 574–610.
Bekerman, Z. (2009). "Yeah, it is important to know Arabic—I just don't like learning it": Can Jews become bilingual in the Palestinian-Jewish integrated bilingual schools? In C. McGlynn, M. Zembylas, Z. Bekerman, & T. Gallagher (Eds.), *Peace education in conflict and post-conflict societies: Comparative perspectives* (pp. 232–246). New York: Palgrave Macmillan.
Bernstein, B. (2000). *Pedagogy, symbolic control and identity.* Lanham: Rowman & Littlefield.
Bourdieu, P. (1977). Cultural reproduction and social reproduction. In J. Karabel & A. H. Halsey (Eds.), *Power and ideology in education* (pp. 487–511). Oxford: Oxford University Press.
Cazden, C. B. (2001). *Classroom discourse.* Portsmouth, NH: Heinmann.
Freire, P. (1999). *Pedagogy of the oppressed.* New York: Continuum.
Jabarin, Y., & Hamdan, H. (2002). *Ha'ezrahim Ha'aravim Ba'arim Hame'uravot.* Jerusalem: Shatil.
McLaren, P. (1997). *Revolutionary multiculturalism: Pedagogies of dissent for the new millenium:* Boulder: Westview Press.
McLaren, P. (1999). *Schooling as a ritual performance.* Lanham: Rowman & Littlefield.
Morris, B. (1994). *1948 and after: Israel and the Palestinians.* Oxford: Clarendon Press.
Morris, B. (2004). *The birth of the Palestinian refugee problem revisited.* Cambridge: Cambridge University Press.

Nasser, I., & Abu-Nimr, M. (2007). Peace education in a bilingual and bi-ethnic school for Palestinians and Jews in Israel: Lessons and challenges. In C. Mcglynn & Z. Bekerman (Eds.), *Addressing conflict through peace education* (pp. 107–120). New York: Palgrave Macmillan.

Varenne, H., & McDermott, R. (1998). *Successful failure.* Boulder: Westview Press.

Wexler, P. (1992). *Becoming somebody: Toward a social psychology of school.* London: Falmer Press.

13

CHALLENGES OF EDUCATION
FOR PEACE IN SEGREGATED
SCHOOLS IN VUKOVAR

Marinko Uremovic and Ivana Milas

Although the recent years in Vukovar, Croatia, have been peaceful it would be incorrect to say that full reconciliation has been achieved. In this chapter, we will take a look at the current educational system in Vukovar and specifically into the problem of segregated schooling. We will try to explain the reasons why and how such schooling came to be, and how the main stakeholders in Vukovar, that is, the Croatian majority and the Serbian minority, view current schooling in the city. We will also present two different approaches that the Nansen Dialogue Centre (NDC) has taken as a possible answer to this problem: The New School Project, an initiative to open an integrated school in Vukovar, and the implementation of the intercultural subject "Cultural and Spiritual Heritage of the Region" (CSHR), that has been introduced in the curriculum of presently segregated schools. Finally, we will talk about the lessons learnt from our work, by presenting both the achievements and the obstacles we have encountered in our journey to promote integrated schooling in Vukovar.

HISTORICAL BACKGROUND

Vukovar is a city in eastern Croatia and is situated at the confluence of the Vuka River and the Danube. For many years it was known for its economy, rich history, and cultural diversity. According to the 1991 census 56.07 percent of population were non-Croats, with Serbs making up 32.3 percent. There were 27 different national minorities living in Vukovar including Hungarians, Germans, Ruthenians, and the Roma. Vukovar also had the second biggest share of mixed marriages (usually between Croats and Serbs) in former Yugoslavia. All these people coexisted peacefully in this region for several decades. The breakup of Yugoslavia in 1991 put an end to this peaceful coexistence, when on August 25, 1991, the Yugoslav People's Army launched the siege of Vukovar, which lasted for 87 days (Popović, 2009). During this period some 1,000 civilians were killed, more than 2,500 wounded, while some 5,000 were transported to detention facilities and prison camps in Serbia. Upon the fall of Vukovar on November 18, 1991, two hundred prisoners of war and civilians from the Vukovar hospital were taken to the Ovčara farm where they were executed and buried in a mass grave (Popović, 2009). All non-Serbs were banished from the city of Vukovar.

Four years later, on November 15, 1995, the Erdut Agreement was signed between the Republic of Croatia and the local Serb authorities. This agreement put an end to war in the region and also brought the region of eastern Croatia back under the sovereignty of the Republic of Croatia within the process of peaceful reintegration from 1995 to 1997. The process of return of non-Serb population in these areas began in 1998 and was long and slow as it depended mainly on rebuilding houses; it was not fully completed until 2011.

SOCIAL COHESION IN POST-CONFLICT REGIONS

In multicultural societies minorities have three options, in our view: segregation, integration, or assimilation. In conflict or post-conflict areas where true reconciliation has still not been achieved these options are often reduced to just two: segregation or assimilation. Since assimilation is the biggest fear of any minority (Ajduković & Čorkalo, 2001) separation or segregation is a common consequence in these societies. In conflict and post-conflict areas the issue of identity becomes even more important than usual and many members of a certain identity retreat to the safety of their own group (Ajduković, 2003, p. 173). Naturally, the safest group is the family but in case of ethnic conflicts belonging to a certain ethnic group becomes a crucial trait as well. In Vukovar the two big ethnic groups, Croats and Serbs, even fifteen years after the Erdut Agreement, still live in the safety of their own ethnic groups. Vukovar's Serbs and Croats live in integrated neighborhoods, but they do all they can to avoid contact and conflicts (Freedman & Abazović, 2006). The separation between these two groups is most visible among children—the educational system is segregated, beginning with kindergartens and ending with high school education. If two pupils who live in the same street attend separate groups in kindergarten and separate classes and shifts in schools, it is inevitable to conclude that they belong to different ethnic groups. The separation between adults is less visible though who will greet you with a "ciao"[1] and who with a "bog"[2] is common knowledge (Mažić, 2009).

SCHOOL SEGREGATION

Upon the start of the process of return in the area of Eastern Croatia, returnee children (non-Serbs) started attending separate classes that were conducted in the Croatian language. Meanwhile, Serb children continued attending classes in Serbian language (since 1998 following the Croatian educational plan and program). Such an educational model was agreed within the Erdut Agreement as many people thought it was the only model for preventing violence between previously conflicted communities. In 2000 the Croatian parliament ratified the European Charter for Education in native language and also passed the Constitutional law on the rights of national minorities that legally regulated the existing segregation designed within the Erdut Agreement.

Based on the Constitutional law on the rights of national minorities there are four basic models for organizing teaching and lessons in the languages of national minorities. In Model A all lessons are in the languages and scripts of the national minorities, with all textbooks translated into the language of a national minority. Model B includes bilingual lessons, that is, the lessons are conducted in the Croatian language, while the national group of subjects (language, history, geography) are conducted in the language of a national minority. Model C includes nurturing minority language and culture as a special program with five lessons per week. Model D includes special programs like summer schools, special programs for inclusion of students into educational system, and learning the national minority language as the language of the region. While models B and C enable children to attend schools together, the implementation of model A causes full segregation in schools.

Currently, there are six primary schools in Vukovar. In three schools Model A has been implemented for the Serbian national minority while in other schools classes are conducted solely in the Croatian language. This division is clear when people refer to classes as "Croatian" or "Serbian." There is one school offering Model C for members of Ukrainian and Ruthenian minorities. Children belonging to other minorities as well as children from mixed marriages are in an unfortunate position because their parents must decide which "side" they will ally with. As a result of the segregation through the educational system, children are showing a tendency to discriminate against other ethnic groups more than their parents (Ajduković & Čorkalo, 2001). Schools in Vukovar have become a place that furthers division among groups of different nationalities, instead of being a place of social contact.

Moreover, as Ajduković and Čorkalo-Biruški (2007) show, the students from the minority groups and their parents hold moderately positive attitudes toward integration of children outside the school, but the students' attitudes are less positive than their parents. Also, the majority group holds negative attitudes toward social integration out of school, with no difference between the students and their parents. Furthemore, Ajduković and Čorkalo-Biruški (2007), show that the parents' attitudes toward school integration are more positive than toward social integration. On the other hand, their children have a clear negative attitude toward school integration. Croatian children hold clearly negative attitudes toward school integration whereas the Serbian children are more neutral. As far as the teachers in Vukovar are concerned, Croatian teachers support school integration, while Serbian teachers are more neutral.

The NDC Osijek, a nongovernmental organization (NGO), conducted a survey in 2004 among 256[3] families with primary school children in Vukovar. The survey showed that 71.4 percent of all parents of all nationalities in Vukovar were dissatisfied with the way the primary education was organized for members of minorities , and that 81.25 percent of parents had a positive outlook toward enlisting children in joint (nationally mixed) classes. Also, the results revealed a large number of parents who felt that the educational needs of their children were not fully met. Many parents felt that segregation was not the right answer to their needs.

The New School Project

As a response to the situation of segregated education and the reactions of parents, the New School Project was initiated in 2003. The aim of the project was to create a curriculum that could better respond to the educational needs of children living in a postwar multiethnic society. The project gathered parents, as primary stakeholders, professionals (teachers, education experts), and official institutions (Education and Teacher Training Agency, local authorities), and facilitated their dialogue into a constructive and applicable framework that could satisfy all those involved in primary education. As a result of this, by the end of 2006 the general curriculum of the New School was designed; the curriculum placed strong emphasis on values that parents and teachers felt the children should nurture: respect for others, and acceptance of differences, inclusiveness, solidarity, equal opportunities for everybody, nonviolence, and peaceful coexistence.

The New School not only enables members of the minority to realize their right to education in their own language and alphabet and to learn about their cultural heritage, but it also goes a step further. The New School enables and encourages *all pupils* to learn about cultural heritage of all ethnic groups that live in the Vukovar region so that they get to know each other and understand and respect their differences, which we see as a precondition for the development of sustainable interethnic relations among groups that share the same space.

A specific characteristic of the general curriculum is CSHR, and the teaching of the mother tongue as a regional language. The CSHR offers an opportunity for pupils to learn about all nationalities and ethnic communities that live in the region. It encourages children to learn and develop insight about different nationalities that live in their region, to learn about the impact these groups have on the development of their region, and to realize how interconnected and interdependent all of them are. The teaching of the mother tongue as a regional language (Serbian, German, Hungarian, Ruthenian, Ukrainian, and so on) should be carried out in the form of an elective subject for all interested pupils (not just respective minority members). In 2007, the Education and Teacher Training Agency issued a positive expert opinion on both the general curriculum of the New School and on the subject curriculum for CSHR, which it also recommended be taught in schools of other multiethnic communities.

Since no existing school in Vukovar would implement the New School curriculum, NDC Osijek, together with parents, started an initiative for opening a school that would implement the integrative model of education—the New School model (2008). A formal request for the establishment of the school was submitted to the Ministry of Science, Education and Sports. The same request was submitted to the government of the town of Vukovar. After a series of meetings with governmental officials and the previous mayor of Vukovar it was up to the Ministry of Science, Education and Sports to promote the initiative. A meeting was held at the ministry in the spring of 2010; however, the opening of the New School was delayed for "lack of financial means."

IMPLEMENTING CSHR IN SEGREGATED SCHOOLS

Given that the opening of the New School is uncertain and long, we have decided to accept the positive recommendation for the implementation of CSHR in segregated schools. As noted before, in most educational systems, the majority learns mostly about itself (history, culture), while minorities (within the scope of minority education) learn about the majority and almost "autistically" about one's own minority. There is no learning about each other, and local specificities are omitted. One of the basic goals of the CSHR curriculum subject is exactly the opposite. It provides an opportunity for all the people of the region to learn about themselves as well as about other people they share their living space with. Naturally, learning about others does not necessarily imply that there will be immediately a better understanding between segregated groups. On the other hand, giving an opportunity for otherwise segregated groups to share their learning environment and engage in a communication process is certainly a step in a direction that can lead to better understanding. In order to achieve this better understanding, people need to be aware of their own cultural background and then be exposed to different cultures in a nonthreatening way. Our belief is that if people feel secure about their own identity and culture they will not be threatened by members of a different culture but will rather see this as an opportunity for exchange and joint learning.

As pupils are predominantly segregated in the city of Vukovar, it is of utmost importance to form groups of children where participants can nurture active understanding of different cultures and establish positive exchange relationships and mutual enrichment. Developing relationships between segregated groups within segregated communities is a nearly impossible task, but if pupils of different cultural backgrounds are placed in a tolerant and nurturing environment, there is a chance of creating better mutual understanding. Learning through differences means focusing on differences and respecting cultural diversity where every culture has its own borders that can only be crossed by showing openness and interaction (Hrvatić, 2009).

During the implementation of our project forming mixed groups of children was at times rather challenging due to mono-ethnic classes at schools and the pressure that those who wanted to join such classes felt from the outside—especially from the members of their own group. Leaving the safety of your own group and engaging with the members of the opposite side demands great bravery and determination and teachers involved with these people always tried to make this clear to those who joined in.

Since the peaceful reintegration in 1997, children in Vukovar have not been given a chance to share their lives and experiences with members of other ethnicities, mainly because they attended separate classes or schools. Therefore, the CSHR project also aims at developing communication skills (active listening, empathy, and so on) in order to enable pupils to get out of their comfort zone and interact with other pupils from different cultural backgrounds. Apart from having positive consequences in school settings, experiencing an ethnically mixed school environment might have long-term effects outside the school. For example, Braddock and McPartland (1989) showed that children who attended desegregated schools were, as adults, more likely to live and work in mixed neighborhoods, compared to children who went to segregated schools. Unlike existing schools in Vukovar, the New School with its curriculum, that is, CSHR, aims at creating a school where education is not merely gaining knowledge but rather gaining a new level of knowledge that can facilitate the development of intercultural community. Only if pupils are educated to be open-minded, tolerant, mindful, and respecting of diversities can an intercultural community be established. In order to make a better future for the city of Vukovar we need to educate children in an environment that provides them with the opportunities to learn together and also provides them with the skills and knowledge to use in their adult life.

When the CSHR curriculum was developed it was decided that it will not be implemented and presented in a frontal way, that is, the teacher will not teach the subject but rather create an environment where interactive learning can take place. Interactive learning puts an emphasis on building networks, learning in a team, learning in a community, and the emphasis is on cooperation, exchange, group activities, and the wish to live and work together (Hrvatić, 2009).

The implementation of CSHR started in August 2007 in the region of Eastern Croatia. For three years it was implemented in three primary schools (all following Model A) as a pilot project, and since November 2010 it has been implemented in seven primary schools in the region. It has been implemented as an elective subject (35–70 hours per year) in each school. In addition, joint meetings of all schools and pupils are organized once or twice a year, to share experiences, present accomplishments, get more visibility, and create a social support network.

ACHIEVEMENTS

The results of the implementation of CSHR are very encouraging so far. First, multi-ethnic groups of pupils have been formed, which has been a challenge considering that pupils attend schools in different classes and shifts. Pupils and their parents have been invited to enroll for CSHR, with a very clear and transparent explanation why CSHR is being implemented, what and how pupils will learn, and presenting teachers who will facilitate the subject. For most pupils in segregated schools this was the first time they had shared a classroom and participated in education with pupils of another nationality, because CSHR became the first joint activity in their schools. Teachers facilitate CSHR work in pairs, with one teacher teaching in "Croatian" classes and the other teaching in "Serbian" classes. In schools where teaching is not divided the CSHR project also aimed at developing intercultural competences but were conducted in a slightly different way: during researches on their small communities and their heritage, teachers would facilitate a process in asking questions about others and different members of family, neighbors, and neighboring villages. These pupils also had opportunities to meet with children of different nationalities and backgrounds during joint networking seminars for schools that took part in CSHR implementation. These networking seminars were organized twice in a school year. During the first three years in three schools, 75 children attended the classes. In 2012 in eight schools over 180 children were involved.

Second, feedback from the children involved has been extremely positive, with a higher number of new children applying every year, high attendance, and no dropouts—an indication of the quality of the program (it is an elective program, so selecting CSHR at the beginning of the school year is completely voluntary). According to the evaluation done by Monika Šimek, an NDC Osijek associate,

> pupils have become aware of connection that exist between how people lived in the past with the present way of life, and a strong impact tradition has on the preservation of national, religious and family affiliation. At the same time, they become aware that everyone is entitled to their own identity, language, religion and the tradition.

The evaluation also showed that pupils mentioned positive experiences, new friendships, development of tolerance, and experiencing diversity as the most positive practices that they gained from taking part in this project.

Main Challenges and Lessons Learnt

During the implementation of CSHR several challenges were encountered. Forming multi-ethnic groups of children in schools that are segregated, and conducting teaching in Croatian or Serbian language for children in separate shifts, was not an easy task. Several schools that joined the project were almost mono-cultural. Teaching and talking about diversity where there is virtually no diversity to speak of within a class proved to be very challenging. However, due to the building of a network of all schools involved in the project this challenge was successfully overcome to a certain extent. This school network allowed the pupils to spend time in a nonformal environment outside schools and we believe it proved to be a successful catalyst for a better mutual understanding and a great opportunity to establish personal relationships among children of various ethnic backgrounds.

The teachers involved in the project felt that an intercultural subject such as CSHR, when offered as an elective/extracurricular activity, usually reaches those children/parents whose attitudes are already more tolerant than average, and that presents a new challenge: how to reach those who are not willing/prepared to take part? On the other hand, if you ask yourself who suffers the most in a segregated community the answer would be those who are more tolerant and those who are willing to live in an integrated community, as they are the ones who have been refused the opportunity to live in such an environment.

Another obstacle in implementing the CSHR curriculum was building teachers' capacities for this work and providing them with continuous support and empowerment during the implementation of the project. Teachers who implemented the CSHR project taught subjects like English, Croatian, maths, music or history in their schools, which means none of them were officially qualified or trained to teach such an interdisciplinary subject. Again, it was down to the teachers and schools network to exchange ideas and experiences and thereby improve the implementation of the subject. Another issue with teachers was encouraging them in their work. Teaching about culture, religion, languages, and customs is a very sensitive work, and in post-conflict areas even more so. During external or internal evaluations teachers often discussed the issue of pressure from head teachers, parents, or community in general. Building an intercultural society in a segregated environment is not easy and will not be easy as long as there is no political will to change the educational system in Vukovar, which brings us to the biggest challenge of all, namely, politics. This remains a challenge yet to be solved.

During the development of the New School project and the CSHR curriculum and its implementation, relevant educational institutions gave support to the project. In 2007, the Education and Teacher Training Agency (an independent, state-funded agency in charge of primary education in Croatia) issued a positive expert opinion on both the general curriculum of the New School and on CSHR, which it also recommended be taught in other schools in other multiethnic communities. Formal recommendations for the New School project have also been obtained from the County of Vukovarsko-Srijemska, Coordination of National Minority Councils, OSCE Field Office Vukovar, president of the Republic of Croatia Ivo Josipović, former president of the Republic of Croatia Stjepan Mesić, Children Ombudsman of the Republic of Croatia, UNICEF Croatia, and others.

What have we learnt during the implementation of the project? First, according to the evaluation done by Dinka Corkalo Biruski,[4] children are, in spite of institutionalized division, willing and capable of cooperating and working with others, if there is a place and time for social contact, and a good catalyst—a teacher motivated and skilled in intercultural education. Second, it is hard for teachers to be motivated and dedicated if they are not supported or are blamed by other teachers and school staff. Nine years after its inception, the New School project has still not been fully implemented although the teachers involved in the project have done all they could. Nonetheless, motivation still exists and until the New School is opened, at least one of its aspects, that is, CSHR is being implemented. Skenderović (2009) states that learning about regional heritage is an important element of every school curriculum and it should be affirmed to a great extent, because it offers actualization of many educational aims. Knowledge of regional heritage can help pupils to develop into responsible people, ready to actively participate in a democratic society. With this in mind, we strongly believe that the CSHR curriculum contains universal values as there are very few regions in the world that are mono-cultural. Due to these values, skills, and knowledge gained through the implementation of its curriculum the CSHR could perhaps be considered in other parts of the world with cultural diversity and conflict.

CURRICULAR APPROACH

As it has already been noted, the New School curriculum was developed in 2006. A few years later, in 2010, Croatia got its first National

Curriculum Framework where all the educational aims were listed. One of the goals listed in the curriculum included the following:

> Modern democracies need working, informed and responsible citizens. The purpose of teaching civil education as an interdisciplinary theme is to prepare students for an active and effective civic life. The more significant elements of this theme include the knowledge, skills, abilities, and attitudes that develop students' democratic awareness and encourage them to help foster democratic relations in school, in the local community and throughout society. Civil education also contributes to the development of personal identity, respect for others, and problem solving skills according to democratic principles. By becoming more familiar with themselves and their roles in society, as well as by accepting the differences of others, students develop independence, personal integrity, and positive relationships with other students and the surrounding environment. Civil education as an interdisciplinary theme will enhance collaboration within schools, families, local communities, and throughout society. (National Curriculum Framework, 2010, p. 26)

If you compare the values of the National Curriculum to the values currently taught in the city of Vukovar the enormous gap is more than obvious. These goals enlisted in the National Curriculum Framework cannot be implemented in segregated schools simply because the majority of pupils are exposed exclusively to the members of their own ethnic groups and have very little contact with members of other ethnicities. If pupils of different cultural and ethnical backgrounds spent more time in daily formal or informal contact with each other, they would have more opportunities for reconciliation (McGlynn, 2004). What we have today in Vukovar is a segregated educational system that focuses exclusively on the heritage of a single ethnic group, either Croatian or Serbian, and thereby disregards the plurality of cultures and ethnicities in the region. This all means that despite the National Curriculum, schools in Vukovar do not play an integrating role but rather a segregating one. It is difficult to develop respect for others if you are rarely allowed to be in contact with them. Obviously, there is a clear need that the educational system in Vukovar needs to be adjusted to the values listed in the National Curriculum.

So how can the educational system in Vukovar be adjusted to the values in the National Curriculum? The National Curriculum offers the schools the opportunity to create their own school curricula in order to implement all the values, aims, and objectives listed in it. These curricula offer the opportunity for various programmes to promote intercultural values in schools. It is up to schools and their staffs to think of programs and subjects, choose direct or interdisciplinary approach to intercultural teaching, implement their ideas, and create a learning environment where teaching diversity will replace segregation. Moreover, these school curricula offer various NGOs the chance to suggest programs aimed at meeting these objectives such as CSHR.

CONCLUSION

Teaching, organized within a formal system of schooling, is a basic tool by which society transmits knowledge, values, and norms to the youth. We believe that the current educational system in Vukovar transmits knowledge, values, and norms to the youth that are not in accordance to the values defined in the National Curriculum Framework. When that is the case we should look for resources that can meet the educational needs clearly stated in the National Curriculum but that would also meet the needs of all stakeholders involved in the educational system. In the absence of political will for any deeper change in educational policies in post-conflict areas the answer is not to give up but rather to put even more effort into developing an intercultural community by implementing projects such as CSHR and thereby offering alternatives to the current system.

NOTES

1. "Ciao," an Italian informal greeting, commonly used by the Serbian population in Vukovar.
2. "Bog," a Croatian informal greeting literally meaning "God," used throughout the Republic of Croatia.
3. This sample represents 14.6 percent of all parents of primary school children in Vukovar . The sample is made of 50 percent of parents of Croatian nationality, 32.4 percent of Serbian nationality, 3.12 percent of other nationalities, and 14.46 percent of undeclared.
4. Associate professor, Department of Psychology, University of Zagreb in Croatia.

REFERENCES

Ajduković, D., (2003). Socijalna rekonstrukcija zajednice (Social reconstruction of the community), Society for Psychological Assistance, Zagreb.
Ajduković, D., & Čorkalo, D. (2001). *Attitudes about education in Vukovar.* Unpublished manuscript. Society for Psychological Assistance, Zagreb.

Ajduković, D. & Čorkalo-Biruški, D. (2007). Separate schools—a divided community. *Review of Psychology, 14*(2), 93–108.

Braddock, J. H., & McPartland, J. M. (1989). Social-psychological processes that perpetuate racial segregation: The relationship between school and employment desegregation. *Journal of Black Studies, 19,* 267–289.

Freedman, S.W., & Abazović, D. (2006). Growing up during the Balkan wars in the 1990s. In C. Daiute, Z. Beykont, C. Higson-Smith, & L. Nucci (Eds.), *International perspectives of youth conflict and development* (pp. 57–72). Oxford: Oxford University Press.

Hrvatić, N. (2009). Intercultural education: New developments. In A. Peko, & V. Mlinarevic (Eds.), *Educational challenges in multicultural communities* (pp.115–130). Osijek: Faculty of Teacher Education.

Mazić, M. (2009). *Vukovar—A divided town.* Vukovar: Youth Initiative for Human Rights.

McGlynn, C.W. (2004). Education for Peace in Integrated Schools: A priority for Northern Ireland? *Child Care in Practice, 10* (2), 85–94.

Ministry of Science, Education and Sport. (2010). *National curriculum framework.* Zagreb: Ministry of Science, Education and Sport.

Popović, D. (2009). *Vukovar—Impunity of Urbicide.* Vukovar: Youth Initiative for Human Rights.

Skenderović, R. (2009). Cultural and spiritual heritage: A model for intercultural education. In A. Peko, & V. Mlinarević (Eds.), *Educational challenges in multicultural communities* (pp.195–205). Osijek: Faculty of Teacher Education.

14

Exploring Controversial Issues Together in Northern Ireland

A View from the Lagan College Chaplaincy

Helen Killick and Sharon Verwoerd

Introduction

Lagan College was established in Belfast in 1981 by a group of Catholic and Protestant parents. With the backdrop of violent conflict and a segregated education system, they hoped that educating children together could contribute to building a peaceful, common future. They founded a school where members of the same family could be educated together regardless of gender or academic ability. As people of faith, they made a Christian response to division, creating a school based on inclusion and reconciliation. The school opened with no funding, in temporary buildings, facing opposition from politicians and churches. Despite these and other challenges, the school grew rapidly and eventually found a permanent home in the Castlereagh hills above the city.

Thirty years later our school community is made up of over 1,250 students (aged 11–18) and around 150 staff members from a range of backgrounds. Each year, new students come from over 60 primary schools from all over Belfast and beyond. Lagan College is now one of 20 integrated secondary schools in Northern Ireland. Despite this growth, the experience of 92 percent of secondary students in Northern Ireland (and their teachers) is of single-identity education (Department of Education, 2012). Although many curricular and extracurricular initiatives are generally supported, segregation remains the norm and strong friendships across cultural, faith, and academic divides are unusual.

In contrast to this experience, our school was founded with an explicit vision for reconciliation, inspired by Jesus's prayer *"that they may be one"* (Gospel of John, chapter 17) as expressed in our school motto, *ut sint unum.* As well as providing a school for Protestants and Catholics, we welcome those of other faiths and none. We aim "to educate to the highest standards Catholics, Protestants and others of goodwill, together" (Lagan College Mission Statement).

The joint chaplaincy is a unique expression of our Christian ethos and is one of the significant ways the school encourages meaningful conversations and engagement with identity, faith, and culture. The Roman Catholic and Protestant chaplains work together for all members of our community, regardless of background, modelling cooperation and unity. We are motivated by the gospel values of inclusion and reconciliation and want to bear witness to faith as a positive influence in drawing people to God and each other, rather than causing separation or alienation.

OUR UNDERSTANDING OF INTEGRATED EDUCATION

Our understanding of integrated education as a response to conflict and segregation is rooted in our experience in the chaplaincy. First, through sharing life and facing controversial issues together as they arise, we believe members of our school community can grow in appreciation of their own uniqueness and their capacity to engage with all kinds of difference, in issues of faith, politics, gender, social class, and academic ability. As well, our shared space and diverse community can provide greater breadth and depth to education than would otherwise be experienced. Another important element of our understanding is that integrated education is deliberately anti-sectarian. In our opinion, exploring religious and political difference positively has to be a priority to equip young people to be agents of change in a sectarian society. We hope students and staff grow to be confident and comfortable with difference, forming genuine friendships. This does not happen automatically by attending school together. Deliberate efforts must be made to develop the capacity of young people and adults to have respectful and honest conversations.

CONTROVERSIAL ISSUES

A topic becomes controversial when it is difficult or emotive for some people. Any issue that evokes strong opinions or emotions can create tension. Some of the controversial issues we face are organizational in nature and can be found in many schools. For example, currently some of the most contentious issues for us as a school are around admissions and academic selection; behavior management and how we respond to serious incidents; and the practice of our founding Christian ethos. Other issues are a legacy of our conflict. Anniversaries, commemorations, official visits, feast days of different traditions, and involvement of representatives of the police and armed forces in school events are just some of the areas that have been seen as contentious at different times. Any issue, political or not, can affect people in different ways, depending on their experience and background. A word, symbol, or action can appear natural to some and offensive to others.

During the years of conflict, people who came to Lagan College from all backgrounds were united in opposition to violence. This and the shared struggle to teach without adequate accommodation or resources, particularly in the pioneering early days, brought people together. Now violent conflict is mostly behind us and we are well on the way to having adequate buildings. Differences that always existed, but seemed less important than the need for a united response to ongoing violence, have become more apparent.

We now explore two examples of controversy among staff and students in our school, which we hope will resonate with people in other conflict-affected societies. One is a specific response to an event where staff engaged meaningfully with difference, navigating a way forward through a process of consensus building. The second example is an encounter regularly offered to students, which challenges them to face their own prejudices and to grow in understanding. Both examples show that, in general, controversial issues can be opportunities to explore difference positively and strengthen relationships.

THE FUNERAL OF POPE JOHN PAUL II

There can be a great deal of misunderstanding about the ways Protestants and Catholics mark the death of a loved one, leading to presumptions about the meaning of traditions and awkwardness around different ways of grieving. In our integrated community, funerals have often become occasions when people step into unknown territory in order to support friends and colleagues of other traditions. Most members of staff have stories of attending funerals in unfamiliar churches, visiting homes or cemeteries in areas of the city that are new to them, and joining in practices and customs that are different to their own cultural background. Bereavements are times when we have a window into the life and faith of our friends, and although some may feel a discomfort, the desire to be with a grieving friend overrides any strong feeling of uneasiness or wariness. Perhaps these experiences prepared us a little for the emotion and tension around the death of Pope John Paul II on April 2, 2005.

When the death of the pope was announced, it was clear that for some this event affected the most precious aspects of their lives: faith, culture, identity, and family. For others the event had little impact. The school community had to find a shared response. From the start it became clear that opinions were varied and deeply held. Some were quickly voiced, which led to frantic and fearful debates, polarizing some staff members. Many Catholic staff felt that the school should be closed on the day of the funeral as a mark of respect and to allow Catholic families to spend the day together and with their faith community. Some Protestant teachers felt that the funeral of a pope was not a good enough reason to close a school. In the background, senior teachers were unsure of the next step and decided to wait and see if any lead was given from education authorities or churches. This "watching and waiting" time was crucial. Although there was some frustration, this interim period gave an opportunity for the original flurry to settle and for important conversations to take place.

Three days after the Pope's death, a letter from the Council for Catholic Maintained Schools (CCMS) was circulated to Catholic schools about the day of the funeral:

> The Northern Bishops believe that the Board of Governors of each school…is in the best position to decide how to mark the occasion…Schools which decide to remain open are encouraged to find appropriate ways to commemorate the life and death of Pope John Paul II. (CCMS Circular No 2205/12)

At the time, it seemed that no clear lead was being given in the circular, but its flexibility freed integrated schools, as well as Catholic schools, to make their own decisions about the day.

As the days went by there were formal discussions in meetings and informal conversations in staffrooms and in the chaplaincy. Staff members made use of the chaplaincy as a place where they could say what they really felt about the issue and share their hopes and expectations.

At one stage we noticed an important shift in the conversations. Having heard the feelings of colleagues, some staff members began to advocate on behalf of those from another tradition. Some Protestant teachers approached the management team on behalf of their Catholic friends, concerned that if the school did not close, those friends would be hurt and feel let down. Some Catholic teachers assured us they would understand if the school had to remain open. The point of tension had been transformed as some began to see things from another's perspective.

The emerging compromise was one example of the richness of opportunity possible within the integrated school. The school remained open and the funeral was shown live in the assembly hall. Students were asked to indicate if they wanted to watch the funeral and, as the list of names grew longer, it became clear Protestant and Catholic students were signing up together. When asked about this, Protestant students explained that they wanted to be with their Catholic friends on this important occasion. Teachers offered to cover classes for their Catholic colleagues to free them to join those watching the funeral. One of the Religious Education teachers prepared a printed order of service, explaining the mass for the many Protestant students who had never witnessed one before. He provided a sensitive commentary throughout the service. Over four hundred students watched the funeral calmly and respectfully.

Although the outcome was not ideal for everyone, there is a consensus that what took place that day was remarkable. This was "a dignified and satisfactory compromise," wrote a Catholic member of staff; "I felt this was a seminal moment in the history of the College; a time when difference was acknowledged and mutual respect was expressed." In the morning briefing the following day, another Catholic teacher movingly thanked Protestant colleagues who had supported the wishes of Catholics, and had spoken up or volunteered to cover classes: "Not only was the situation well handled but out of it something important was achieved, a deepening of understanding, a sealant on the growing bond between us."

The lessons we learned in April 2005 have stayed with us, giving us confidence to face other contentious situations as they arise. Good relationships are fundamental to finding a way through such times. In our busy school, we often find it difficult to create opportunities to strengthen relationships among staff and students, even though we know from experience how important that is.

We learned that decisions should not be rushed and time should be allowed for people to be heard and understood. There was a shape to the conversations in the time between the pope's death and the funeral mass. As the days progressed there seemed to be less speaking and more listening and the conversations became more meaningful.

The time people took to listen to one another was crucial in the consensus process.

As chaplains, sometimes our role is to accompany people through difficult discussions like these, being present without pushing our own opinions or expectations. At that time, some people expressed appreciation for the chaplaincy as a place where they could speak honestly and freely, on their own or with others. Significant conversations can happen anywhere, but an intentional space can provide opportunities to acknowledge explore and accept difference. A welcome to all and the sharing of food and drink can create a foundation for a meaningful exchange of views.

On this occasion, it was important that different views were represented in our conversations together. We have learnt that we need to be prepared to include anyone in the conversation, including those with controversial views, even though that may be uncomfortable for us. If we are serious about building consensus, we must include those whose opinions seem extreme to us, making the choice to speak to those we find difficult and giving a voice to those we disagree with. This calls for a generosity of spirit, which can be a challenge when we feel strongly about an issue.

Even though this event took place some years ago, its impact continues to be felt today. It has become part of the story of our school and is often mentioned when staff members recall good experiences of integration. Through the process of navigating an initially controversial issue, many experienced a growth of trust and the deepening of friendships. Some of the most encouraging and inspiring occasions are when someone unexpectedly "steps into the shoes" of another and speaks up on their behalf. These moments cannot be planned or expected but when they happen they build community. A level of understanding has been reached where there has been a change of perspective. Something powerful happens when we stop speaking just for ourselves and our own tradition, but advocate instead about an issue that is important to our friend.

VISITS OF EX-PRISONERS

The second example is about how we engage directly, and in an ongoing way, with issues related to the violent conflict in and about Northern Ireland. In addition to responding together to particular events or anniversaries as they occur, we aim to provide opportunities for our staff and students to engage with people whose experiences of the Troubles were very different from their own. Northern Ireland's small population and geographical size means that very few were not affected (at least indirectly) by death, injury, riots, imprisonment, fear, and sectarian hatred.[1] All members of our school community have been touched by the violence in different ways. Some of our students continue to be affected by the ongoing division and conflict in their areas. There are others for whom it has little conscious impact. As another year passes since ceasefires and peace agreements were signed, we find that more students have not needed to consider the Troubles and its legacy. There is an increasing generation gap between those who directly experienced the conflict and those whose understanding is secondhand. There is also a widening gap between those who live in divided communities in which stories and ongoing effects of the conflict are daily realities and those who live in mixed, socially advantaged neighborhoods in which the past is not spoken of. While some suggest it's no longer needed, we believe these gaps in experience increase our responsibility to intentionally explore the conflict together in an honest and respectful way.

Over the years we have found, like many others, that sharing our stories can be a very effective way of connecting with each other on a human level. Personal life stories cannot be debated in the way politics or theology can, and it is very difficult to dismiss them as unimportant or as lies or propaganda. With this in mind, we invite a variety of people to come and share their life story with different groups in the school. Even though they may present a challenging worldview or story to the group, most visitors are not controversial.

However, lively debate is sparked each year when we invite a loyalist and a republican ex-prisoner, who were both involved in paramilitary violence, to come and share their personal life stories together with Year 13 students.[2] We have now been welcoming Alistair Little and Gerry Foster to the school for four years.[3] Their visit forms part of a course that explores diversity and the legacy of the Troubles.

Two weeks before the session, we open conversations with class groups about who the guests will be, what they will be talking about, and why we invited them. We encourage students to continue those conversations among themselves and with us. We ask them to come and talk to us if they have concerns about it, creating space for those who feel strongly opposed to have their thoughts and feelings heard.

On the day of the session, we introduce the speakers and facilitate their storytelling in a structured way, following themes of early, formative life experiences; how they got involved in violence and their experiences in prison; and experiences that led to personal transformation and peacemaking. The visitors take turns with each theme, allowing students to compare the experiences and actions of the speakers at each stage of the journey.

A number of common themes become apparent as they tell their stories in this way. The basic, human feelings and responses of the speakers were very similar at each stage of their journey, despite the different experiences and views they grew up with. It is also often noticed that they became involved in violent organizations because of personal experiences during their mid-teen years—about the same age as the students sitting in front of them. This leads to questions about who are "victims" and who are "perpetrators," and why many people who became involved were so young.[4] The stories highlight a common myth about the motivations of people involved in the paramilitaries: their participation was not because of strongly held, developed political views, but was a very personal reaction to trauma. It is also meaningful that the ex-prisoners speak together and listen to each other. In addition to the words they speak, their respectful and honest interactions are testament to what is possible. Many students later remark that it gives them hope, and indeed challenges them to do the same with people they dislike or with whom they disagree strongly.

The storytelling section of the session is followed by a time for students to talk together in small groups and then to ask questions. Some questions that are often asked include, "How did your family react?", "Are you sorry for what you did?", "How have you been affected by your actions?", and "Have you ever met the victims of your actions?" Questions like these are not easy to answer because they raise sources of pain and trauma for the speakers and for some of the audience. They require a high degree of honesty and vulnerability about their own lives and sensitivity to the experiences of others in the room. These moments often pave the way for deeper connection and understanding of the human side of the conflict.

There are always strong and varying reactions to this encounter. We spend time over the next few weeks informally asking students for their thoughts and debrief fully with the students in class. The chaplaincy remains open for the young people to come by to discuss it. Other staff members support the process by asking students about the visit and this has proved invaluable for some students who do not want to raise their concerns directly with us. Some of the issues raised during this stage range from believing that the ex-prisoners should still be in jail, to being surprised (and a little disconcerted) by how much they liked the men. Students with family involved in the state forces or in the prison system sometimes struggle to reconcile the stories they grew up with about paramilitary organizations and prisoners with the stories they have now heard. Other students whose families have been hurt by paramilitary action question why we invite them into our community "after what they've done." Some are simply faced with their stereotypes of what someone who was involved in paramilitary organizations might look like and say, "I thought they'd be huge and have loads of tattoos and be really tough-looking..." We try to ensure as many perspectives as possible can be heard and affirmed and to explicitly connect the uncomfortable thoughts and feelings this experience raises with the real challenges we face if we are to include all in our society.

An informal consensus is reached by most students after a few days:: it is good to talk about these things rather than avoid them; it is alright to be uncomfortable and to disagree; and we have learnt something about the human side of this conflict. Of course, this consensus does not include everyone, which would be impossible if we are —and not desirable either. We must be able to differ on these things, too. Listening to, and accepting, those who see things differently and express strong minority opinions is an important element of the process for us. We know that some students quietly disagree, but they do not raise this with us for their own reasons. Some are simply not interested and so don't engage with others about it. However, the majority come to this consensus through conversations with different people over a period of time (including the students a year ahead in the school who remember the same encounter). It is not an easy process. However, we believe that students grow in confidence in having honest and respectful conversations about divisive, even painful, issues about which they disagree.

Alongside those who find the encounter uncomfortable, there are those whose reactions are of genuine curiosity and desire for deeper understanding.

> We found their stories shocking, yet inspirational at the same time. It was reassuring for us to see how people can reform and this gave us all a sense of hope. The personal and touching stories from each of our guests really helped to put the Northern Irish conflict into context. It was very rewarding to see two men, with conflicting beliefs, now able to sit in the same room and share their individual experiences. (Lagan College student)

In response to conversations with these students, we now offer a year-long course of study and a residential. Throughout the year we explore the legacy of the Troubles, make connections with people from other conflict-affected societies, and reflect on conflict and peacemaking in our own lives.

In these and similar situations, one important lesson we have learned is to hold the space for difficult conversations with patience and sensitivity. It is not easy to listen to people who strongly disagree with others or who are expressing pain. However, these moments are opportunities to learn, to develop our capacities in dealing with conflict, and to nurture the roots of real community, building confidence that we can face new challenges together in the future. If we can hold that space when a controversial issue first arises, similar situations that follow tend to be less contentious, though they still may be emotive for some. For example, when we first invited ex-prisoners to meet students, we invested much time and care in preparing both staff and students for their visit. Now we have been through the process a few times, we find that people are less fearful of the issues and emotions triggered by discussions about the violence of the Troubles.

Another important lesson has been about hospitality and who we welcome into our community. Henri Nouwen (1975) expresses our intentions beautifully:

> Hospitality…means primarily the creation of a free space where the stranger can enter and become a friend instead of an enemy. Hospitality is not to change people, but to offer them space where change can take place.

The gospel values of inclusion and reconciliation are at the heart of our approach. This does not mean, however, that we give a public voice to all who visit. We have learnt that some conditions must be placed on inclusion to protect our basic values of nonviolence and mutual respect. For example, we do not invite anyone who advocates continued violence connected to the conflict in and about Northern Ireland. We are cautious about giving public voice to any individual who derides the faith or political views of others. This is a balancing act that we do not always get right. We constantly rely on goodwill from staff and families. We want to create a protected space for all as well as opportunities to learn and be challenged.

Challenges Ahead

The young people now starting secondary school were born after ceasefires and peace agreements were signed. Though sporadic

violence has continued and sectarianism and division remain a reality, it seems increasingly likely that lasting peace is within our grasp.
It is in this context that we have embarked on a decade of significant
anniversaries. We are faced with the question of how to mark these
anniversaries in ways that honor their symbolic importance for some
and respect the opposition (or lack of interest) of others. In 2011, our
thirtieth anniversary coincided with commemorations of the Hunger
Strikes of 1981.[5] At assemblies, we highlighted the changing social
backdrop against which we have grown as a school. In September
2012, we will be marking one hundred years since the Home Rule
for Ireland Bill and the signing of the Ulster Covenant[6] by many
thousands of people in response. Throughout the coming decade, we
will also be marking one hundred years since World War I (including
the Battle of the Somme[7]), the Easter Rising, and the Partition of
Ireland.[8]

As we write, there is much debate about the future structure of
the education system in Northern Ireland. The two major political
parties, which are opposed along the Catholic/Protestant divide, are
advocating very different education structures for the future. These
negotiations present an opportunity for all schools and churches to
reflect on their vision of education. For an integrated school in particular, this adds a political layer to any discussion about how we
respond to proposed changes.

As a 30-year-old institution, Lagan College has reached a significant threshold. The founding parents and teachers, who were instrumental in developing the vision and ethos of the school, are moving
on. A new generation will be leading our school, making choices
about what we take with us and what we leave behind. For some, this
is a source of anxiety because they treasure the founding vision and
the journey that has brought us here. In particular, in an increasingly
secularized and multicultural society, the relevance of our Christian
ethos is being questioned by some but increasing in importance for
others.

For us in the chaplaincy, an important challenge in the coming
years will be to continue to hold space for people to respond together
to controversial issues as the demands on time and money in schools
becomes increasingly difficult to manage.

CONCLUSION

For any integrated school, how we respond to controversy is very
important. It is the way in which many people form their opinions

about the sincerity of our mission, the resources we have to fulfill it, and our relative success in achieving it. The deep emotions and strong opinions evoked at such times can seem daunting. However, in our experience, these times have also been an opportunity for our community to grow in resilience and goodwill.

The lessons we have learned can be gathered together in the word "space." By space we mean time and physical places in the school as well as openness in the minds, hearts. and spirits of people. We have come to treasure space in our school, making a determined effort to preserve it. As one of the older integrated schools in a growing movement, we hope our experiences and the lessons we have learned may be helpful to others seeking a way forward through and beyond violent conflict.

NOTES

1. Fitzduff and O'Hagan (2009) estimate that more than half of the population are closely associated with someone seriously injured or killed in the Troubles. In addition, about 25,000 people were imprisoned as a result of paramilitary activity.
2. Year 13 students are 16–17 years old. They are in the first of two post-compulsory years of schooling.
3. We are grateful to Irish Peace Centres for their financial support of this initiative and to Alistair Little and Gerry Foster for their time and willingness to engage honestly with us and each other. The story of their friendship is recounted by Alistair in his autobiographical work *Give a Boy a Gun: From Killing to Peacemaking* (2009).
4. Sixty percent of the people killed were young men between 18 and 35 (Smyth, 1998).
5. The Hunger Strikes were significant in developing both local and international sympathy for the Republican cause. In prisoners' efforts to achieve "political status," ten people starved themselves to death.
6. The Home Rule bill of 1912 offered some measure of local autonomy to the people of Ireland. In protest, almost half a million Ulster Unionists signed the Ulster Covenant and Declaration.
7. The Battle of the Somme during World War I was infamous because of the large number of casualties, including more than 2,000 Ulster Protestants.
8. The Easter Rising refers to the uprising against British rule in 1916. The Irish War of Independence continued after World War I and eventually led to the partition of Ireland in 1921.

REFERENCES

Department of Education, Northern Ireland. (2012). *Summary data, 2011–2012*. Belfast: Department of Education.

Fitzduff, M., & O'Hagan, L. (2009). *The Northern Ireland Troubles: INCORE background paper*. Londonderry: INCORE. Available online at http://cain.ulst.ac.uk/othelem/incorepaper09

Little, A. (2009). *Give a boy a gun: From killing to peacemaking*. London: Darton, Longman and Todd.

Nouwen, H. (1975). *Reaching out*. Garden City, NY: Doubleday & Company.

Smyth, M. (1998). *Half the battle: Understanding the impact of "the Troubles" on children and young people*. Londonderry: INCORE. Available online at http://cain.ulst.ac.uk/issues/violence/cts/smyth1.htm

15

Embedding Integration through the Antibias Curriculum

Paula McIlwaine

Introduction

This chapter is written from my perspective, as a staff member at Northern Ireland Council for Integrated Education (NICIE) who has worked, over the last six years, with a focus on providing opportunities for teachers to consider why and how their role places an onus on them to maximize on the diversity within their integrated environment in order to create a rich, meaningful, and valuable educational experience.

This is rendered particularly poignant as I cast my mind back to the challenges and opportunities presented to me as a 25-year-old English lecturer arriving at Gashua'a College of Education in Yobe State, Nigeria. I had chosen to work in the predominantly Muslim Hausa/Fulani part of Northern Nigeria because of a desire to experience and gain insight into a completely different culture. However, I made assumptions that my students would be a largely homogenous group while, in reality, they came from an array of social backgrounds and ethnic groups indigenous to Nigeria and other West African countries, varied in age and gender, and differed in their practise of the Islamic and Christian faiths. I realized, through tailored professional development in the months before and during the first period in Nigeria, that such diversity (in a society that had historically experienced conflict and division related to ethnic, religious, and political differences) provided opportunities to add value to the trainee teacher experience but only if careful thought was given to choices of literature, exploration of pertinent themes from a range of perspectives, consideration of the use and power of language, and modeling teaching methodologies designed to stimulate dialogue and reflection. In the process, I learnt a lot about myself through reflection on my personal experience of education as a Protestant brought up within a Northern Ireland education system that denied me the opportunity to study alongside young Catholics, until I attended university. In Nigeria, I understood what my shortcomings might be and was greatly supported by colleagues and students as I learnt along the way and personally benefited from exposure to such rich diversity.

As I reflect on my experience within the integrated education movement in Northern Ireland I am struck by these words, often attributed to Nelson Mandela: "We are all meant to shine as children do. It's not just in some of us; it is in everyone. And as we let our own light shine, we unconsciously give other people permission to do the same. As we are liberated from our own fear, our presence automatically liberates others" (Williamson, 1992, p.165). My view is that the proliferation of fear in Northern Irish society, underlying and reinforced by years of conflict, emanates from and is reinforced by a distrust and wariness about difference and being different, and is often manifested as fear of being in a minority group or as fear of expressing personal opinions that go against the grain. In its essence, my understanding of integrated education is that it challenges this notion that we should remain fearful, keeping our mouths firmly closed and saying nothing about the issues that divide us. Rather, integrated education embraces the concept that education should be about exploring differences (as well as similarities) through engaging in dialogue as a means of contributing toward the healing of societal wounds. It involves consciously and carefully creating environments and conditions in which all of those involved in integrated education can be liberated from fear and allowed to shine.

Those founding parents who held the vision for integrated education, as well as those teachers, parents, and governors who have turned it into a reality, have often articulated it as "education together in a school of children and young people drawn mainly from the Protestant and Catholic traditions, with the aim of providing for them an excellent education that gives recognition to and promotes the expression of these two main traditions" (Statement of Principles for Integrated Education, 2009). However, such emphasis on a single aspect of identity labeled as "Protestant" or 'Catholic' does not fully elaborate the focus and potential of integrated education in terms of the multiple aspects of identity. Rather, this is given fuller expression in the affirmation: "Children and young people of all religious, social and cultural backgrounds, regardless of ability, race, gender or sexual orientation have a right to an education which respects and gives expression to their individual identities, while providing opportunities for them to explore the diversity of the world in which they live" (Statement of Principles for Integrated Education, 2009). Integrated education is, therefore, about creating an educational environment where various aspects of each young person's identity are acknowledged and given the opportunity to grow and flourish. Moreover, it is also about supporting and enabling young people to recognize and appropriately challenge when others are being denied the right to express aspects of their identity or being discriminated against because they belong to a minority group.

NATIONAL POLICY / CURRICULUM

In the wider educational and political arena, the importance of Northern Ireland schools developing an approach that takes account of issues of diversity and equality has been widely recognized. Indeed, the Northern Ireland Programme for Government (2008–2011) stressed the necessity of tackling the ongoing problems of sectarianism, racism, homophobia, and intolerance in its various forms within Northern Irish society. While education is certainly not the only way to address such deep-seated prejudices, there has been recognition by government, and specifically the Department of Education, that education/educators must make an attempt to tackle these issues. Recently, this was made explicit in the Community Relations, Equality and Diversity Policy (CRED Policy, March 2011) in which the ministerial foreword begins with the statement: "Aas our society emerges from the period of conflict into a new and hopeful phase, and we become more diverse in our communities, I want to ensure our children and young people have the skills and attitudes to ensure a society where equality and diversity are valued and relations within and between communities are strong' (CRED Policy, March 2011). Indeed, this policy embraces some of the long stated aims of integrated education and it is positive that, through extensive consultation and response, the integrated movement appears to have significantly influenced the content and language of the final draft of the CRED Policy. This can be detected in statements such as the following: "Children and young people need opportunities to learn about themselves and their culture, and about others and the similarities and differences in their culture. They need to build positive relationships with young people from different backgrounds (across the range of section 75 groups[1]) and to dispel negative perceptions and images about those who are different from them; the self-confidence to have pride in their own tradition; and the resilience to deal with intolerance and prejudice" (CRED Policy, March 2011).

Moreover, more recent changes to the Northern Ireland Curriculum (2007) introduced Personal Development and Mutual Understanding (PDMU), at the primary school phase, and Local and Global Citizenship for the postprimary, with the specific aim of providing opportunities within the curriculum for developing young people's knowledge and understanding of opportunities and challenges they may encounter in an increasingly diverse society. It is positive that PDMU and Learning for Life and Work offer curriculum-based opportunities for exploring similarity and difference but the potential shortcomings of restricting an exploration of diversity to these areas of the curriculum are highlighted later in the chapter.

Adopting an Antibias Approach within Integrated Education

The Statement of Principles for Integrated Education recognizes that in an "inherently segregated and contested society," it is through meaningful and sustained engagement with those who are different, that children and young people can learn to respect difference. My role in NICIE has involved providing integrated schools with support to enable such "meaningful" and "sustained engagement" to take place child to child; between adults and children as well as adult to adult. One of the most effective means of enabling such deep learning has been developed, over a number of years, within the integrated education sector under the banner of developing an antibias approach to education.

Background to NICIE's Antibias Document

In 1995 a group of passionate academics, parents, and practitioners gathered together with the aim of producing good practice guidelines for leaders and teachers working in integrated primary schools and preschool environments. The outcome was the original *Anti-Bias Curriculum* document, produced through funding provided by the Esmee Fairbairn Foundation. By 2008 it was felt necessary to redraft the document and ensure it would have broader relevance. As with previous incarnations of the *Anti-Bias Curriculum*, the focus of the redrafted document *ABC: Promoting an Anti-Bias Approach to Education in Northern Ireland* (2008) remained on the development of inclusion, respect, sharing, and openness—essential aspects of a school's ethos and practice in the delivery of the formal Northern Ireland Curriculum and also the more informal and hidden curricula that exist in schools. This resource is firmly aimed at all aspects of the holistic development of children and young people and the ABCs of this approach relate to the fundamental elements of understanding, respecting, and valuing difference, being inclusive and challenging prejudice and discrimination.

However, these guidance materials were extensively redrafted to take into account the (then) newly revised Northern Ireland Curriculum at primary and postprimary levels. Where the previous focus of the antibias resource had been on early years and primary, the redrafted resource was designed to be useful to all individuals involved in the learning process, from early years through primary school to second level education.

The revised document was also enhanced to reflect changes to Northern Ireland's equality legislation. As a consequence, each chapter provides an opportunity for reflection on different aspects of diversity and inclusion. While Chapter One gives an introduction to the antibias concept, its application to issues of culture, religion, and ethnicity is the focus of Chapter Two. Chapter Three is devoted to pertinent issues relating to gender and sexual orientation and Chapter Four places specific emphasis on the inclusion of children and young people with special educational needs. The final chapter is devoted to the important partnership between schools and parents in reinforcing the antibias approach.

Antibias Training for Teachers

The desired outcome of integrated education is that the young person develops a confident/strong identity as an individual and member of a cultural group and also develops skills to negotiate the day-to-day natural discomforts, tensions, problems, or conflicts that can arise from difference. While the expressed aim is that they should also "be encouraged to recognise those less fortunate than themselves, the oppressed and victims of injustice" (Statement of Principles for Integrated Education, 2009), the antibias approach, promoted by NICIE, goes further in recognizing that it is also essential to equip young people with the means to challenge prejudice, discrimination, and injustice.

It seems clear to me, however, that developing young people's positive attitudes and behaviors toward difference cannot occur before teachers have been supported to engage in a process of examining their own attitudes to difference. Therefore, deep levels of self-awareness need to be created (and attitudinal change to occur) if schools and teachers are to be prevented from reinforcing (often unconsciously) those stereotypes/prejudices that have proliferated within Northern Ireland's deeply divided society. Developing self-awareness, generating attitudinal change, and providing teachers with the tools, skills, and impetus for delivering an antibias approach in their teaching is the focus of NICIE's accredited professional development course Anti-Bias in Education (along with the document *ABC: Promoting an Anti-bias Approach to Education in Northern Ireland*). The development of this training was made possible through funding from the Esmee Fairbairn Foundation. Thanks to this financial support NICIE has developed not only a three-day Continuing Professional Development (CPD) course for teachers but also a range of other training courses that incorporate an antibias approach to education. This training is designed to encourage teachers to revisit the core aspects of the ethos of integration in a Northern Ireland context and integration on a global level. Teachers are also taken through a process, sometimes uncomfortable, that encourages them to explore their own, personal experience of and response to difference and uncover some of their more hidden and unconscious biases and/or prejudices. Such learning is summed up in the words of a teacher who took part in the March 2009 training: "I have had to address my own bias and recognise that I cannot ask children to deal with bias if I have not dealt with my own". Participatory, experiential, and reflective processes are led by experienced facilitators to provide training that goes beyond the superficial and encourages deeper levels of reflection. Considerable time is spent creating an atmosphere of safety in which participants (in groups not larger than 20) are encouraged to express their concerns about tackling sensitive issues and the challenges involved in dealing positively with diversity. Course materials, resources, and content are presented in a very professional manner in order to stimulate confidence and encourage participants to fully embrace the process.

Antibias Training Content

Antibias training has been designed to be highly interactive. It moves from participatory tasks focused on assumption making (and the relationship between assumptions, bias, prejudice, and discrimination) to exploring the development of antibias in a local and global context.

For many the emotional impact of watching video clips (such as *Little Rock 9*) from the US during the time of Civil Rights on Day 1 stimulates a deeper reflection on the nature and impact of segregation and integration within education, not only at a particular time and place in history but also with specific reference to their own Northern Ireland context, during the remaining days of the course. A reminder of the historical journey of the integrated education movement within Northern Ireland places greater emphasis on the role they have to play within a type of education that provides a challenge to the long-established norm of segregation within education.

On Day 2, participants are encouraged to consider their own education and map their personal experience of bias, prejudice, and discrimination during their primary and postprimary schooling. They are then facilitated through a process of drawing conclusions about the negative impact of the latter on young people within the current education system. The use of language for diversity and equality is discussed and examples are touched upon that are relevant to disability, special educational needs, sexual orientation, ethnicity, and religion.

The impact of segregation, within our society today, is brought into stark relief by the visit to West Belfast, to areas still clearly divided along sectarian lines, on the evening of Day 2. Qualified tour guides who were born and brought up within the respective Catholic and Protestant communities in West Belfast provide an insight into the social and political history of the Falls and Shankill Roads, and the surrounding areas, through reference to landmarks and murals. For many educators, even those brought up in Belfast, it is the first time they have visited this part of West Belfast. During the tour they are asked to pay attention to their emotional reactions to this experience and register any strong emotions generated by sight or sound. Afterward, considerable time is spent debriefing this experience and giving consideration to the differences in perspective and narrative presented on "each side" of the "divide." Thought is also given to the content and purpose of murals and the impact and meaning they have for those who view them daily. Participants are facilitated to identify relationships between this experience and their experience as educators. This ranges from emphasis on the power of the visual messages presented around the walls of their classroom and school (e.g., do those visuals convey positive messages about equality and diversity?) to recognition that the language we use and the perspectives we present have been conditioned by our own cultural backgrounds/

identities and therefore careful thought may have to be given to how we present lessons in history, literature or religion so that differing perspectives are presented. The residential nature of days 2 and 3 provides participants (who are drawn from a range of integrated schools) with an opportunity to reflect, debrief fully, and chat deeply about this experience.

A change of pace on Day 3, with an emphasis on application to practice, begins with case studies of dilemmas faced by some of our integrated schools in relation to sexual orientation, cultural and ethnic difference, religious provision, and symbols and emblems (and each school's desire to be inclusive). Time is also devoted to sharing antibias interventions, approaches, and practices. Examples include giving regular attention, by the whole school, to equality/diversity auditing of resources and the use of classroom, corridor, and foyer space for visual images that are inclusive and promote equality. Whole staff approaches to challenging the use of prejudicial and discriminatory language are also discussed. Development of a school protocol, for reacting to potentially controversial events as they occur, in the form of a school response that encourages dialogue rather than avoidance, is recommended. In terms of the delivery of lessons, within the curriculum, encouragement is given to the planned, conscious exploration of differing perspectives (political, religious, and cultural) in history, Religious Education (RE), and English. Consideration is also given to the appropriate use of "discomforting pedagogies" (Zembylas & McGlynn, 2012). This follows up on a session earlier in the course that uses a video clip of Jane Elliott's "Brown Eyes, Blue Eyes" to discuss the ethics around using experiential learning (i.e., designing a lesson that puts young people in the shoes of those who are experiencing prejudice or discrimination in order to help them develop empathy rather than just knowledge). Beyond that, specific training for young people to enable them to challenge prejudice and discrimination is also discussed. This provides a catalyst for thinking about application to their own contexts and the action planning process (which forms the final part of the course) for their future work back at school.

Throughout the three days, participants are given time to reflect and record their thoughts on each session in a reflective log. These reflections and the notes from discussions feed into the content of their portfolios that are submitted for accreditation. No academic content is required for their final, written work. Rather, they are encouraged to express their personal learning and how it relates to and will influence their practice as educators.

Teachers' Responses

On the subject of personal learning, many participants, at the end of the course, comment on their increased awareness and understanding of their own bias and the need to challenge it on both a personal and professional basis. Comments, such as the following, are frequently expressed by participants during the evaluation process: "I have been challenged to look at my own bias and prejudice and how it affects both the judgements and assumptions I make about others and even the children in my classroom" (Primary school teacher, March 2009).

However, the process that induces such learning, for many, is challenging and sometimes uncomfortable. Teachers, at the beginning of the course, often deny holding any biases/prejudices and are immediately challenged by the first activity, which asks them to make assumptions about the unknown person sitting facing them, in terms of their religion, political viewpoint, and the type of school they attended (as well as personal preferences for hobbies, holiday destinations, films, and so on). During the debriefing process there are always some participants who comment that they never stereotype or categorize people from the North of Ireland, on first meeting, as Catholic or Protestant. Further discussion, and insights offered by other participants, explores how and why our society has conditioned us to primarily seek to identify local people as fitting into either the Protestant of Catholic traditions. We discuss the cues that we use to assist us in this identification process. Interestingly, by the end of the course, those who expressed most resistance to the idea of holding biases are often those who identify this as an aspect of personal learning: "I didn't realize I was biased and made assumptions as readily as I do. It has taught me to be more sensitive and aware of others—and how assumptions and bias can impact..." (Postprimary teacher, June 2008).

The pace and learning model embraced by the course often leads to revelations around the use of language. One memorable example occurred for an RE teacher in a postprimary integrated school. Several teachers from Catholic backgrounds vocalized how prefacing "Catholic" with "Roman" had taken on negative connotations for them as a consequence of the vitriolic tone adopted by Unionist politician Ian Paisley in the 1970s when he decried Roman Catholicism. "Roman," for them, was used by Paisley to denote something foreign that must be viewed with suspicion. This came as a huge surprise to the Protestant RE teacher who shared how she had always used the term "Roman Catholic" in her classroom as it was the technically precise and correct use of terminology. She was shocked to hear from others the powerful negative associations this technically precise language had assumed. She was also surprised to learn that she was betraying her own background each time she chose to preface "Catholic" with the word "Roman."

The experience of delivering the course has also revealed that each cohort of participants consists of some teachers who are openly resistant to the notion that their pupils would have any awareness or experience of sectarianism. Rather, they tend to express the view that exploring issues around difference will only heighten negative awareness and potentially lead to distrust and division. Often justification for this is that their pupils are mostly drawn from middle-class areas that are free from visual indicators of sectarianism, such as murals and peace walls (found in the communities visited on Day 2 of the course), and that their families have chosen an integrated school because they want their children to be educated in a "neutral" environment. The antibias concept, however, challenges the view that it is positive to attempt to create an environment that is neutralized, where everyone is regarded as being the same. Instead, schools should strive for "equality" rather than uniformity or neutrality. The course presents this challenge and encourages exploration of the different ways in which sectarianism is manifested and how it touches people's lives. An example is derived from a training course run in June 2011 where several teachers, from integrated schools in small towns, asserted the need to focus on counteracting gender bias and bias related to special educational needs but expressed the necessity to avoid references to sectarianism, regarding their towns as being untouched by such issues. Interestingly, discussion revealed that these small towns had a higher than average number of residents working in the armed forces. The course facilitators felt it was important to raise participants' levels of awareness of the prevalence of sectarianism in the wider society and how it touches everyone's lives. At an appropriate point in the course a poster of a young Catholic police officer called Ronan Kerr[2] (who had been murdered by dissident Republicans in April 2011) was shown to participants. A few months earlier this poster had been inserted into every copy of the *Belfast Telegraph* (sold widely throughout Northern Ireland) and every reader had been asked to display it in their home windows or places of work as a means of exhibiting their disapproval of this murder. The poster was also held by all those who demonstrated against this atrocity at a rally held in Belfast. Participating teachers were asked if their schools had, when the murder occurred, created age-appropriate opportunities to explore the motivation behind this murder and its impact at a family, community, and national level. Some schools had made reference to this in assembly but the majority had not created opportunities for discussion about an incident that had dominated the local news. This provoked discussion about the confused messages children and young people pick up from the media and how integrated schools can and should dispel some of the confusion and create opportunities for learning related to integrated education's core purpose of contributing to peace and reconciliation.

The examples above relate to increase in personal awareness as well as attempts to dispel teacher fear about tackling sensitive issues and build levels of confidence. Beyond end of course evaluations, there has been a need to ascertain the longer term impact of the training and whether learning is actually applied.

While it is positive to note that the quality and impact of antibias training has been widely recognized (and it has been cited within the Department of Education's CRED Policy, March 2011) as an example of good practice in building teacher capacity and confidence to deal positively and proactively with issues of equality and diversity, it is disappointing that by the end of 2011 only 27 out of 60 integrated schools have actually sent staff to participate in the three-day training. The lack of willingness within some schools to adopt an antibias approach appears to be borne out by past research evidence suggesting an avoidance of issues around religion and politics in some integrated schools (Donnelly, 2004; Hughes and Donnelly, 2007, McGlynn and London, 2011). Moreover, a review of integrated education practice observed a sometimes adopted passive approach to integration (Montgomery et al., 2003). Later studies revealed that integrated school principals adopt a range of approaches to integration (McGlynn, 2008, McGlynn and London, 2011) that place different emphases on cultural similarities and differences, and different degrees of emphases on intergroup relationships. Therefore, there is still much work to be done within the integrated education sector to encourage integrated schools to proactively adopt NICIE's recommended antibias approach.

I believe that in order to feel confident in an integrated school environment, teachers should be guided through a process of examining their own attitudes to difference and be facilitated to discover their own biases. The "Anti-Bias in Education" training provides such opportunities for teachers (who have received no initial training or CPD in this area) to work meaningfully and consciously in integrated schools. This may be more difficult to achieve for teachers with limited opportunity to engage with difference themselves because they received their initial teacher training in segregated institutions and spent their teaching career in largely single-identity school environments. It is essential, therefore, that teachers are given the opportunity to experience professional development, in this area, with a mixed group of colleagues to personally explore and challenge their own beliefs, traditions, and perceptions. The type of personal learning provided by this course is necessary in readiness for working with young people around their attitudes, skills, and behaviors.

Beyond integrated schools, NICIE has delivered, and is keen to promote, antibias training to teachers in other sectors, particularly as the number of shared education initiatives increases. This training could be extremely beneficial but, ultimately, teachers and the wider community may be deterred from engaging in this work as a consequence of a genuine lack of confidence and/or fear of tackling such issues, as demonstrated by the views expressed to NICIE. Therefore, until teachers have the necessary understanding and skills it is unlikely that community relations, diversity, and equality will be taught effectively in schools. Indeed, past research into the implementation of curricular initiatives and contact schemes and their impact on pupils' identities and attitudes suggests that good practice has tended to be outweighed by a tendency for schools to avoid more controversial issues (Smith & Robinson, 1992, 1996; Kilpatrick & Leitch, 2004). However, there is now a requirement placed on all schools to develop young people with "an understanding of their role in working for a more inclusive, just and democratic society where equality is fully accepted and discrimination actively discouraged" (CRED Policy, March 2011).

CONCLUSION

In my opinion, changes to the national curriculum, with the introduction of PDMU and Local and Global Citizenship, could be rendered meaningless if teachers are not taken through a process of realization that our education system in Northern Ireland has conditioned us to think very narrowly from the position of our own cultural backgrounds and identities. The outcomes from antibias training demonstrate that teacher professional development, which gives teachers the opportunity to realize and reflect on this, can be extremely valuable and enriching for their subsequent practice. The latter is essential if future opportunities are to be created by teachers for young people to step into the shoes of the "other," fully appreciate alternative perspectives, and develop empathy as a consequence.

The main lesson gleaned from this work is that integrated school environments have prided themselves on being inclusive and a lot of extremely good work happens around inclusion (McGlynn & London, 2011). However, tackling prejudice and discrimination consistently, across all equality areas, presents a much greater challenge and one that not all integrated schools have embraced. The antibias approach provides a framework to assist with bringing about such consistency but significant funding would have to be sought and staff resources provided by NICIE to enable that to happen.

Finally, in an increasingly global world, it is important that our young people do not fear but are willing to embrace diversity. The concepts and methodologies incorporated in NICIE's antibias training are transferable to other contexts. Training such as this should *not* be considered an optional luxury in culturally and ethnically diverse contexts that have historically experienced division and conflict. Rather, teacher education and continuing professional development should be as much about personal development as about the ability to complete lesson plans, control young people, and ensure a national curriculum is followed. Experience within the integrated sector in Northern Ireland has demonstrated that teachers can and should be encouraged to develop a passion about issues of diversity and equality.

NOTES

1. Section 75 of the Northern Ireland Act 1998 came into force on January 1, 2000, and placed a statutory obligation on public authorities in carrying out their various functions relating to Northern Ireland, to have due regard for the need to promote equality of opportunity

   - between persons of different religious belief, political opinion, racial group, age, marital status, or sexual orientation;
   - between men and women generally;
   - between persons with a disability and persons without; and
   - between persons with dependents and persons without.

   In addition, without prejudice to this obligation, public authorities are also required to have regard for the desirability of promoting good relations between persons of different religious belief, political opinion, and racial group. The statutory obligations are implemented through Equality Schemes, approved by the Equality Commission, and by screening and carrying out Equality Impact Assessments on policies.

2. Police Constable Ronan Kerr (25 years old) was a Police Service of Northern Ireland (PSNI) officer killed by a booby-trap car bomb planted outside his

home on April 2, 2011, in Killyclogher, near Omagh. Responsibility for the attack was later claimed by dissident Republicans claiming the mantle of the Provisional IRA and separate from other dissident Republican groups. Roman Catholic police officers at the time constituted approximately 30 percent of PSNI officers (a proportion recruitment policies were trying to increase). Kerr was a member of a Gaelic Athletic Association club, the Beragh Red Knights. The guard of honor at Kerr's funeral was formed of club members and PSNI officers, a funeral also attended by the leaders of Ireland's four main churches. His murder was condemned by almost all sections of Northern Irish politics and society as well as condemned internationally. On April 6, a peace rally was organized in Belfast by the Irish Congress of Trade Unions, which was reported to have been attended by up to 7,000 persons. Similar events were held in Omagh, Enniskillen, and London. BBC Ireland correspondent Mark Simpson commented, in relation to the unified response of the community, "A murder designed to divide people has actually brought them closer together."

REFERENCES

Department of Education Northern Ireland. (March 2011). Community relations, equality and diversity in education policy. Accessed online at www.deni.org.uk on January 30, 2013.

Donnelly, C. (2004). Constructing the ethos of tolerance and respect in an integrated school: The role of teachers. *British Journal of Educational Research Journal, 30*(2), 264–278.

Hughes, J., & Donnelly, C. (2007). Integrated schools in Northern Ireland and bi-lingual / bi-national schools in Israel: Some policy issues. In Z. Beckerman & C. McGlynn (Eds.), *Addressing ethnic conflict through peace education* (pp. 121–134). New York: Palgrave Macmillan.

Kilpatrick, R., & Leitch, R. (2004). Teachers and pupils' educational experiences and school-based responses to the conflict in Northern Ireland. *Journal of Social Issues, 60* (3), 563–586.

McGlynn, C. (2008). *Integrated education: Case studies of good practice in response to cultural diversity.* Research report, Queens University Belfast, School of Education.

McGlynn, C., & London, T. (2011). Leadership for inclusion: Conceptualizing and enacting inclusion in integrated schools in a troubled society. *Research Papers in Education*, iFirst article, 1–21.

Montgomery, A., Fraser, G., McGlynn, C., Smith, A., & Gallagher, T. (2003). *Integrated education in Northern Ireland: Integration in practice.* Coleraine: UNESCO Centre, University of Ulster.

Northern Ireland Council for Integrated Education. (2008). *ABC: Promoting an anti-bias approach to education in Northern Ireland.* Belfast: NICIE.

Northern Ireland Council for Integrated Education. (2009). *Statement of principles for integrated education.* Belfast: NICIE.

Smith, A., & Robinson, A. (1992). *Education for mutual understanding: Perceptions and policy.* Coleraine: Centre for the Study of Conflict, University of Ulster.

Smith, A., & Robinson, A. (1996). *Education for mutual understanding: The statutory years.* Coleraine: Centre for the Study of Conflict, University of Ulster.

Williamson, M. (1992). *Return to love: Reflections on the principles of "a course in miracles."* New York: Harper Collins.

Zembylas, M., & McGlynn, C. (2012). Discomforting pedagogies: Emotional tensions, ethical dilemmas and transformative possibilities. *British Educational Research Journal, 38*(1), 41–60.

CONCLUSION TO PART 3

Michalinos Zembylas

This part includes five chapters focusing on curriculum and pedagogy issues in different integrated education settings. Although this part is not wholly inclusive of all the multifaceted and complex issues that arise in such settings, the personal experiences of authors from Israel, Croatia, and Northern Ireland echo the serious challenges of those involved in efforts to develop and implement curricula and practices in integrated schools. Our task here, then, is not to outline all of these numerous challenges but rather to highlight some important issues that emphasize the *historicized* and *theoretical* character of curriculum efforts (Kliebard, 1975) in integrated education settings. That is, as distinguished curriculum historian Herbert Kliebard made clear, a historical and a theoretical understanding of curriculum development processes enables efforts to understand the history of the present and the future prospects in the current moment. We want, therefore, to focus on three issues that permeate the chapters in this part and, through them, illustrate the promise of integrated education in challenging segregation.

The first issue is the importance of reconstructing the subjective and sociopolitical spaces in curriculum and pedagogy developed in integrated schools. As Helen and Sharon show, for example, exploring controversial issues in sensitive yet critical ways provides opportunities to staff and students to carve new spaces that transform the school ethos. Integration, in this manner, is not viewed as simply an institutional arrangement, but rather as constituting a culture that gradually reconstructs the individual and social spheres of integration. In their chapter, Marinko and Ivana show the slow and sometimes painful process of reconstructing the subjective and sociopolitical spaces in integrated settings, highlighting that one of the most powerful challenges is the mentality of segregation that "governs" curriculum thinking and pedagogical practices. Similarly, Julia and Bob discuss the consequences of identity-based curriculum and its ideological components that threaten to reproduce rather than reconstruct the spaces that are necessary to transform segregated spheres to integrated ones. Finally, Paula suggests that an important aspect of reconstructing the subjective and sociopolitical spaces in curriculum and pedagogy developed in integrated schools is teacher professional development for antibias approaches. Paula points out that innovative and specialized curricula and pedagogies in integrated schools do not mean much if teachers are not trained to deal with their own biases and prejudices; this issue is not merely a task of personal professional development but rather an effort that concerns teachers as a community that struggles to change its ethos.

The second issue concerns how the past influences the present and the role of the politics of conflict in curriculum efforts. Many hope that "correcting" the curriculum—for example, developing a curriculum for integrated education—might influence the larger society. Although this may be a major step in the right direction, it has to be clear that a commitment to school integration is not enough to temper societal segregation. This idea is shown very clearly in the chapter by Marinko and Ivana in which the hegemonic culture of segregation prevents the realization of the New School project in Vukovar; instead, the Nansen Dialogue Centre is forced to adjust to the harsh reality of ongoing segregation and introduces part of the curriculum of the New School to presently segregated schools. Despite some positive results, Marinko and Ivana acknowledge that in the absence of political will for structural changes, the progress will be slow; yet, it is important to not give up the effort. Similar ideas are emphasized in the other chapters in this part that also show how the past haunts the present in numerous day-to-day encounters—from unexpected events that raise controversy to school curriculum choices and the content of teacher training. The important point of these chapters is *understanding* the relation among school curricula, the conflict in society and its consequences, the processes of reconstructing new and hopeful spaces of integration, and the character of the historical moment in which all these are taking place. It is understanding that informs the ethical obligation to push for integration efforts, that enables us to think and act with intelligence, sensitivity, and courage in the context of integrated schools.

Finally, the last issue that permeates all chapters is the need for *recapturing* the curriculum and pedagogy of integrated education as an ongoing process of development. The different settings of these chapters—Israel, Croatia, and Northern Ireland—show that there are essentially multiple sites of (ongoing) curricular experimentation in integrated education. There is no educational reason why all integrated schools within a society must develop the "same"curricula and pedagogies, as there are different challenges in each setting. It is therefore important that the process of curriculum development for/in integrated schools be kept open and ongoing, emphasizing specific and challenging issues that are pertinent to particular individuals and groups. For example, the introduction of the intercultural subject entitled "Cultural and Spiritual Heritage of the Region" in Vukovar provides opportunities for all conflicting groups to intensify their study of their histories and cultures and construct a curriculum linked specifically to the overall integration project. Similar efforts are described in the remaining chapters of this part that also show the need for innovative approaches that capture the imagination and the concerns of those involved rather than mirror bureaucratic compartmentalization of knowledge according to traditional curricula. Integrated schools can break new ground by developing curricula that go beyond banal designs and carve spaces that truly promote a new ethos and a new culture. The present historical moment in many conflicted societies continues to be defined politically by segregation practices. What is needed, therefore, is to reconstruct the curriculum and pedagogy by confronting—directly or indirectly—the segregated structuring of education for the social reproduction of conflict.

REFERENCE

Kliebard, H. (1975). Persistent issues in historical perspective. In W. Pinar (Ed.), *Curriculum theorizing: The reconceptualists* (pp. 39–50). Berkeley: McCutchan.

4

MOVING FORWARD—DEVELOPING AND SUSTAINING SUPPORT FOR INTEGRATED SCHOOLS

INTRODUCTION TO PART 4

Michalinos Zembylas

The fourth and final part will focus on what is currently needed to develop and support integrated education for the future. It will reflect on what has been achieved already and what has yet to be done. For this purpose, this part includes two different accounts that look back at the integrated education system and consider what has been achieved so far and what is needed to move forward. The first account comes from a young individual, Richard Wilson, who went through the integrated education system in Northern Ireland and reflects on his experiences as a student; the second account comes from Colm Cavanagh who is currently the chairperson for the Northern Ireland Council for Integrated Education and has been connected with the integrated educational movement for over 25 years. Both accounts will bring to light the importance of constant renewal and persistent effort that any initiative toward integrated education needs to face the new barriers to the establishment of integrated schools in conflicted societies. The part will also consider what support new initiatives, which have been presented in earlier chapters, might receive from those involved in such initiatives for a long time. Although initiatives toward integrated education are at different stages in the societies of Bosnia and Herzegovina, Cyprus, Macedonia, Israel, Croatia, and Northern Ireland—the different sites that have been looked at in this book—there are opportunities to develop support networks across sites that might be influential in the success of integrated education.

The part will begin with a reflection from a former student on what he has gained from his school experiences. In his chapter, Richard Wilson, tells us the story of how he experienced integrated education. Writing seven years after his graduation, Richard reflects on the various benefits and limitations that integration symbolized during his secondary school years. The major benefits include the encouragement of confident, well-rounded, and tolerant members of societies; Richard recalls various incidents from his life at the integrated school that show how he gradually developed what he calls an "integrated mentality"—a process that takes place daily and it is not always obvious until years later. Richard also refers to the limitations of integrated schooling, emphasizing that the integrated system of schooling must learn to reach out to those groups in society that have been so far resistant to integration. In other words, Richard identifies the dangers that come with the "institutionalization" of integrated schools and warns that there should be a continual renewal of the efforts that are undertaken in integrated education. At the same time, as he points out, integrated schools should remember their roots and retain as much radicalism as possible. His suggestion, then, is that greater innovation, experimentation, and passion for integrated education should be constantly nurtured.

The concluding chapter by Colm Cavanagh relates the stories of three integrated schools in Northern Ireland. Each story allows Colm to draw conclusions regarding the challenges that those interested in developing integrated educational settings will have encounter in their path. Colm reminds us that integrated schools in Northern Ireland, over 30 years after the first integrated school opened its doors, count for only 7 percent of all schools in that area; he sees this indeed as a great achievement but the lessons he has learned, he believes, can help us in moving forward in trying to achieve more allies to the integrated cause.

16

MY EXPERIENCE OF INTEGRATED EDUCATION IN NORTHERN IRELAND

Richard Wilson

I attended Northern Ireland's first integrated secondary school, Lagan College, between 1998 and 2005, eventually becoming the "head boy" during my final year. However, my connection with integrated education began long before this time as my parents had put me and my brothers on the school's waiting list as young children in the hope of securing a place when we were older. We grew up in a largely Protestant area in rural County Down and as children attended the local Non-Subscribing Presbyterian church. This was as much social as religious, and as primary schoolboys we each decided that we would stop going.

Given this ambivalence toward church it is unsurprising that the divisive politics of religion were never a preoccupation of my childhood. I went to the local state-sector primary school, which wasn't integrated but was friendly, and I do not remember any moments of sectarianism while I was there, although this may have been a product of the fact that we were all, for the most part, from similar backgrounds. Also, living in the countryside provided a natural shield from the worst effects of the Troubles. My generation are lucky that as we grew up violence in Northern Ireland was receding. This was particularly true for those of us who lived away from the most conflict-affected areas. So while I do have some memories of things like army checkpoints and recall once hearing a bomb going off, these events did not have an overbearing influence on my identity or outlook. Of course, had I grown up elsewhere this might not have been the case. Furthermore, I have Catholic family members and friends so by the time I started at Lagan College I viewed the basic concept of "integration" as natural and right.

I believe it is important that my personal background is recognized in order to understand the context in which I experienced integrated education. Many different factors including class, wealth, religion (or lack of it), gender, and geography (rural or urban upbringing) impact upon each person as they enter any education system, contributing to—but not binding—the expectations and prospects of each individual. These must also affect the views and characteristics of the adults emerging at the other end of the system. Therefore, my outlook on integration will not be the same as everyone else in my peer group, nor do I believe it is one that many practitioners of integrated education would necessarily subscribe to. It is, however, formed on the basis of personal reflection on the various benefits and limitations that integration symbolized during my secondary school years.

I have spent most of the years that followed my time at Lagan College in Scotland and still live there. The distance of time and geography that my current circumstances offer allows me to view the issues of integration with fresh eyes, and on assessment I believe that my experience and that of my schoolmates was one of great value, even if we did not know it at the time. The impact of this system can only grow exponentially as increasing numbers of Northern Irish people gain the social benefits of being educated with all children, regardless of their background. In a society like that of Northern Ireland that still suffers the malaise of underlying sectarianism and mistrust of the "other," integrating increasing numbers of children could eventually prove to be socially and politically reconstructive.

It should be noted that it is now almost seven years since I last set foot in Lagan College, the same length of time that I spent there as a pupil. Inevitably some of the forthcoming analyses of my experience will not be as relevant as they were at the time when I was there. It would be remarkable, indeed, if nothing had changed. This chapter is based on my experience of a period of time that has long passed, but I believe that useful lessons can still be drawn from it. Any criticism offered here is intended to be constructive and is not a reflection on the way the school currently operates, with which I am not familiar.

UNDERSTANDING OF INTEGRATED EDUCATION

My understanding of integrated education has been fluid over the years from before I started at Lagan College, during my seven years within the secondary school system itself, and now looking back years after I moved on to university. An academic interpretation of integrated education gives us strong theoretical grounds to understand the rationale behind the system. It sets the boundaries for scholarly debate and study but may not say very much about the experience of the pupils within the system and how they understand their education. As I will expand further in this chapter, from the context of the pupil integration is a moving concept. This is unsurprising because as a pupil you do not have the ability to stand back and observe. Rather, you are an active participant and unaware of all the benefits or limitations of the education you are experiencing. Indeed, unless a child attends both an integrated and a nonintegrated school, we should not expect them to have a particular awareness of the experience of either system at the time. They just experience "school" in general. For this reason, the impact of integrated education will likely be subtle and a pupil's understanding of their education will not be complete until after they have moved into adulthood.

I have arrived at a more concrete understanding of integrated education as someone who has experienced the system and had time to assess its merits and problems. From the perspective of a participant I understand the purpose of integrated education to be to encourage and facilitate the mixing of the many different types of children that make up our whole society, removing both the obvious sectarian barriers to social interaction in Northern Ireland that created an education system where Catholics and Protestants were mostly educated separately, as well as engaging with other less-publicized underlying causes of division including class, geography, and race. I believe that the interactions resulting from bringing children together from this wide range of backgrounds do not represent a zero sum game where some benefit at the expense of others. Instead it is a win-win situation where each pupil has the potential to develop socially *and* academically in a more holistic approach to education than that offered in other schools. Particularly in this social context, it is much more constructive for children to learn to work with *and about* others from different backgrounds and cultures as they grow up, for once they enter the world of work or university they have to deal with this situation anyway. It also equips them, if they are open to it, to have a more nuanced and intelligent understanding of the history, politics, and traditions of their country, providing a safe arena in which to question and challenge received wisdom while learning through necessity to see issues about which one feels strongly from opposing perspectives.

The aim of integrated education in this context should be to encourage the talents in each child, whatever they may be, and to equip them to enter the adult world as confident, well-rounded, and tolerant members of society. It should not be about social engineering or compelling everyone to become middle-of-the-road Alliance Party voters. Indeed, compulsion is probably a poor substitute for curiosity when it comes to integration. The best lessons in terms of tolerance for those from "other" backgrounds are not learned by rote but absorbed by osmosis. This reasoning forms the backbone of my contention that the direction the integrated movement should in future be toward a more secular understanding of the divisions in our society, beyond Christian religious conflict. Bringing children together from both sides of a divided society is a huge and laudable achievement, but as I see the aim of integration as being to increase overall social tolerance, not just in the religious context, focusing on the divisions between Catholics and Protestants may eventually stifle the greater potential for integration to ultimately lead to a more well-rounded and cohesive society in general.

Lessons from Integrated Education

My outlook on integration has grown more sophisticated as I have matured. To begin with, attending an integrated school meant traveling twice as far each day, leaving the house earlier in the morning and arriving home later at night than if I'd gone to my nearest grammar school. It was also not really my choice—rather integration was a decision that, as noted above, was taken by my parents when I was very young. So although I was reasonably happy to go to Lagan College, to do so meant a certain amount of sacrifice (of time and leaving behind friends from primary school) without much agency in the decision itself. This set of circumstances put me into a certain group of pupils found in integrated schools—one in which the presumed value of integration was the overriding parental motivation behind attending the school. However, I do not believe that this was the main concern for all parents/pupils (perhaps not even the majority) during my secondary school years.

Furthermore, I already considered myself to have an "integrated mentality" before I started at Lagan College. I did not see myself as being in any way sectarian, nor did I believe for this reason that it would personally make much difference which school I attended, integrated or otherwise. This was predominantly my opinion as I moved up through the school, but as I matured and learned more, I began to understand how being part of an integrated community would be transformative for those of my peers who came from the other group whose parents' choice of attending an integrated school was not based primarily on values or principles but rather on any number of other reasons—including because the school was close to home or that it had a better academic reputation than the alternative secondary school in the area, for example. By the time I left the integrated education sector, I felt I had a firm understanding of its value—it brought together, for a variety of reasons, children whose backgrounds and outside influences could otherwise incline them toward sectarianism on both sides of a divided society. Pupils like me, I felt, saw less benefit in this sense, perhaps analogous to the way that an economist can show that distributing a set amount of money has a greater impact proportionately to the incomes of the poor than the rich—I felt I was "more integrated" in the first instance so profited less than others.

However, I have increasingly come to view this perspective as flawed, particularly having observed the education of my youngest brother who did not go to an integrated secondary school but to the local grammar school. While this example may not be academically robust it is probably as good an illustration of a real-life counterfactual as is likely to be found. Despite sharing the same background, I now realize that no matter what the atmosphere is at home, the culture of the school you attend and the views of your peer group there have an impact on how you interpret the world. This is not to say that he is so very different from me, but he has not had the benefit of learning to see the world through diverse eyes, which is intrinsic to integrated mixed-ability education, with all the class and cultural divides that are bridged. So while I would strongly argue that he is not particularly worse-off for lack of an integrated education, he did not gain from the value-added element of mixing with a greater diversity of people that I enjoyed and benefited from in my secondary school education. There is much to be gained from integrated education, I now believe, regardless of the opinions you bring with you to school.

Of course, while I contend that all the participants in integrated education benefit from the system, it would be wrong to argue that the impact is not potentially greater on those who attend *despite* the deeper prejudices that may linger within their communities and family backgrounds, which were absent for me. It is not hyperbole to state that as well as the moderate, integration poster boys and girls that Lagan College attracted, the school also educated pupils who held more extreme opinions, including even support for the violent paramilitary groups that would seek to undermine the progress of law, order, and normality in our country. And while some pupils paraded during the marching season, others (their classmates) even threw stones at the marchers. Even the inevitable graffiti scrawled on desks was often sectarian. The point is that the school was not populated by a certain type of model integrated child. Rather, it was a bubbling cauldron of divergent cultures, traditions, and backgrounds. The beauty of this situation was that no matter what went on at the weekend, in school everybody had to come together for lessons. This idea echoes the theory of the contact hypothesis, described in Tomovska (2010, p. 127), whereby face-to-face meetings with those from the "other" side of a divided community are argued to help "alter participant's hostile views of each other and promote mutual understanding." Slowly, over time, it seems impossible that even the most hardheaded bigot would not see the irony—and the futility —of fighting with people over some small supposed differences that seem so important to those on the inside, but inexplicable to people with the broader worldview that integrated schools should endeavor to foster. It was these silent lessons that were the most powerful, although most of us did not even know we were learning them at the time. This is a far more potent message than the somewhat forced, set-piece examples of political correctness that can potentially creep into integrated education, symbolized for me by the Lagan College PE calendar—to ensure balance we played only two weeks of rugby and two weeks of Gaelic football in the year. Not only does this timid cultural oversensitivity serve to reinforce stereotypes that Protestants play rugby and Catholics play Gaelic football, the end result was that you never had long enough at playing either of these games to get any good!

Yet, despite the divergent backgrounds of the pupils who attended the school, it is interesting to note that in my experience of my peer group (certainly those in my close circle of friends but I suspect much wider) not many seemed outwardly very religious. This anecdotal evidence may be suggestive of a shift away from the traditional place of religion in our society and could explain to some degree the growth of the integrated sector. Perhaps we were more open to integration along religious lines because those divisions were less meaningful in the modern world? Was religion simply a fig leaf for a more primal tribalism that is the real problem in our country? This could pose wider questions for the international applicability of the Northern Irish model of integration, especially for societies in which religion is an even more dominant force. Alternatively, it could be argued that strong religious values—"love thy neighbour as thyself" perhaps— could bolster more than undermine attempts to integrate. From a personal perspective, holding no religious faith, I sometimes found the overriding ethos of the school, which was couched within the safe terms of Christianity, to be somewhat stifling. I have no problem with Christian teachings being delivered at school assemblies, but why not other moral lessons from different religions, philosophies, and great thinkers? There is a world of opinion on the big issues of our day out there and we do no justice to ourselves by insisting on always looking out through the same Western, Christian lens. The earth as a whole is increasingly interconnected, competitive, and uncertain than the one our parents and teachers grew up in. The more we look inward, the less prepared we are to meet the challenges of tomorrow's globalized planet. Therefore, I believe that the process of integration should be driven by a passion for pushing boundaries and challenging received wisdom, harking back to the early, more radical days of the integrated movement but not being bound by the constraints that these pioneers imposed on the system they created or had imposed upon themselves.

Through recent experience of working in the Northern Irish education sector I have learned that there are still many parents who value having their particular version of religious instruction as the backbone of their children's education. This is a potential problem for the future of integrated education—how to persuade those who currently disparage or are ambivalent about integration of its merits for individuals and society in general. The realization that other ways of thinking *do* exist, that my views may *not* be correct, and that children from very different backgrounds can be just like me after all is liberating and is the best way that I can see to heal the divisions that still plague Northern Ireland. Yet, unless we seek to address the situation where most children are educated separately, we'll never create a healthy, normal society that all our people will want to live in and raise their families in.

Winning this argument means persuading parents of the benefits of integration for their children but it is made more difficult by the questions over academic results in integrated schools. When I first went to Lagan College much was made about the perceived lower standards of education in the integrated sector in comparison to grammar schools. There may be some truth to this, but how do you compare two entirely different systems? This becomes more a matter for a debate on the merits or not of academic selection. However, this is a difficult issue for integrated secondary schools as in the process of bringing children together from different religions and backgrounds they must also balance the range of academic abilities of their intake of pupils—without equilibrium across the academic spectrum some children could be left behind while others are held back. Certain members of staff at my primary school greeted the news that I was heading to Lagan College, after getting an A in my 11 plus, with barely concealed dismay, perhaps for academic reasons, perhaps religion. Yet, with the right mixture of people from all abilities there is nothing to fear in terms of academic results provided you take personal responsibility in achieving them—which is a good lesson for life in itself. We had the opportunity to attain the highest marks we were capable of, but this did not come at the price of focusing entirely on academic excellence like in more traditionally results-focused schools—this way there is a better chance of bringing out the best in *all* pupils, not just the ones who are good at exams. If well managed, this can be to the benefit of everyone.

This is not an apology for lower results—personally I did well at school and have had success at university also. But equally, people who were less academic had the opportunity to apply themselves in other ways and excel at their own talents. An education system that exists just to churn out fresh recruits for universities does not necessarily benefit pupils or the wider society if these young adults only take degrees because it is what is expected of them. The situation today increasingly resembles an educational analogy of the military-industrial complex—maybe less dangerous but just as wasteful of resources, with schools mechanically channeling children toward a university education without paying close attention to the other opportunities that may exist for each individual pupil. And just as we cannot deduce the wellbeing of a society based solely on the average wealth of the population, neither should we judge a system of education entirely on the academic results that are produced. Of course, we want all our young people to be well educated and interested in learning useful skills and information. It is hoped that this will translate into success at examinations, with success itself being subjective to the individual sitting the test. However, equally important—if not more so—to the grades achieved by those in education are the unquantifiable outcomes that are reflected in the happiness, ambitions, and ability to *think for themselves* of the pupils who pass through it. These are the qualities gained during a child's education that echo long after the euphoria or disappointment of opening examination results has been forgotten. It is this independence of mind that integration is best placed to unveil and that can mark it out most from alternative school systems.

And, while it would go somewhat against the philosophy of educating "all children together," there is nothing intrinsic about formally integrating religious groups that would preclude either grammar or high schools from doing so, although this may be anathema to some in the integrated movement itself. Indeed, it could prove to be a popular option, particularly for parents who feel unable to—as some see it—gamble with their children's education by choosing a mixed-ability integrated school despite believing in the underlying values of integration. The mixed-ability model may not be right for everyone, and in every education system there will be those who fall through the net as they struggle in their learning. But as I've shown, the argument against integration based on academic achievement in general is very often a straw man. The positive personal development from being put into strange and challenging situations with people that you would not otherwise meet is also undeniable. So what is holding back faster progress to integration?

CHALLENGES AND PROSPECTS FOR INTEGRATED EDUCATION

The biggest obstacles to greater integration throughout Northern Ireland remain the resilient and pervasive attitudes of mistrust and division that have existed here for longer than living memory. In order to progress, the integrated system must learn to reach out to those groups in society that have so far been resistant to integration. This will be the defining challenge of the integration movement in future years and as difficult but important as any it has so far faced. In order to do this, an open and inquiring mind is required, and questions need to be asked not just in negative form—why don't these parents choose integrated education—but also from a positive perspective—what is it that these parents value in their current school of choice.

As the integrated system naturally favors mixed-ability education, I see the biggest impediments to reaching more children currently coming from two sections of the education sector in Northern Ireland—the support for grammar schools and the support for Catholic schools. The grammar school system is favored by many from all sides of the religious divide for the results it achieves, and perhaps integrated schools do need to learn from their attitude of pushing children on to achieve their academic potential and having high expectations of everyone. I dealt earlier with the argument against integration on academic grounds, positing that if it is well managed mixed-ability education can produce strong academic results. I am certain that it does neither the pupil nor the school any good to settle for mediocrity. Of course, a balance should be struck between academic achievement and personal development, a distinction that the grammar school system itself does not always get right. What is most important is to instill ambition into each child, the confidence that with hard work they can achieve their goals, and the knowledge that they are just as entitled to go onto successful careers as pupils from any other school or background. I do not see this challenge as unique to integrated schools, but in a society where many still favor academic selection and grammar schools, the integrated system needs to show definitively that all its children can achieve academic success right up to the highest levels.

I see the challenge of the position of Catholic schools in the Northern Irish education system as being even more fundamental to the future progress of integration than fears over academic standards. Having worked for about a year within the Catholic-maintained schools sector I gained a rich insight into many of the issues that the integrated sector must address to continue to grow. I witnessed the passion and pride that many of the actors in this system take in delivering Catholic education to the children in their community and it is clearly widely supported. Certainly some of the reasoning behind this is the religious messages and ethics that are espoused in these schools and that many parents and teachers find favorable. Just as integrated schools need to convince parents worried about academic standards that their pupils can achieve great results so too do they need to explain to parents concerned about moral values that their children will be catered for in this respect. While my own instincts emphasize the importance of broad moral instruction as opposed to a strictly religious version, the main challenge is to show that the integrated system produces just as well-rounded and upright adults as any other—except that the benefit of daily interaction and free discussion of difficult issues without fear with people from very different backgrounds is unique to the integrated system. Persuading more representatives of churches from across the community of the benefits of integration is probably also necessary. While the majority of Catholic children attend Catholic schools, and the majority of Protestants go to the therefore de facto Protestant state schools the integrated sector will remain a less significant player in Northern Ireland's education, which is why this challenge is so important for the future of our country's experiment with integration. It is encouraging therefore that more politicians seem to be tentatively engaging with the idea of integration, seeing it as a way of normalizing a still somewhat dysfunctional society (BBC, 2011).

It is laudable also that attempts are being made to learn the lessons of the last 30 years of integration, analyzing the subject from the perspective of academics, practitioners, and participants. In my opinion, one of the best life-skills I developed through necessity from my integrated education was the ability to step back from difficult issues and view them from opposing perspectives. This does not mean believing in nothing; instead it teaches you that most opinions are valid and hold a certain amount of truth. With this in mind I contend that the integrated education system itself needs to harness the same kind of vision—it should take heart from its growing support and the progress it has made in the last 30 years, but it must also engage in honest self-reflection about what it can do better in terms of both attracting more children (and their parents) and making sure that each child attains their potential, both socially and academically. Furthermore, I also believe that integrated schools should remember their roots and retain as much radicalism as possible. In the scheme of our modern history they were revolutionary and they should celebrate that with greater innovation, experimentation, and passion in educating the children that pass through them. If they follow the path of simply emulating every other school they lose a wonderful opportunity for creating a true alternative to the current divided education system. The challenge is to take the most attractive parts of all systems, the parts that currently still retain support among wide sections of Northern Irish society, and fuse them together to make even better schools.

If there is one lesson that I would choose to emphasize from my time in integrated education it is this—the real process of integration takes place daily, but is imperceptible to the pupil. It is not two weeks of rugby, then two weeks of Gaelic football. It is five or seven years of sitting in classrooms with people you would probably never have met if you went to the school most children in your community attended. Tolerance is harder to teach than intolerance, but it is this lesson that is most keenly absorbed by the pupils of integrated schools, even without the help of teachers. And while you might not always remember how to calculate the area of a circle or the French word for "pencil case," I think most former pupils will take the silent messages of integration—tolerance and respect—with them into their adult lives.

The integrated sector in Northern Ireland should be proud of its achievements so far but with this success comes responsibility, placing it at the vanguard of a growing international movement. Having studied global development, I see the potential for integration to be utilized as a positive tool for reducing conflict in some of the most troubled societies in the world. Education by itself is thought to have terrific benefits to other sectors in developing countries, including health and gender equality improvements, and a recent report from the World Bank (2011, p. xii) calculated that civil conflict "costs the average developing country roughly 30 years of GDP growth," stunting development for at least a generation—we could also wonder about the cost of our own conflict. The benefits of seeking to develop the Northern Irish model of integration for use at the grassroots level in other countries could therefore be globally beneficial and an inspiring, innovative achievement to have come out of our troubled recent history.

REFERENCES

BBC. (2011). End sectarian division, Peter Robinson tells DUP conference. *BBC News, Northern Ireland.* Accessed December 15, 2011. http://www.bbc.co.uk/news/uk-northern-ireland-15897047

Tomovska, A. (2010). Contact as a tool for peace education? Reconsidering the contact hypothesis from the children's perspective. *Journal of Peace Education, 7*(2), 121–138.

World Bank. (2011). *World Development Report 2011: Conflict, Security, and Development.* Washington, DC: World Bank.

17

THIRTY YEARS TO ACHIEVE 7 PERCENT

WORKING TO DESEGREGATE SCHOOLS IN NORTHERN IRELAND

Colm Cavanagh

What is my own, personal experience of encouraging integrated schools in Northern Ireland? Let me tell you three stories of parents starting different integrated schools here—the stories of three groups of Catholics and Protestants who refused to let their children be educated apart. My wife Anne and I were involved in two of these school start-ups. Then let me talk about the special challenges of running an integrated school in a segregated society. But first let me highlight some issues about Northern Ireland's divided school system:

1. Does integrated education work? My personal experience says "Yes." And joint research by Queen's University, the University of Ulster, and Oxford University says that students from integrated schools are more prepared for life in a pluralist society than are students from segregated schools. In addition, research by Queen's University Belfast shows that students from integrated schools have fully cross-community friendships that students from integrated schools tend not to have.
2. Most Northern Ireland churches, politicians, and the Northern Ireland Assembly *do not actively* encourage integrated schools.
3. In the 1830s, when the government was setting up the national school system across Ireland, it wanted all children to attend the same schools together. But the Christian denominations—primarily Catholic, Anglican, Presbyterian, and Methodist—all wanted to have their own schools and so a denominational system soon emerged, funded by the government.

4. There are about 1,200 primary and second level schools in Northern Ireland.

5. The religious segregation of our schools is not compulsory. It is not required by the government. It is self-selected and mirrors the British-Irish/ Protestant-Catholic identity divide within the community.

6. Apart from about ten evangelical Protestant primary schools that self-fund, the government funds 100 percent (salaries and running costs) of the "Protestant" schools and the "Catholic" schools in Northern Ireland.

7. All schools are open to children of any, or no, religion.

8. Only 61 schools—about 7 percent of all schools—are now formally "integrated". All of these have been created by parents since 1981—some are completely new schools and some are existing schools that have voted to become integrated.

9. Of the remaining 93 percent of schools, about half are attended by Catholic children and the other half are attended by Protestant children. Less than one hundred of these schools have any significant degree of mixed attendance by both Protestant and Catholic children.

10. In Britain, Ireland, Australia, and the United States some Christian churches have created joint Protestant-Roman Catholic schools. But this example has not been tried by churches in Northern Ireland.

11. In 1989, during the Troubles period when Northern Ireland was being ruled directly by the UK government, a new law imposed on the Northern Ireland Department of Education the duty to encourage integrated education. It gives core funding to the Northern Ireland Council for Integrated Education.

STORY 1: CREATING OAKGROVE INTEGRATED PRIMARY SCHOOL (DERRY~LONDONDERRY), 1990–1991

It was 1990. The year would see 84 killings in Northern Ireland.

Oakgrove Integrated Primary was the fourteenth integrated school in Northern Ireland. (There are now 61.) Parents in Derry~Londonderry opened it in 1991, ten years after Belfast parents opened Lagan College, the first planned integrated school in Northern Ireland.

But on a sunny day in June, a casual conversation took place among some local parents, including teachers, in the park at Crawford Square,

Derry. The "11+" results had just been published by the Northern Ireland Department of Education. ("11+"-type examinations still exist in Northern Ireland dividing children at the age of 11 every year into groups of more academically able and less academically able.

"Why do we divide our children on the basis of an examination at 10 years of age?" someone asked. "Why do we divide many of our children on the basis of gender at 10?" added someone else. "Why," came a third comment, "do we divide our children on the basis of their church at the age of 10?"

The conversations continued into the autumn. The parents determined to follow the example of the new integrated schools and figure out how to avoid these divisions for their own children. They contacted other people they thought might be interested. They held two or three meetings in the local Everglades Hotel because it was a neutral venue. Then they rented a room at Lisnagelvin Leisure Center—another neutral venue—advertised it publicly, and more than one hundred people turned up. Some people present wanted an integrated primary school; some wanted an integrated college; some wanted an integrated nursery. A committee was elected. Geoff Starrett (Protestant) and I (Catholic) were elected co-chairs. Several people were delegated to go and visit some of the handful of new integrated schools opened by parents since 1981. The committee then had to find pupils, staff, and a building. They spoke to the Northern Ireland Council for Integrated Education (NICIE). They went to Belfast to meet the Department of Education. They decided that the simplest way forward was first to open a primary school.

Of almost 30 possible sites, the parents preferred a vacant temporary office building belonging to Londonderry City Council at Limavady Road. (It had been used temporarily as the offices of the City Council from 1972–1977 after its Guildhall was bombed in 1972). Getting use of this publicly owned premises would, we realized, be much more complicated than signing a simple lease for a privately owned site.

I went and spoke to an Social Democratic and Labour Party (SDLP) nationalist councillor I knew. I well remember his reaction. "Oh, Jesus!" he said. "Don't ask us to support integrated education! If you want our support, ask us for money—but don't ask us to support integrated education!" Another nationalist councillor was supportive, but said, "I don't think integrated education will solve the problems of Northern Ireland. But at least you won't make them worse!" One councillor cautioned us to treat this as a simple commercial request for lease—not to ask the council to support the principle of integrated education.

We wrote to the City Council and were invited to meet its Marketing Committee. (The rules gave us ten minutes for not more than two speakers to make our case.) About half a dozen of us attended. Geoff Starrett and I set out our "purely commercial" request to rent the empty council offices. There followed 45 minutes of questions from councillors after which we were requested to leave. We were later notified that the matter had been forwarded, without any recommendation, to the full monthly meeting of the City Council. We were again invited to make a ten-minute case—this time to the full council. We accepted the invitation and had another 45-minute discussion with the city councillors. We were later notified that the council had agreed to lease us the premises for 12 months.

When the school opened in September 1991, 69 children turned up. In the preceding weeks, with £90,000 that NICIE had raised from charities—the Nuffield Foundation, the Rowntree Trust, and the Community Relations Council—the dilapidated premises had been refurbished and equipped as a school. Some of this work— clearing the site, cutting back the hedges, and so on—was done by the parents themselves.

Among the families who founded the school were those called "mixed marriages" in Northern Ireland, where one parent is Protestant and the other Catholic. The daughter of one of these mixed marriages gave the best description of integrated education that I have ever heard.

> The little girl was eight years old and had already attended an existing "normal" segregated school for four years. A few days after she started at the new integrated school, the eight-year-old arrived home and her mother was chatting to her as she took off her schoolbag and coat.
>
> "How did you get on today?"
> "Fine," replied the little girl.
> "How do you like your new school?"
> "It's fine," replied the little girl.
>
> And then her mother casually asked, "What is the difference between your new school and your old school?" The mother was quite taken aback when the little girl said to her, "Mammy, I never told you this before—but at my old school I never talked about you. I talked about Daddy; but I never talked about you. At Oakgrove, I can be proud of both of you".

And this is what integrated schools allow us to do—they let us be proud of both main traditions in Northern Ireland, of their religious, cultural, and historical cultures. It also demonstrates that in a divided society, even an eight-year-old knows that there are things one is free to talk about, and things that are better left unspoken.

The year 1991 saw 102 more killings in Northern Ireland.
Some lessons learned from this story?

• *You will find support for reconciliation*— and it may not be public or visible. (Even individuals from existing segregated schools were personally supportive.)
• *Do not wait for someone else to provide leadership.*

STORY 2: TEN FAMILIES—£250,000— CREATING OAKGROVE INTEGRATED COLLEGE (DERRY~LONDONDERRY), 1992

It was January 22, 1992. Already 13 Northern Ireland people had died violently in the Troubles that month. By the end of the year, this figure would rise to 91.

Some parents met in Derry~Londonderry to discuss opening an integrated college for 11–18 year olds. For the first time ever, we had circulated advance notice of a motion for discussion. It was so important. The resolution for discussion stated simply: "We will open an Integrated College in September 1992 even if the Department of Education will not finance it." This was a hugely important issue because we needed to appoint staff who would be resigning their posts in existing schools long before September. We would have to take responsibility for those staff regardless of whether the Department of Education would agree to finance the college or not. It was going to cost about £250,000 to finance the college in its first year.

Ten families were represented at that January meeting: Jim and Kathy Laverty; Rita and Andy Meenagh; Bert and Anne Montgomery; Derek and Nuala MacLochlainn-Row; Vincent Brown; Marie and Ronnie Cowan; Bernie and Tim Webster; Jim and Jen Simpson; Mary and Gerry Walpole; and Anne and Colm Murray-Cavanagh.

The discussion was focused, very serious, and went gravely back and forth. All angles were talked out. We were just a group of ordinary parents. We did not have £250,000. Would the Department of Education agree to finance it? How could we possibly raise £250,000? £25,000 per family! Fund-raising? Charitable foundations? A bank loan? Mortgages? And if the department didn't approve the college, then the following year could cost a further £500,000!

We knew we had to decide that night. We did not want to live in a divided society. We wanted integrated, not segregated, schooling for our children. Would we take on the commitment? *Could* we take on the commitment? Eventually we went right around the circle of parents and each gave their vote. It was unanimous: "Let's do it!"

Six months later the Department of Education *did* approve the college, a few weeks before the school opened in September 1992 with 79 students—Northern Ireland's fifteenth integrated school.

Oakgrove Integrated College now has 850 students. But it was seven years later, in 1999, that I first discovered the personal cost to the original students. Two Catholic and Protestant sixth form students in 1992, told me that initially they did not wear the college uniform in the city center; and that each had been called a "traitor" within their respective community. But now, they said, they were proud to wear the Oakgrove College uniform in public. And no one calls them "traitor" any more.

- *By the end of 1992, there had been 91 killings in Northern Ireland.*

Some lessons learned from this story?

- *You do not have to wait for government support.* (And government embarrassment can be just as important as government sympathy.)
- *Do not underestimate the commitment of the pupils or the parents.*

STORY 3: CREATING ULIDIA INTEGRATED COLLEGE

In 1995 there were nine killings in Northern Ireland's Troubles.

Some parents in Carrickfergus wanted to open a new school, Castle Integrated College, in 1995. Their efforts failed because of local opposition. But, led by Tom Pennycook, the Castle College steering group refused to give up and started planning again for an integrated college in East Antrim. In early 1997 they lodged with the Department of Education a proposal for a new college. This time they proposed opening a brand-new integrated college in Whitehead, a few miles north of Carrickfergus. The Department of Education refused the request and refused financial assistance. But Tom Pennycook and the local parents and friends steadfastly refused to give up hope and decided to open the proposed new integrated college, independently, without any assistance from the Department of Education.

In February 1997 the steering group approached NICIE who agreed to help and act for the parents. NICIE's sister organization, the Integrated Education Fund (IEF), obtained funding for the college for a period of three months only, with the promise that the IEF would fund-raise for the college to help maintain it throughout its first year. With this guarantee of three months' funding, the steering group went about enlisting the necessary 60 students (with a 30 percent balance from the minority religion) and recruiting a principal and staff.

Later that year, September 1, 1997, Ulidia Integrated College finally opened in mobile classrooms on hockey pitch that had fallen into disuse in Whitehead. The new principal was Eugene Martin, who had formerly taught in Lagan College, Northern Ireland's first integrated school. Ulidia College began with 63 students (with religious balance) and six teachers in a secondhand, temporary accommodation and with secondhand furniture and equipment.

At this time there were no less than *three* integrated schools in the Belfast region that had been opened by local Catholic and Protestant parents despite government refusal to finance them. These three integrated schools were Oakwood Integrated Primary School, Lisburn, 1976; Strangford Integrated College, Co Down, 1977; and Ulidia Integrated College, Carrickfergus, 1977. It was subsequently stated that not only had the government refused to finance these schools but also that because the children were no longer in government-recognized schools, the Department of Education had actually *saved* over £1 million!

Subsequently another Development Proposal was submitted to the Department of Education. Again the government turned it down. The department did not feel that such a school in such an area was viable. The college had to survive on its own finances for another year before a new Development Proposal could even be submitted.

On February 26, 1998, a deputation travelled to London from the three integrated schools opened by Protestant and Catholic parents (Oakwood Integrated Primary, Strangford Integrated College, and Ulidia Integrated College) but refused any public funding. At 10 Downing Street we submitted a 15,000-signature petition to the UK prime minister Tony Blair MP, asking for funding for the three schools. The petition was received and, apparently, forwarded to the Northern Ireland Department of Education. Ulidia was not approved.

But, with additional financial assistance from the IEF, Ulidia Integrated College did survive. Interest in this new integrated college from local parents in the area was very strong. Yet another Development Proposal was submitted to try and obtain full government funding

for the 1998–1999 academic year and once again the Department of
Education turned down the college. The department was "not convinced about the viability of an integrated college in an area where the
minority religion represented only 9 percent of the population".

Again, the college approached the IEF for financial assistance for
1998–1999 and once more both NICIE and the IEF pledged their
support.

On October 19, 1998, a remarkable meeting took place in Castle
Buildings, Belfast. The education minister John McFall met with one
person from each of the three non-recognized schools supported by
no less than *seven* of the nine political parties elected to the new
Northern Ireland Assembly. This was said to be the widest cross-
party support for any single issue since the election of the members for the new assembly the previous June. Three small Northern
Ireland political parties, Alliance, the Women's Coalition, and the
Progressive Unionist Party, had policies to encourage integrated
schools. The other party representatives in meeting Minister McFall
came from the Ulster Unionist Party, the UK Unionist Party, the
SDLP, and Sinn Fein. But the government still did not give approval
to Ulidia College.

Ulidia continued independently in 1998–1999 with over 130 students and ten staff and, of course, additional mobile accommodation.
The religious balance was completely in line with government recommendations, yet the government of the day "was not convinced." The
teachers continued to teach the students and the IEF continued to
fund the college from its slender resources.

For the academic year 1999–2000, a new Development Proposal
was presented to the Department of Education. Since the college now
had over 130 students, with over 600 students on its waiting lists for
the incoming years, everyone at the school was confident of approval.
But for the seventh time, the government refused approval. Again the
college sought help from the IEF and its sponsors. The IEF assured
Ulidia that it would "go to the wall" before it would cease funding
the college.

With the help of the American Ireland Fund and the EU Peace
funding, finance was found to allow Ulidia to continue in existence
for yet another year. The college now moved to its present site in
Carrickfergus because it could not expand at its site at Whitehead.
Ulidia now had 240 students and 17 staff, with religious balance,
and, in addition, temporary accommodation.

In December 1999, Ulidia sent its eighth Development Proposal to
the new secretary of state, Dr. Mo Mowlam. Finally, it was approved

and the government undertook to fund the school from September 2000—Northern Ireland's forty-fourth integrated school.

During its time in the wilderness as an independently funded college, Ulidia students were victim of many sectarian incidents. The school suffered three petrol bomb attacks and two arson attacks, one of which destroyed the library.

Today the college stands overlooking Belfast Lough, in new, hi-tech buildings, with an enrollment of 500 students. The parents and staff are justly proud of their achievements—being proved right in suffering the three long years of isolation and rejection, and refusing to live segregated lives. They felt that an integrated college in such a troubled area was not only needed but also essential. The college is now oversubscribed each year by seven percent, that is, seven percent more students apply that it has places to offer. The future of the college is now secure and the college's website offers public thanks "to those who stood by the college in its time of need especially the Northern Ireland Council for Integrated Education and the Integrated Education Fund."

From 1995, the year the parents started to campaign for the college, until 2000, when the college achieved public funding, 135 people were killed in the Northern Ireland Troubles.

Some lessons learned from this story?

- *Do not depend upon getting political or civil service support.* Take what you can and be prepared to let politicians use you afterward. (Prime Ministers of the UK and Ireland often visit integrated schools to show their support for reconciliation.)
- *Success may not come quickly.*
- *No school has failed solely due to lack of money.* Support can always be found for reconciliation. (UK charities and Irish-American charities supported integrated schools here before the Northern Ireland government did.)

THE ONGOING CHALLENGE OF RUNNING AN INTEGRATED SCHOOL: CONTENTIOUS ISSUES?

There is a real dilemma for teachers who wish to embark on this type of work—by its very nature it creates discomfort; challenges mind-sets; tackles sensitive issues. The truth is that individually and collectively we need to take responsibility for this work. We are all part of the problem and we can all be part of the solution.

(Marion Matchett, former Chief Inspector of Schools, Department of Education of Northern Ireland)

Do not expect that integrated schools will not have community problems. The principal of Oakgrove Integrated Primary School illustrates the importance of dealing with contentious issues in integrated
schools. In her primary school the Primary 3 children were looking
at a topic entitled "People Who Help Us." This included the school
road crossing ("lollipop") lady, the veterinary surgeon, the nurse, the
police officer, and so on. In the mid-1990s (at a time of sustained
civil confrontation with the police) a police officer arrived in full riot
uniform. The children, especially the boys, were fascinated by the
police officer. However a parent with a strong Irish nationalist background happened to be present when the officer was in the building
and became extremely angry. She demanded to meet the principal
and expressed her anger at riot police being regarded as "people who
help us"! The principal noted the parent's concerns and promised
to respond to her. The principal was unaware that the police officer had decided to bring riot gear. She expressed her unease to the
police community liaison officer and was assured it would not happen
again.

Then, however, the principal organised a series of workshops for
parents, staff, and governors to look specifically at contentious issues
and to find an agreed way forward in terms of policy. This particular
principal felt it was important not to avoid these types of issues but
also understood the importance of the process of engaging in dialogue with all the people involved so that they could all have their
voice heard. As she said herself this was an uncomfortable time to
be the leader but also a very important time for leadership to be
demonstrated.

The workshops proved very useful and beneficial, but at times
awkward and uncomfortable. But they demonstrated overall why
integrated education was so important—because it could provide a
safe space for different people within our divided community to come
together and discuss issues of difference in a nonviolent way. The
school principal commented: "If I do not have difficult, awkward or
some kind of contentious issue to deal with in the course of my job,
what are we as a school avoiding?"

As our community grows, our new members need induction every year.
That local principal recently declared the importance of reminding
people—parents, staff, and governors—about the importance of integration. As schools become more established, there is great danger in
avoiding talk of diversity and differences in our society. At her annual
induction session for parents she reminds people of how and why the
integrated school started and also why it is still so important today.

She intentionally shows images of Orange Order marches, "Bloody Sunday" murals, sectarian slogans, and so on, in order to let parents know that the school takes its integration remit seriously and that children *will* be involved in discussion on issues such as sectarianism, and will be encouraged to develop skills and attitudes to help them deal with the diversity in our society.

Another annual challenge for this principal is to engage all her school staff at the beginning of each school year in different kinds of presentations and experiential activities that help them to develop the skills necessary for life in an integrated school in a divided society. Teachers do not always love coming to these sessions because they can be uncomfortable, says the principal. But for that very reason these discussions are vitally important in terms of staff training to enable, empower, and upskill staff to deal with contentious issues that can arise. Teachers need to understand the open ethos and they also need to feel supported. The challenge is keeping this training fresh each year.

Afterword

When Protestant and Catholic parents opened Northern Ireland's first planned integrated schools (Lagan College, Belfast) in 1981, they had 28 pupils. From those 28 pupils in one school, there have now grown 21,000 pupils in 61 schools. This is an immense achievement. But they still comprise only 7 percent of all Northern Ireland's school pupils. "But if we had waited," say the parents, "for the Government, the Department of Education, the churches, the politicians, or the Education and Library Boards to create integrated schools, we would still be waiting."

CONCLUSION TO PART 4

Michalinos Zembylas

The last two chapters of this edited collection show most powerfully how integrated education is a dynamic, multilevel process that often starts on the ground ("bottom-up"), yet to be effective it requires the participation of all stakeholders at all levels both from above and from below. The stories narrated by Richard and Colm show the different ways that the roles of students, teachers, parents, community leaders, and school administrators are entangled in the process to develop initiatives toward integrated education. Clearly, the whole sequence of developments surrounding integrated schools is embedded in the specific circumstances of Northern Ireland but it also raises more general issues relating to political and governmental involvement, parental participation, and policy formulation (Morgan & Fraser, 1999). Perhaps most importantly, write Morgan and Fraser, the experience of Northern Ireland

> highlights the difficulty all participants face in attempting to develop and sustain a system which reconciles principles of equity, long-term educational needs of a whole society and the desire to involve and accommodate individuals and groups whose concerns focus on the more immediate and local issues which impinge directly on their lives. (p. 376)

This experience, as shown in many chapters of this edited collection, resonates with the experience in other societies. Therefore, struggles to address the numerous issues raised in this collection—from regional challenges about how to develop a new integrated school to national and global concerns related to the long process of rebuilding trust and reconciliation after traumatic conflict—can certainly benefit from each other's efforts taking place in different countries. The experience of Northern Ireland, for example, teaches the new initiatives (e.g., Bosnia and Herzegovina, Cyprus, Macedonia, and Croatia) that establishing integrated schools is a long, often painfully discouraging process, so there should be perseverance and patience. Effective integrated education can only be realized in partnership between the whole range of stakeholders, especially regional political authorities; yet, someone has to take firm leadership of the process and this seems to be close to the local level. The experience of Northern Ireland also teaches initiatives that have been taking place for some time (e.g., Israel) that developing clear goals, "appropriate" curricula, and evaluation and self-reflective mechanisms to adjust school curriculum, evaluate progress, and communicate the gains is also part of the process.

If integrated education is to be a genuine, dynamic, multilevel process that involves all stakeholders, then the stories by Richard and Colm urge us—especially those initiatives taking place for the first time—to consider concretely the following questions:

- How do we realize in practice the participation of all stakeholders in the process of formulating integration policies, curricula, and pedagogical practices?
- How can we create the necessary ground and specific frames ensuring that these integration policies, curricula, and pedagogical practices become effective? How can we make sure that good integration practices are developed, new initiatives are encouraged, and creative synergies between different settings are enhanced?
- What could be the role of local and regional authorities (municipal, political, and so on) in the process? How could these authorities better support initiatives toward integrated education while giving them space to retain some of their concerns? How could integrated education initiatives better involve local communities and different organizations?
- How do integrated education and its vision reach out to those who do not have the resources, power, or even willingness to participate in new initiatives?
- How do integrated schools constantly renew their policies, curricula, and practices so that they enhance opportunities and access for all students?

To address the challenges ahead, the initiatives in different countries can benefit from the development of *supportive networks* or *communities*, a crucial element that can help us build on each other's experiences and lessons learned. The question "Does the initiative have the potential to be one that others can learn from (what and how?) and that can be transferred to other settings?" is central in the effort to move forward and enhance integrated education in different settings around the world.

REFERENCE

Morgan, V., & Fraser, G. (1999). When does "good news" become "bad news"? Relationships between government and the integrated schools in Northern Ireland. *British Journal of Educational Studies, 47*(4), 364–379.

GENERAL CONCLUSION

THE FUTURE OF INTEGRATED EDUCATION IN CONFLICTED SOCIETIES

Michalinos Zembylas and Zvi Bekerman

In March 2012, a team of academics, practitioners, and nongovernmental organizations gathered in Belfast to discuss the current status of integrated education in various conflicted societies—Bosnia and Herzegovina, Croatia, Cyprus, Israel, Macedonia, and Northern Ireland. A driving concern for this group was the need to review the different frameworks and approaches in the developing field of integrated education in conflicted societies, where children who are more normally educated apart are deliberately educated together. Indeed, it was that concern, or rather the recognition that integrated education was "happening" in different conflicted societies, that led to the urgent need to learn from each other's experiences and reconceptualize how integrated education initiatives could be fostered through supportive networks for practice and research. To that end, the academics, practitioners, and nongovernmental organizations from these conflicted societies began a critical dialogue that resulted in what we believe is a valuable effort to sustain an international network of integrated education. For, as has been demonstrated in this book, it is through critical reflection on existing initiatives in different societies that more effective modes of integrated education can be enunciated.

Although attempts at integrated education have a considerable history, especially in Northern Ireland where these efforts enter their fourth decade, many initiatives in other conflicted societies struggle to develop the ground, resources, and mechanisms to support integrated education. Northern Ireland's remarkable attempts for integrated education in the middle of the Troubles have captured the imagination of those who are inspired by the vision of integrated education and have become symbolic as a model that could be utilized in other conflicted societies. The fact of the matter though is that Northern Ireland's experience is grounded in the political context of a religious conflict and may fail to capture the "qualitatively different contexts" of conflict in other societies and how those influence the prospects and challenges of integrated education. Speaking about Northern Ireland and Israel, Gallagher (2007) emphasizes:

> The experience of some of these other contexts…have advanced the idea that shared schooling provide an important basis for promoting shared living, but their efforts have been characterized by a commitment to the idea that shared schools should be more than places where different students come together. Rather they should be *qualitatively different contexts* within which the curriculum and ethos of the school deals directly with the issue of diversity. They are contexts, in other words, where there is a commitment to addressing the cognitive and affective every bit as much as the behavioral. (p. 18, emphasis added)

One of the major challenges of integrated education then, as shown in many chapters of this book, is how to create this qualitatively different ethos of integration, given that initiatives for integrated education take place within the societal structures of the nation-state in which segregated identities, policies, and practices are highlighted. The desire to initiate forms of integrated education in other settings can be duly informed by Northern Ireland's experience, especially in terms of the manner in which nation-states and governments engage with the idea of public schooling in conflicted societies. But the question of what kind of places integrated schools should become in the existing hegemonic structures of nation-states and what theoretical concepts and approaches should or could inform these initiatives are issues that need to be addressed more carefully (see Bekerman & Zembylas, 2012).

For example, the question of whether new concepts should be introduced into existing discussions about integrated education that would lead to more effective approaches needs to be on the agenda. Where integrated education is discussed as the deliberate coeducation of children who are normally educated apart in conflicted societies, a strong link should be made with wider issues of integration such as the socioeconomic situation, race, gender, ethnicity, and structural conditions for social cohesion, equality, and democracy. In these discussions, sufficient attention should be paid to the position of particular groups (e.g., immigrants, minorities, indigenous groups, diaspora groups, special needs groups, and so on). This means that new concepts will need to be introduced to ensure that these issues are adequately addressed. In other words, integrated education is not a "technocratic" process where different students come together in a conflicted society; integration is a multifaceted, long-term and open-ended process in which ideally all stakeholders come together and benefit from it. This realization demands careful theoretical and practical considerations that will strengthen long-term commitment to the process of integrated education and will address explicitly the concerns of those who are not only positively inclined but also those who oppose it or are not convinced of its merits. A recent European report on "integration beyond migration" emphasizes some ideas that are very much relevant to our discussion here and can strengthen the prospects of effective integrated education:

- Acknowledging that integration is and can be more driven by competent and empowered individuals and organizations acting toward the goals they value and negotiating on the means to achieve them will emphasize their role in integration processes by calling on their responsibilities and building on their capabilities.
- Identifying key policy areas and frameworks as well as the main public, private and third sector actors and analyzing their mandates, roles and the concepts they use. This will help to assess the merits of an approach that values equality, diversity, openness and inclusion. (Kirchberger & Niessen, 2011, p. 15)

Furthermore, more attention should be paid to the theoretical grounding of integrated education initiatives. For example, in our recent book (Bekerman & Zembylas, 2012), we raise questions about the psychologized grounding of many peace education efforts within a nation-state framework—including integrated education initiatives. Our argument is that if the framing of an initiative—let's say "integrated education"—takes for granted notions of identity, education, and integration as those are situated within a nation-state framework, then our vision for the new ethos that Galllagher (2009) talks about will be limited. Central to the analysis of integrated education, therefore, are the ways in which notions of identity, education, and integration are entangled and perpetuate or challenge the depth of attachment to essentialist ideas about conflict, reconciliation, diversity, and so on. More specifically, one could notice that even in some of the integrated education initiatives described in this book, there is still a certain grounding on artificial categorizations of identity—be this religious, cultural, ethnic, national, or other—as the basis on which "integration" takes place. Many chapters in this book make an attempt to widen the discourse knowing too well that (integrated) education cannot magically change things within a deeply divided and segregated society, yet for the ethos of integrated education to develop, there have to be some more fundamental theoretical and practical changes. Admittedly though, we are well aware of the challenges confronted by those who want to promote integrated education initiatives, especially when trying to negotiate among their understanding of students' needs, their personal commitments, and their commitments to the larger society within which they are asked to educate.

Let us be a bit more specific. When discussing integration we need to ask questions of politics and power relations, of dominance and marginalization, and also questions about self-positioning and belonging. "Integrated education" is entangled with life processes for which individual and collective identifications are or are made to be highly relevant. When discussing integration we need to confront complexity and abandon educational perspectives that remain atheoretical and ahistorical. To grasp complexity means much more than realizing the importance of accounting for the multiple social, political, and economical contexts within which different individuals and groups "come together" to survive, and thus "integrated education" might be criticized that it creates an artificial "bubble" within which all groups become suddenly "equal" when societal structures are grossly unequal and unjust. It means also to realize the centrality of historical evolving contexts to current social conditions, a historicity that belongs to all of the different groups in a conflicted society and the degree to which they feel attached to a particular belonging. And yet it is very interesting to notice that the stories told in this book about the integration of conflicting groups in schools of different conflicted societies are often presented as "their" stories and not as "our" stories, that is, the whole society's stories. National entities seem to need these groups disentangled and separated from what we call the "majority" or "dominant" society and yet be in dialogue with it. This dialogue of negation is needed for it feeds and strengthens the dominant sense of togetherness without which a nation will not be.

Furthermore, critical perspectives have pointed at the lack of educational theorizing in integration efforts geared toward social cohesion, harmony, and peaceful coexistence that, to this day—as in most of the education field—is being guided by functional, psychologized, and idealistic perspectives when articulating its aims. The reader will notice that even some of the initiatives described in this book cannot evade such criticisms; thus, some of these educational initiatives are guided by essentialized conceptions of human rights and idealist perspectives about the results of integrated education and its potentiality within a segregated society. It is questionable, however, if working through the same premises that are constituted and constitutive of the modern nation-state under which much of the lack of social cohesion, harmony, and peaceful coexistence, which integration is expected to help smooth and ultimately overcome, have flourished is the right direction such an education should take.

Integration is often set as a universal idealist goal; and yet we should remember that integration/segregation are reveled and are dependent on their absence. This striking duality bears remarkable similarities to the paradigmatic dichotomies set by Western epistemology (male/female; bad/good; us/them) and as such seems only to be able to replicate past outcomes. Inasmuch as there is a "true" way of "doing" integration, a critical dialogue with alterity becomes a difficult task. This is what comparative studies with other conflicted societies can offer to the "integrated education movement"—the perspective of comparability and criticality that is often missing from understanding integrated education as something self-evident or a utopian noble achievement. When integration is set in the ground as a universal utopia it stops its potential productivity by representing its values as universally self-evident. More importantly, this self-righteousness disregards the tight entanglements among conflict, nation-state, and the present capitalist order; in short, it disregards the social and political arrangements that institutionalize inequality and injustice. Avoiding questions such as "Who are we?," "What perceptions of justice do we hold to?," "How do we understand and practice "integration" in general?," "What dialogue do we want to sustain? And under which conditions?" cannot be a good formula to encourage integration and peaceful accommodation. If indeed integration efforts are serious about the verbiage that sustains them—the affirmation, recognition, and rehabilitation of that which is "other"—they need to start by critically approaching the various epistemological, social, political, educational, and metaphysical certainties that are held. There needs to be a clearly articulated insertion of the epistemological, social, political, educational, and metaphysical questions into discussions about integrated education.

Toward a Future of Integrated Education Studies

Integrated schooling has developed in recent decades in response to segregation practices that have been occurring, not only in conflicted societies but also around the world (Mickelson & Nkomo, 2012). The issue is not so much about defining what is meant by "integrated education" in different settings but rather *how* it is practiced and *what* its consequences are. So there has to be a systematic examination of what integrated education *does* in specific settings and under certain circumstances. Such an examination is urgently needed in a sociopolitical context inflected by conflict and post-conflict implications that raise numerous complex issues about the future prospects of a society that is truly "integrated." Given that there has been little scholarly work that theorizes the different stories and accounts of integrated education, more systematic research is needed on the practices and the results of integrated education. Developing and sustaining an international network of integrated education creates spaces for such research to enrich the policies and practices of integrated education and learn from each other. But for this to happen, deeper theoretical work is also needed at the same time; the stories narrated in this book offer the point of departure to begin doing so and for this reason they make an important contribution to the field of integrated education studies.

By providing opportunities to critically analyze stories from different integrated education settings, academics, practitioners, and nongovernmental organizations are invited to inhabit renewed learning spaces and form alternative networks of support. Alternative options, in general, are enabled and invigorated by efforts that do not remain stuck in taken-for-granted assumptions about integrated education initiatives. Although transformations are not always achieved in the examples that are offered in this book, it is important to reflect on both the failures and the successes of the efforts that are undertaken. This book, then, does not limit itself to the description of the complexities of integrated education and their intricate relations to various ideologies; it also shows how under some circumstances these complexities may indeed create opportunities for alternative understandings of identity, education, and integration—understandings that are not bounded in the limitations imposed by the nation-state. These examples show the way for a different sort of theorization of integrated education, for a limited understanding of the multiple complexities involved can erode even the strongest will or the greatest aspirations. This idea implies a relentless critique of our own positions and taken-for-granted assumptions about integrated education and suggests the need for constantly renewing our framework, vision, planning, organization, policies, and practices.

REFERENCES

Bekerman, Z., & Zembylas, M. (2012). *Teaching contested narratives: Identity, memory and reconciliation in peace education and beyond.* Cambridge: Cambridge University Press.

Kirchberger, A., & Niessen, J. (2011). *Integration beyond migration: Kicking off the debate.* Brussels: European Network Against Racism.

Gallagher, T. (2007). Desegregation and resegregation: The legacy of Brown versus Board of Education, 1954. In Z. Bekerman & C. McGlynn (Eds.), *Addressing ethnic conflict through peace education: International perspectives* (pp. 9–19). New York: Palgrave Macmillan.

Mickelson, R., & Nkomo, M. (2012). Integrated schooling, life course outcomes, and social cohesion in multiethnic democratic societies. *Review of Research in Education, 36,* 197–238.

EDITORS AND CONTRIBUTORS

Maria Asvesta is assistant head at the English School in Nicosia, Cyprus, with special responsibilities in the areas of Diversity and Student Voice. She has taught Economics at the Jewish Free School in London before moving to Cyprus to teach at the Falcon International School. In 1992 she took a position at the English School to teach Economics and Business. Since 2003 she has undertaken a vast range of training courses in the field of Intercultural Education and gained a Postgraduate Certificate in Education for Democratic Citizenship from the Institute of Education (2010). She has been involved in the development and implementation of school policies such as the School Anti-Bullying Policy and the Equal Opportunities Policy as measures to help promote the creation of a more culturally responsive school. More recently she has been responsible for the introduction of Citizenship Education and Global Perspectives into the school curriculum.

Zvi Bekerman teaches anthropology of education at the School of Education and the Melton Center, Hebrew University of Jerusalem. His interests are the study of cultural, ethnic, and national identity, including identity processes and negotiation during intercultural encounters and in formal/informal learning contexts. He is the editor of the journal *Diaspora, Indigenous, and Minority Education: An International Journal.* He has been widely published and among his recently published books are (with Michalinos Zembylas) *Teaching Contested Narratives: Identity, Memory and Reconciliation in Peace Education and Beyond* (2012) and (with Thomas Geisen) *International Handbook of Migration, Minorities and Education: Understanding Cultural and Social Differences in Processes of Learning* (2012).

Noreen Campbell is chief executive officer of Northern Ireland Council for Integrated Education (NICIE). She was appointed to this role in September 2009. She has been involved in integrated education since its beginning. She was a founder parent and teacher of Hazelwood Integrated College, where she served as vice principal from 1986 to 1996 and as principal from 1996 to 2006. During this time, Hazelwood College was featured in the National Commission on Education's book, *Success against the Odds*. Noreen has served on a range of educational panels advising on educational issues including DE's Specialist Schools Panel and QUB Sharing Education Advisory Panel.

Paul Caskey is campaign director of the Integrated Education Fund (IEF) in Northern Ireland. A graduate of the Queen's University Belfast and Trinity College Dublin, where he completed a Masters in Peace Studies, Paul has worked in fundraising and campaigning in the not-for-profit sector for over 21 years. With the IEF he is responsible for leading the fundraising development campaign to help increase the growth of integrated schools in Northern Ireland working along-side the board of trustees and campaign volunteers. Paul is married with three children, two of whom attend Forge Integrated Primary School in Belfast.

Colm Cavanagh is president of NICIE. In 1991, he and his wife Anne were among the Protestant and Catholic parents who opened an integrated primary school, high school, and nursery in Derry~Londonderry. In 1998 he joined the cross-community Alliance Party of Northern Ireland. With others he encouraged research into the financial cost of Northern Ireland's divisions—now quantified as up to £1.5 billion every year. He edited the first *International Directory of Joint Catholic-Protestant Schools, Colleges & Universities*. In 2007 he gave NICIE's Dunleath-All Children Together Lecture, "Thy People Shall Be My People: The Community Impact of Integrated Schools."

Inas Deeb is currently the educational director at the Hand in Hand Center for Arab-Jewish Education (HIH) in Israel. In 1997 Inas completed a Master's degree in Language Education from the Hebrew University, in 2000 a second Master's program in Adult Education and Organization Development from St. Joseph University, Philadelphia (USA), and in 2010 earned a PhD degree in social psychology from Bar-Ilan University. For 15 years, she worked as a teacher counselor in schools and organized various teacher training programs in different pedagogical areas. Her PhD research was on the impact of integrated education on Jewish and Arab children's conception of ethnic categories and essentialism. Her research interests include bilingual and integrated education, multicultural education, and diversity.

Ljuljjeta Goranci-Brkic is general manager at the Nansen Dialogue Centre (NDC) Sarajevo (Bosnia and Herzegovina). She completed an MD at the medical faculty at Tuzla University (Bosnia and Herzegovina) and MA in Conflict Transformation Studies in regions affected by intractable conflicts (ACTS—Applied Conflict Transformation Study). She has been working in (NDC Sarajevo since 2000. Ljuljjeta is actively involved in various associations, networks, and activities that contribute to the development of integration of divided communities throughout the country.

Helen Killick is one of the chaplains at Lagan College in Belfast, where she also teaches music. She is interested in ecumenical dialogue and engaging young people in the areas of peacemaking, conflict resolution, and social justice. In her 20 years' experience in integrated education she has been particularly interested in the development of ethos, providing opportunities for students and staff to explore issues around integration.

Nadia Kinani is the headmistress of the elementary school of HIH, the Arab-Jewish bilingual school in Israel. She completed her BEd in special education at David Yallin Collage, Jerusalem, in 2000 and her Master's degree from the University of Durby. She has been teaching in HIH for eight years. In 2007 she became a vice principal, and in 2010 she was appointed as the headmistress. She has three daughters enrolled at HIH; her oldest daughter graduated last year.

Biljana Krstevska-Papic is employed as manager for education, training, and development at NDC Skopje. For the last five years, she has been working on the promotion of the Nansen model of integrated education in Macedonia. Her interests are integrated, intercultural, and inclusive education. She is currently preparing her PhD thesis, "Program Basis of School Pedagogues' Work." Biljana has prepared a manual for promotion of children rights and three interactive picture books. She is also the author and coauthor of some articles in pedagogical journals.

Kevin Lambe is the founding principal of Shimna Integrated College, Newcastle, County Down. He completed a BA (Hons) in Spanish from Queen's University Belfast followed by a PGCE and subsequently a Masters in Educational Management. He began his teaching career in St. Louise's Comprehensive College, the first comprehensive school in Northern Ireland, before moving on to teach in Lagan College, the first integrated, all-ability school. He became the first development officer of NICIE when it was founded in 1990, in which role he assisted 13 parent groups to open new, planned integrated schools and where he worked with Tony Spencer in drafting the NICIE statement of principles. He has been principal of Shimna Integrated College since it opened in 1994.

Bob Mark is a long-time resident of Neve Shalom / Wahat al-Salam, an intentional community of Jews and Palestinians in Israel who promote dialogue and equality between the two peoples. Bob is an English and history teacher with 23 years of experience in a bilingual Arab-Jewish primary school. Research for both his master's thesis and doctoral dissertation at the Hebrew University is based on critical examination of mundane classroom interactions between teachers and children in the Jewish-Arab school. He is particularly interested in how group participation patterns in the school are shaped and rationalized through multicultural structures and discourse.

Peter McCreadie has a Bachelor of Education (English and Drama) (1976), a Diploma in Advanced Studies in Education (1986), and a Masters of Education (1988) from Queens University Belfast. He has worked for 37 years in postprimary all-ability education. His initial appointment was as a founding teacher at Northern Ireland's first community school where he worked for 14 years. A ten-year period at a rural high school followed before his appointment to Priory Integrated College in June 2000 where, initially as vice principal and then principal, Peter led staff through a process that placed integration at the heart of the college. He is currently employed in a part-time capacity as an associate by NICIE with a remit to promote positive pathways toward integration in the wider educational community.

Claire McGlynn is lecturer at the School of Education, Queen's University Belfast and her research interests include integrated education, multicultural and intercultural education, education for social cohesion in conflict and post-conflict societies, and teacher education for diversity. She has been researching the integrated schools in Northern Ireland for more than 15 years. Her last edited book, with Michalinos Zembylas, Zvi Bekerman, and Tony Gallagher, *Peace Education in Conflict and Post-Conflict Societies: Comparative*

Perspectives (2009) won the Comparative and International Education Society Jackie Kirk Outstanding Book Award in Montreal in 2011.

Paula McIlwaine has a BA Hons in English, and BSc Hons and MSc in psychology. She is interested in child development and organizational psychology. Paula has taught English and psychology and has also worked in an international development role, as a teacher trainer, in a College of Education in Northern Nigeria. Paula's formal qualifications plus training in education and leadership skills, conflict mediation / transformation, and diversity awareness complement her diploma and practice as a professional life and business coach. Paula is passionate about integrated education, and has worked with NICIE for over seven years in the design and delivery of professional development training for teachers in fostering positive attitudes toward diversity and inclusion alongside skills and strategies for constructively challenging prejudice and discrimination.

Ivana Milas finished medical studies at Osijek University. In 1996, she became involved in peace activities and projects of peaceful reintegration and return in the region of eastern Croatia that was greatly affected by the 1991–1997 war. From 1998 to 2001 she worked for the Centre for Peace, Nonviolence and Human Rights on the project, Building Civil Society and the Culture of Nonviolence. From 2001, she worked on educational projects in NDC. In 2003, NDC started the New School project, aiming to open the first integrated school in Vukovar. She also leads a project of intercultural education implemented in eight primary schools in eastern Croatia, and a project of joint education in segregated kindergartens in Vukovar.

Vilma Venkovska Milcev is country director of Search for Common Ground (SFCG) in Macedonia and Kosovo. She has a GSP in Civil Society Initiatives in Peacebuilding and Conflict Transformation at the School for International Training, Vermont, USA, and a BA from the University St. Cyril & Methodius in Skopje, Macedonia. For the past 18 years, she has been involved in designing and implementing national and regional civil society initiatives integrating respect for cultural diversity and multicultural understanding, using specific SFCG-designed tools such as informal education, arts, and media. Her expertise is in working in the fields of conflict transformation, organizational management, local capacity building, and participatory community development. She has given numerous presentations at international and local conferences and led workshops and trainings in conflict transformation, consensus and team building, facilitation, cross-cultural communication, fundraising, and NGO management.

Mary Roulston is the founding principal of one of the grant-maintained primary schools in Northern Ireland. She has experience of working in French and English schools before she moved to Northern Ireland in 1978. Prior to taking up her post in the integrated sector she worked in the controlled (mainly Protestant) sector and in the Rudolf Steiner Holywood Scchool. During a career break when her three sons were young she was very involved in cross-community work and was chairperson of her local parent and toddler group and the community association. She was also a volunteer in the local cross-community youth club. She is particularly interested in peace education and the inclusion of all children within schools.

Julia Schlam Salman is lecturer and teacher trainer at the David Yellin Academic College of Education in Jerusalem. She also works as an English language teacher at the Max Rayne Hand in Hand School for Bilingual Education. Julia's research interests include language education, critical pedagogies and language learning, identity negotiation processes and language acquisition, and English language learning in areas of intractable conflict. Most recently, Julia has been working on teacher training initiatives focused on integrating language education methods, twenty-first century skills, and information/communication technology.

Marinko Uremovic is teacher at the Blago Zadro primary school in Vukovar where he teaches English and German. He gained his Masters degree in English and German language and literature from the Josip Juraj Strossmayer University of Osijek in 2004. The same year he started working with NDC Osijek on the New School project and is also one of the creators of the curriculum for Cultural and Spiritual Heritage of the Region. As a part of the Intercultural Navigators, a program designed by the British Council, Marinko was one of the cofounders of the ConSol organization, which uses scientific methods to promote tolerance and to empower children for everyday challenges in areas of conflict. He is also currently active as a treasurer in the Croatian Association of Teachers of English.

Sharon Verwoerd has a Masters in Peace and Conflict Resolution from the University of Queensland and has worked in a range of positions in secondary schools in Australia, England, and Ireland. She is part of an international Franciscan group, Pace e Bene, whose mission is to foster justice and peace through nonviolent education, community building, and action. She was chaplain at Lagan College in Belfast from 2008 to 2012 and now lives in South Africa where she is involved in community-development programs.

Richard Wilson currently works in the Humanitarian Department of Oxfam GB based in Oxford, England. He grew up in County Down, Northern Ireland, and experienced integrated education at Lagan College Belfast before moving to Scotland to study International Politics at the University of Stirling followed by Development Studies at the University of Glasgow. He has a deep interest in international development, politics, and history.

Veton Zekolli is program manager at NDC Skopje. He has been working with the Nansen Dialogue Network and Nansenskolen Academy in Lillehammer, Norway, from 2004. He has a BA in Law Studies from the State University of Tetovo and he is part of the inter-university MA Tempus program on international relations between the University of Gothenburg and South Eastern Europe University. He is the coauthor of the handbook *Instruments for Improvement of Inter-ethnic*. From 2007, his activities and work were mostly focused on integrated education in the Republic of Macedonia, and he is also a delegate of the Secretariat for Implementing the Ohrid Framework Agreement for consultancy regarding the Strategy for Integrated Education in Macedonia. Veton has participated in many national and international conferences as an NDC delegate.

Michalinos Zembylas is associate professor of education at the Open University of Cyprus. His research interests are in the areas of educational philosophy and curriculum theory, and his work focuses on exploring the role of emotion and affect in curriculum and pedagogy. He is particularly interested in how affective politics intersect with issues of social justice pedagogies, intercultural and peace education, and citizenship education. Michalinos is the author of numerous articles and books. His most recent book (with Zvi Bekerman) is entitled *Teaching Contested Narratives: Identity, Memory and Reconciliation in Peace Education and Beyond* (2012).

Index

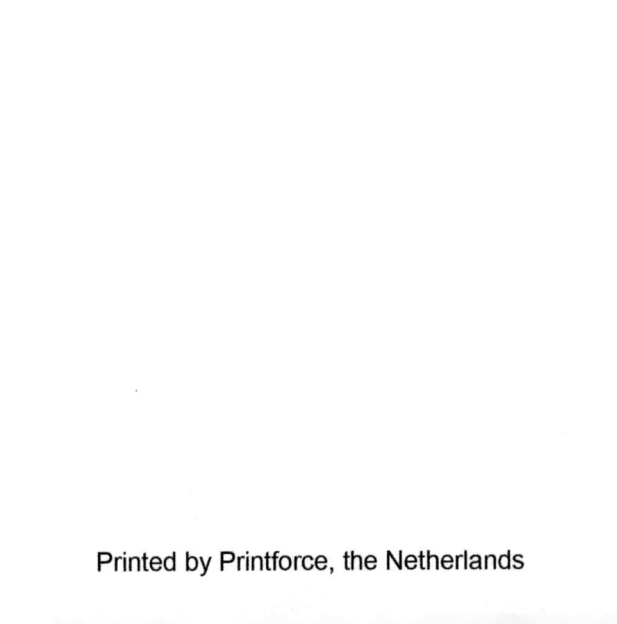

Printed by Printforce, the Netherlands